The author and the bell from the *Manuela*.

Gary Gentile started his diving career in 1970. Since then he has made more than 1,000 decompression dives, over 80 of them on the *Andrea Doria*.

Gary has specialized in the fields of wreck diving and shipwreck research, concentrating his efforts on wrecks along the East Coast, from Newfoundland to Key West, and in the Great Lakes. He has compiled an extensive library of books, photographs, drawings, plans, and original source materials dealing with ships and shipwrecks.

Gary has written dozens of articles for such magazines as *Animal Kingdom*, *Sea Frontiers*, *Sterns*, and *The Freeman*. He has published thousands of photographs in books, periodicals, newspapers, brochures, advertisements, corporate reports, museum displays, film, and television. He lectures extensively on wilderness and underwater topics, and conducts seminars on advanced wreck diving techniques and high-tech diving equipment. He is the author of twenty-one books: ten novels, and eleven nonfiction works on diving and nautical and shipwreck history. The Popular Dive Guide Series will eventually cover every major shipwreck along the East Coast.

In 1989, after a five-year battle with the National Oceanic and Atmospheric Administration, Gary won a suit which forced the hostile government agency to issue him a permit to dive the USS *Monitor*, a protected National Marine Sanctuary. Media attention that was focused on Gary's triumphant victory resulted in nationwide coverage of his 1990 photographic expedition to the Civil War ironclad.

The epic battles of the *Monitor* are the subject of a separate volume.

Above: The *Yancey* being prepared for her new career as an artificial reef.

Below: An example of the types of marine life that grow on or frequent shipwrecks.

THE POPULAR DIVE GUIDE SERIES

Shipwrecks of North Carolina

from Hatteras Inlet South

by Gary Gentile

GARY GENTILE PRODUCTIONS
P.O. Box 57137
Philadelphia, PA 19111
1992

GARY GENTILE PRODUCTIONS
P.O. Box 57137
Philadelphia, PA 19111

Additional copies of this book may be purchased from the same address by sending a check or money order in the amount of $20 U.S. for each copy (postage paid).

Picture Credits

The front cover photo of the *Dixie Arrow* is courtesy of the National Archives. Every attempt has been made to contact the photographers of pictures used in this book where the name was known, and to ascertain the name of the photographer where unknown; copies of many pictures have been in public circulation for so long that the name of the photographer has been lost, or the photographer's present whereabouts are impossible to trace. Any information in this regard forwarded to the author will be appreciated. Apologies are made to those whose work must under such circumstances go unrecognized. Uncredited photographs, including all marine life examples typical to the area, were taken by the author.

The author wishes to acknowledge Jon Hulburt for his expert advice in reviewing and editing the manuscript, Drew Maser for proofreading the galleys, and Richard Lawrence, of the North Carolina Department of Archives and History, at Fort Fisher, Kure Beach, for his valuable research assistance.

International Standard Book Number (ISBN) 0-9621453-5-1

First Edition

Printed in Hong Kong

CONTENTS

Ocracoke light.

INTRODUCTION

Many people believe that North Carolina is a virtual graveyard of wrecked ships, as if more vessels have come to grief on these lonesome southern strands than on any other coast in the world. While this idea may be an attractive selling point for the tourist trade it is far from the truth.

There is no doubt that in the past—say, prior to the Great War, and particularly before the turn of the century—the North Carolina coast was a desolate and desperate place to wreck. Until the establishment of the Life-Saving Service, shipwrecked mariners usually had to fend for themselves. Until the advent of the wireless, ships in trouble offshore were in the same predicament. Nor were the seas hospitable.

The Diamond Shoals is where the cold Labrador current from the north collides with the warm Gulf Stream current from the south. This creates a turbulence in the sky that is the result of sharp temperature gradients in the attendant air masses. Storms are frequent, weather unpredictable. For that reason the adjacent stretch of coast became a place to be avoided. And that, for the most part, is what ships did.

Only when blown off course or lost in fog did windjammers and steamships find themselves stranded in North Carolina. But stranding is not an accident peculiar to the Tar Heel state: during the golden age of sail, when ships were at the mercy of the wind, they ran aground on beaches the world over. North Carolina experienced no more or less than its share. So why the stigma?

Because of the way Cape Hatteras juts out into the Atlantic, strict attention to navigation is required to round the cape without hitting it, or piling up on the Diamonds Shoals that are the extension of the cape. In the nineteenth century mariners relied upon the stars to steer their courses, sun sightings to work out their positions, and dead reckoning to compensate for wind and drift. A sextant, a chronometer, and nautical tables were their only navigational aids. Long periods of rain, fog, or overcast skies (conditions commonly found off North Carolina) make navigation by such antiquarian means imprecise. If you do not know where you are, you are likely to end up where you do not want to be. The consequence is grounding.

That ships often found themselves riding the dunes instead of the waves is not in question. It is the statistics that have been slewed over the years. *An Oceanographic Atlas of the Carolina Continental Margin* lists nearly 700 wrecks in North Carolina waters (although, some of those mentioned either never existed or occurred elsewhere.) The popular National Geographic chart sold in gift shops today looks impressive because a large ship silhouette is placed wherever a ship is suspected of having come ashore; the silhouettes are so close together that they appear to draw a solid line along the coast. Yet a count reveals only 300 named vessels.

By contrast, the incredible concentration of shipping in the New York/ New Jersey bight, where commerce has been funneled into New York harbor for more than three hundred years, has resulted in innumerable ships lost to marine casualty and the forces of nature. Deb Whitcraft has documented six *thousand* shipwrecks off the New Jersey shore alone. Even the Great Lakes can boast of more ships lost than North Carolina, with over 1,100 just in Lake Huron.

In the eighteen hundreds, local newspapers touted North Carolina as the "Graveyard of American Shipping" because of the number of tall ships that made it their last port of call. This descriptive phrase evolved into "Graveyard of the Atlantic," possibly borrowed from Sable Island—that shifting patch of sand off Nova Scotia—that goes by the same name. Then, David Stick immortalized the expression when he wrote a book with that title in 1952. The reputation stuck, and is now a cliche that sells charts and T-shirts. What was once a fresh notion has become banal by overuse. But then, advertising hype and commercialization are not known for originality of ideas. Glamor sells, and must therefore be perpetuated.

Despite these caviats that destroy the myth of numbers, there is no question that what wrecks there are make up in quality what they lack in quantity. The shipwrecks of North Carolina are among the most beautiful, most colorful, most inhabited of any on the east coast. Visibility ranges from great to spectacular. The chance of encounters with large marine animals is an exciting probability. The brightly-hued tropical fish that swarm in and around the wrecks create a kaleidoscopic panorama with hypnotic effect. North Carolina wrecks are not just hulls to explore, they are painted microcosms that should be experienced.

This profusion of marine life is natural to the area. Off the southern portion of the state, natural ledges—once littoral shores formed by lower water levels when much of the ocean was bound up in glaciers and polar floes during the Ice Age—stretch for miles. Drop-offs as high as ten or fifteen feet have created great colorful reefs that abound with fish. They are sportfishing and spearfishing paradises. Lobsters are the exception rather than the rule, but divers can find fossils—such as shells and jawbones—in the surrounding sand.

In order to encourage the growth of marine organisms in areas without naturally occurring ledges or ships sunk through catastrophe, the North Carolina Division of Marine Fisheries has developed an aggressive plan to establish artificial reefs by creating dumping grounds for non-degradable trash (such as railroad boxcars and concrete slabs) and by scuttling obsolete ships. The purpose of the program is to enhance sportfishing opportunities. Coincidentally, these sunken vessels present opportunities for exploration by diving enthusiasts. But this is a book about flesh and blood, not wood and steel. There is no human drama in these artificial reef wrecks, so they are not included within these pages.

Other wrecks not covered are the many blockade runners lost during the War of Secession. Quite a few of these fast steamships (driven by paddlewheels or screw propellers) hit the beach accidentally while evading the federal blockading squadron, or were forced ashore by naval gunfire as they attempted to run the gauntlet. There are dozens of such wrecks, some of whose upper parts protrude above the surface like iron tombstones. Their story would fill a book of its own. Because their remains lie in the surf zone they are exceptionally difficult to fish from small boats, and the mud and sand is usually so stirred up that divers must resort to feeling the wrecks rather than seeing them. Divers are free to explore these sites with the understanding that they are protected by the National Register of Historic Places, and that no artifacts may be saved from the sea. For more information visit the Underwater Archaeology Unit at Fort Fisher, Kure Beach.

Conspicuous by their absence are some wrecks whose names may be found in various publications as if they were real, or significant. Local belief is strong that during World War Two the tanker *Tennessee* was lost south of Cape Lookout, off Morehead City. In fact, it was the Army transport *Santa Rosa* that radioed that she had sighted a U-boat. No attack was made. But in accordance with standard operating procedure during the heyday of the U-boat blitz, nearby vessels retransmitted all sighting and distress calls in order to warn other merchantmen traversing the area. The *Tennessee* did so, but the message was garbled upon receipt, and for two days was carried in the Eastern Sea Frontier War Diary as torpedoed, presumed sunk. Later, researchers who read no further assumed that this was the case and perpetuated the notion of the lost tanker. The Enemy Action and Distress Diary for April 13, 1942 clears up the misconception: "S.S. *Tennessee* (our 0726 April 10) previously reported torpedoed, now reported safe. Arrived Delaware Capes 1945 April 12. Sailed Delaware Capes for New York 0630 April 13." (1945 and the other four digit numbers refer to military time, not the year.)

The Civil War paddlewheeler *Governor* is sometimes placed off Hatteras Inlet, but that ship actually went down off Georgetown, South Carolina. The *Amagansett* and the *Fenwick Island*, popular dive sites, are large fishing trawlers. The tug *Marjorie McAllister* sank on November 2, 1969. For several years divers visitied the wreck, and even recovered portholes and other souvenirs. Do not go looking for it today, however, for it was subsequently raised and towed to port. The *Ella Pierce Thurlow* is a schooner barge whose only claim to fame is that she has been tentatively identified; these dismasted sailing ships were towed as coal barges when steam propulsion came into its own. Hundreds of them litter the sea bed. For the most part they are uninteresting wooden snags, good for fishing and observing marine life.

The virtual absence of offshore snags is peculiar when compared, for example, to the New York bight. There, hundreds of "head" boats fish wrecks on a daily basis. In North Carolina the mainstream of sportfishing is for pelagic fish, or game fish, which do not congregate on wrecks but roam freely on the surface. Add to this the comparative sparsity of boating traffic and one can understand why the number of known wreck sites is relatively few. The loran list at the back of the book reflects this quantative difference. If it were not for the number of artificial reefs in the list, it would be meager indeed.

I have also included a loran list of "hang" numbers that were given to me by a couple of trawler captains. I have kept this list separate from the named wrecks because they are somewhat unverified. Trawl boats stay away from potential hangs, and circulate the positions among their fellow captains. They could be rock piles or natural geologic formations, the positions could be approximate (that is, dart board numbers), or they might not even exist. But they are worth checking out.

Beware of the UNC Sea Grant publication *Hangs and Obstructions to Trawl Fishing*. While the extensive collection of hang numbers was an admirable project, I am told time and time again by many experienced captains that the published numbers are totally unreliable, and that the list is virtually worthless for locating shipwrecks. I pass this caution on to the reader in search of unfound wrecks.

Much to-do has been made about the large schools of sand tiger sharks frequently observed on the wrecks off Ocracoke Island. For more on this topic I refer you to the chapter on the *Tarpon*.

The stories of some wrecks recounted in this book are interrelated to other wrecks lost elsewhere. For that reason I have noted in parentheses after the name of such a ship, in which volume of the Popular Dive Guide Series additional information may be found. A shipwreck is often not an isolated event, but a single thread woven into a vast tapestry. Only by standing back far enough to see all the fabric at once can one appreciate the grand design.

During my research in the National Archives I continuously came upon war records that were still stamped "Secret" and "Confidential." That I had to have these documents declassified was an indication that the files had never been accessed. Since primary source materials are vitally important for a book of this nature, it makes me wonder what sources other researchers have used.

In the preparation of this work there were people who showed me the way through official records, who helped provide information or sources, and who granted interviews. They are, in alphabetical order, Gina Akers, Laura Brown, Wynne Dough, Art Kirchner, Steve Lang, John McCarley, Bob McIver, Steve Nichols, Dewey Preast, George Purifoy, Bill Quinn, Hellen Shore, Wayne Strickland, Charlotte Valentine, Angie Vandereedt, Mike Walker, Anne Wilcox, and Barry Zerby. Thanks to all.

Erik Heyl drew this picture of the *Alliance* as the *Caledonia*. (From *Early American Steamships*)

ALLIANCE

Built: 1853

Previous names: *Caledonia*, USS *Mohawk*

Gross tonnage: 459

Type of vessel: Wooden-hulled propeller

Builder: Teas & Birely, Philadelphia, Pennsylvania

Owner: Latherby, Wickersham & Company; William M. Baird; Alexander Purvis; Charles Purvis; all of Philadelphia, Pennsylvania

Port of registry: Philadelphia, Pennsylvania

Cause of sinking: Ran aground

Location: One mile south of Hatteras Inlet

Sunk: March 4, 1869

Depth: Unknown

Dimensions: 162' × 24' × 12'

Power: Coal-fired steam

The *Alliance* entered service as the *Caledonia*, and was one of ten sister ships built to transport coal and freight along the northern east coast. With an average speed of six knots and a maximum of nine, she fit into this plodding route admirably. She went through four owners during the first five years of her career before being chartered by the U.S. Navy for an expedition to Paraguay. Afterward, the Navy took an option to purchase the vessel. The sale price of $23,459 was certainly no bargain since the ship had cost only $13,000 to build.

She was acquired on June 14, 1859, armed with five guns, and commissioned on September 19 as the USS *Mohawk*. The duty assigned to her was that of cruising for slave runners in the West Indies. It might seem that a steamer of such slow speed was not suited for chasing slavers. But steamers were at a premium in those days, and most ships pressed into the slave trade relied upon the wind for motive force. Indeed, within two months of her new assignment the *Mohawk* captured the brig *Cygnet* on her way from Baltimore to Africa for another human cargo. The *Mohawk* continued to ply Caribbean waters as a deterrent to the slave trade. On April 28, 1860 she captured the slave ship *Wildfire* in Old Bahama Channel; in the *Wildfire's* dark, smelly holds were 530 chained Africans on their way to Southern plantations.

At the outbreak of the Civil War the *Mohawk* was transferred to blockading duty along the eastern seaboard, principally off the coast of Florida. Now, instead of patrolling for slaves she kept a sharp watch for blockade runners bringing sorely needed goods and munitions to the beleaguered Confederates. Initially the *Mohawk's* armament consisted of six 32-pounders and a 24-pounder Howitzer, but in 1862 the Howitzer was replaced with a 30-pounder Parrott rifle.

Blockading duty for the most part was relatively boring. For the *Mohawk* it was even moreso. British built blockade runners were designed for speed, and against them the *Mohawk* was no match. Still, she managed to make one capture during her wartime career, the sloop *George B. Sloat*, which, being under sail, was closer in speed to that of the *Mohawk* than the paddlewheel steamships that usually outran her.

For reasons which Naval records fail to document, the *Mohawk* was decommissioned while the War of the Rebellion was still raging. She was disarmed, of course. On July 12, 1864 she was put up for public auction, and bought by a consortium of seven Philadelphia men. Her new owners renamed her *Alliance*.

Returning to freight service, for the next five years the *Alliance* ran between Boston, Massachusetts and Charleston, South Carolina. During that time four of her owners sold out of the consortium, while Lathbury, Wickersham & Company bought in.

Particulars of her loss are slim. According to *Early American Steamships*, by Erik Heyl, "In the night of March 4, 1869 en route from Boston to Charleston she went ashore about one mile south of Hatteras Inlet, N.C. The storm which had driven her onto the beach developed during the night into a full gale from the south-east and during the next day completely wrecked the hull. The wrecking steamer *Resolute* despatched to the site of the wreck returning to Norfolk, Va., on March 9, 1869 and reported her abandoned to the underwriters. The wrecking commissioners ordered that all materials saved from the wreck to be sold at auction on the beach on March 8, 1869; the salvage consisted of boots and shoes, bales of hay and a portion of the machinery."

The remainder of the *Alliance* lies patiently under the sand awaiting discovery.

Courtesy of the U.S. Coast Guard.

ARIO

Built: 1920
Previous names: None
Gross tonnage: 6,952
Type of vessel: Tanker
Builder: Bethlehem Ship Building Corp., Sparrow's Point, Maryland
Owner: Socony-Vacuum Oil Company
Port of registry: New York, NY
Cause of sinking: Torpedoed by *U-158* (Kapitanleutnant Rostin)
Location: 34-14N

Sunk: March 15, 1942
Depth: Unknown
Dimensions: 435′ × 56′ × 31′
Power: Oil-fired steam

76-08W

Because the *Ario* was steaming from New York to Corpus Christi during the height of U-boat activity, her voyage was anything but routine. Captain Thorolf Hennevig received routing instructions to "proceed from buoy to buoy, as close inshore at all times as safe navigation would permit." Although the *Ario's* tanks were empty the lumbering ship could never outrun a determined U-boat; nor did she have any guns with which to fight.

The night of March 14, 1942 found Second Officer Francis Doudreau standing watch atop the bridge as the *Ario* rounded Cape Lookout. Doudreau had been serving aboard the *Rochester* only six weeks before when she had been running from New York to Corpus Christi. The *Rochester* never made it because she had been torpedoed and sunk off the Virginia coast. This time Doudreau hoped to complete his cruise. Even though the skipper had already done so, Doudreau made doubly sure that the blackout rules were strictly enforced.

After passing the lighted buoy at Cape Lookout, Captain Hennevig ordered the helmsman to steer 235° true, and rang the engine room to get up to full speed. The *Ario* zigzagged at eleven knots. "The sea was calm, and the night dark but clear; visibility was excellent."

Shortly after one a.m., the lookout on the forecastle head "sighted a small vessel 200 to 300 yards off the ship's port bow. She was passing directly across the *Ario's* bow, port to starboard, at a speed of 15 knots, and from his point of vantage the lookout could not say whether she was a patrol craft or an enemy vessel. The skipper . . . ordered a right rudder for the ship, and sounded general quarters."

Five minutes later "a torpedo crashed into the tanker's starboard side at about the No. 9 tank. Quickly the engines were stopped as she began to list heavily to port." The radio operator sent a distress call, "giving the ship's position as 10 miles east of Cape Lookout."

Below decks, several crew members who were playing a late night poker game, "Ran for the lifeboats in such haste that they left a pot of more than $25 untouched on the table." However, "before the boats could be lowered, shells were poured into the tanker, not alone from the starboard but also from the port side. . . .

"In the midst of a sparkling array, the abandoning ship went forward in the blackness of the Atlantic night. The submarine on the starboard side, firing at a distance of less than 1,000 feet, lighted up the tanker with the flashes of gunfire. Both raiders used tracer shells and parachute flares of pinkish, reddish, deep orange hues as 35 of the *Ario's* crewmen of 36 left the ship in two lifeboats." Some men were forced to jump overboard for their lives.

Captain Hennevig estimated that "the shelling lasted for ten minutes and that each submarine fired about fifty shots." One shell "shot away the falls of the No. 1 lifeboat. Another struck the No. 3 boat aft, setting it afire and dropping it and its occupants into the water. . . .

"Men in the No. 1 boat proceeded to pick up those who had jumped and those who had escaped the flames in the No. 3 boat. Two bodies of men who had died of shock were pulled from the water. Of the others from the shelled boat, many were injured. One of these died later in a Charleston hospital of wounds in his skull and body; at least two of the five missing men were believed killed when the shell hit the boat."

Still aboard the *Ario* was the assistant engineer. At daybreak he launched a raft, and at 7 a.m. he was picked up by the U.S. destroyer *Du Pont* (DD–152). Shortly thereafter, the *Du Pont* came upon the *Ario's* lifeboat; she took off the men and cared for the wounded.

Then, "A boarding party consisting of the skipper, first and second officers, chief engineer and some seamen reboarded the *Ario* at 0930 to secure her instruments, codes, and secret papers." They also hoped to save the ship, but she was too badly holed and in imminent danger of sinking with the men still aboard. "When the party left the *Ario* for the last time (at approximately 1000) they had a chance to view the damage done by Axis shells. Several large holes were visible along both sides of the vessel—one by the No. 2 tank, two abaft amidships, one in the engine room on the starboard side, one in the No. 6 tank. Small holes could be seen at the engine room on the port side, and the ship's smokestack was badly perforated. The boarding party made its last exit directly from the lower deck to the waiting motor launch. When they last saw the *Ario*, she was still above water.''

The final death toll was eight. Three months later, insurance underwriters paid $94,900 for constructive total loss of the hull.

According to official documents, the ''Navy Salvage Service of New York reported to the owners of the *Ario* on April 28, that from information received it was doubtful the vessel could be raised. Coastal Information lists the present position of the ship as 34-14N; 76-08W.'' A photograph purporting to be the *Orio* (note spelling) shows two masts in the distance sticking out of the water; the position given in the caption is 34-37N/79-19W (about sixty miles inland, on I-95; I have seen smashed up cars on the highway but never shot up ships.) A revised estimation identified the *Ario* as the wreck later determined to be the *Dixie Arrow* (q.v.). Finally, in 1944, the USCG *Gentian* located a wreck at 34-19N/76-27W which ''is believed to be that of the tanker *Ario*'' because ''it is located about ten miles along the line of reasonable drift from the attack position, and less than five miles from the position at which she was last sighted afloat. Unfortunately the survey was made on a day when high winds and heavy seas impeded Sonar work and made underwater photography impossible.''

Plotting this latter position in light of today's knowledge, it appears that the *Gentian* actually located the *Bedfordshire*. The meaning of all this contradictory information is open to interpretation. The wreck of the *Ario* has not yet been found.

Erich Rostin and the *U-158* also sank the *Caribsea* and the *John D. Gill*, described in this volume. On its next patrol, the *U-158* was lost with all hands, including two captured merchant marine officers, in the Gulf of Mexico.

Courtesy of Mobil Oil, via Anne Willeman.

ARIOSTO

Built: 1887
Previous names: None
Gross tonnage: 2,920
Type of vessel: Freighter
Builder: Russell & Company, Greenock, Scotland
Owner: Ariosto Steam Ship Company, Ltd. (R. McAndrew & Company)
Port of registry: Glasgow, England
Cause of sinking: Ran aground
Location: 2 miles south of the Ocracoke Life-Saving Station

Sunk: December 24, 1899
Depth: 15 feet
Dimensions: 320' × 40' × 19'
Power: Coal-fired steam

On the morning of Christmas Eve most people have thoughts of remaining home with their families, of stockings hanging above the fireplace, of turkey dinner on the table, of warmth, good cheer, and the prospect of happy times soon to be shared with friends and loved ones. Not so for the men of the merchant marine, whose duty calls them to sea without regard for holidays. It is a lonely life that beckons them to the far reaches of the world so that those more fortunate can go to the store and purchase food and clothing so often taken for granted. Those hardy sailors, those rugged men of iron, suffer through heat and cold, through rain and snow, through storm-tossed seas, all to deliver cargoes to landlubbers who comprehend not what travails may overtake the wayward mariner, who think little of lives that often end on some lonely foreign strand.

In the early morning hours of Christmas Eve, 1899, as most people still lay snug in their beds, the thirty men on the *Ariosto* were encountering heavy frigid showers and a pounding sea. The British freighter's holds were filled with wheat, lumber, cotton, and cotton-seed meal that she had picked up in Galveston, Texas. The ship was bound for Norfolk, Virginia to recoal before making the long Atlantic crossing for Hamburg, Germany.

Captain R.R. Baines, master of the *Ariosto*, was lying down in the chart room when he heard the telegraph bells ringing. It was 3:45 a.m. As he dashed into the wheelhouse he bumped into the second mate, who was coming to get him. Despite the dim lights of the bridge Captain Baines could see the fear reflected in the mate's eyes. When he looked through the windows he saw that the ship was entirely surrounded by white water.

Since the order had already been given to reverse engines, there was little more to do other than listen to the strain of the pistons. The propeller churned up the sea and fought to bring the ship to a halt. But heavily laden freighters do not stop quickly. Despite the working engines and the madly spinning propeller, the ship's forward momentum carried it relently forward until the hull grounded out on the sandy bottom. There the *Ariosto* remained, as Captain Baines put it, "bumping and thumping in such a manner that it seemed probable her masts would come down."

"All hands on deck!" went the command. Ascertaining at once that their predicament was hopeless, Captain Baines ordered distress rockets fired.

At the same time Surfman Guthrie, bundled in woolen clothing and huddled in his rain hat, southwester, and rubber boots, plowed through the soft wet sand of Ocracoke Island. He was not beachcombing, however, or out on a midnight mid-winter stroll in order to enjoy the fury of the storm. He was a member of the United States Life-Saving Service, and he was patrolling the desolate beach for signs of vessels in distrees. Despite the wind and whipping rain he kept an ever-vigilant eye turned toward the sea. Thus he saw at once the *Ariosto's* signal of distress. He immediately pulled out a Coston flare, ignited it, and held it high over his head.

Courtesy of the Outer Banks History Center, Manteo.

Said Captain Baines, "While still firing, a red flash was seen in the north, which was taken to be from some source whence assistance might come."

An official investigation later resolved that, "Believing his ship to be among the Diamond Shoals, the master feared she might work off into one of the numerous deep holes or channels and founder there, and besides he was seriously worried by the fact that the heavy seas on the starboard side broke away the three starboard boats, while the ship was constantly heeling over to the starboard, making the destruction of the boats on the port side likely to take place at any moment. He therefore held a consultation with the chief officer, which resulted in a determination to launch the port boats. Here was where the fatal mistake occurred. Signals indicating that assistance would be afforded from the shore had already been seen and correctly interpreted. As subsequent events proved, to a demonstration, if all had simply stood by the ship every soul would have been rescued by the life-saving crews. Nevertheless, it must be remembered that Captain Baines supposed his vessel to be stranded on the Diamond Shoals, a place of extreme danger, so far from shore that he might well have doubted the ability of any boat to reach her, and of course miles beyond the range of any life-saving gun or rocket. Having in view these facts, it may not be a matter of great surprise that he should deem it the part of wisdom to save his two remaining boats and man them alongside until the dawn of day should make it possible to determine his true position and the proper course of action then to be taken.

"This he asserts to have been his purpose. Accordingly the pinnace was first got out and manned by eleven men, including the chief and second mates, who were placed in charge with instructions to 'get away clear' and then lie by until daylight. As soon as the pinnace cleared the ship the lifeboat was successfully put over and manned by fifteen men. Twenty-six persons were now in the boats, while there still remained on the ship four others who were also to go in the lifeboat. These were Captain Baines, Third Officer Reed, Chief Engineer Warren, and Carpenter Peltonen. Fortunately for them the lifeboat got away before they could embark in it. To this providential accident, which probably then seemed to them the worst of ill luck, they owed their lives. It would appear that these entire operations were conducted with such haste that they were completed in less than thirty minutes from the moment the vessel stranded. Meantime she was entirely intact (as indeed she remained for several days) and the life-savers were constantly firing signals of assurance that aid would be afforded. It would therefore hardly seem unreasonable to suppose that the officers of the *Ariosto* should have realized that they were on the shore and not on the Diamond Shoals. However, the boats were now afloat, and the entire crew in them, save four men. In obedience to the master's instructions they lay under the lee of the ship, the men at the oars backing and pulling to keep them head to the waves. It was an awful position, the sea constantly growing rougher and rougher, while the suction of the water around the bows and stern of the steamer was getting to be irresistible."

Meanwhile, the life-savers were doing more than just setting off flares. Surfman Guthrie ran all the way back to the Ocracoke Life-Saving Station and roused the crew from their sleep. In moments they were galvanized into action. Keeper James Howard "having gained some ocular information of the status of affairs, at once set the international code signal 'M K' (Remain by your ship)."

Howard realized that the surfboats could not be launched through the towering combers crashing upon the shore. He ordered the crew to get the

beach apparatus, but, "as soon as they started from the Station the front shaft broke off the beach cart which detained him about one half hour as it was necessary to transfer the gear to the other carts." Then they had to drag the beach apparatus two miles over the sand to a point opposite the stranded steamer. "The hurricane of August 16–18 had cut an inlet, and the keeper was obliged to secure the aid of five citizens in the vicinity to help his crew get the gear to the wreck." Then they set up the Lyle gun and faking box, and fired a shot at the *Ariosto's* still-burning masthead light.

By that time, however, two thirds of the steamship's crew were already dead.

First the lifeboat was dragged by the current into the breakers, where it overturned. Then the pinnace was capsized by waves next to the ship. "Twenty-six persons were now battling for their lives in one of the worst seas with which desperate men have ever contended." With incredible strength and will to survive, Seaman Elsing swam to shore and dragged himself up onto the beach. Two other men, C. Peterson and C. Saline, managed to beat their way back to the ship where they grabbed onto dangling boat tackle and were hauled on board.

Imagine the surprise of the life-saving crew when they pulled in that first shot, which had fallen short of the ship, and found a man clinging to it for dear life. Boatswain Andersen was indeed lucky, for, as his companions drowned all around him, the line shot toward the ship fell directly across his back. He wrapped the line around his arm, then passed out. He was pulled in like a hooked fish, unconscious and more dead than alive. He was resuscitated by the life-saving crew, whereupon he told them about the others who had been dumped out of his boat.

Wrote Keeper Howard: "Then proceeded to look after the men in the surf as he observed some more struggling in the breakers; saving another man by forming a line and running into the surf and pulling out of the water three other men who were found lifeless. Tried efforts to restore them to life but all was unavailing." The other man saved was Fireman Henroth, and he only because the life-savers went into the freezing water up to their necks to pull him out.

The dim light of dawn played down upon the scene of such awful tragedy. There were now three men safely ashore and six still on the ship. Because of her deep draft the freighter had grounded some six hundred yards from shore. With a southwest breeze forming a head wind the shot from the Lyle gun kept falling short. The rising tide ate up the beach, forcing the life-saving crew to retreat to higher ground with the apparatus— farther away from the target. Every time a shot was fired, the crew had to pull in the line, carefully clean the sand off it, and fake it back into the box. The life-saving crew was soon exhausted. The crew from the Durants Station arrived and relieved them. Shot after shot was fired, but the wind beat each one back. Finally, one man ran back to the station to get a thicker line. By this time the ship had worked another two hundred yards closer to the beach. This coupled with a larger measure of powder and a thicker line made the necessary difference. At nine o'clock a messenger line flew across the freighter's heaving deck.

Fearing that the line was so light it would break while pulling in the hawser, it was used only to haul in a heavier line, which in turn was used to haul in a still heavier line, which then was used to haul in a whip line. Only then could the hawser be pulled aboard the *Ariosto* and secured so the breeches buoy could be gotten out to the ship. At eleven o'clock the first man from the *Ariosto* reached shore.

Help arrived from Hatteras village in the form of eight willing men "who rendered valuable assistance." The laborious task of pulling in the breeches buoy needed every available hand. Now the crashing waves forced the ship to roll from side to side. A taut line would threaten to part, or go slack and dump the breeches buoy with its occupant into the frigid sea. The rescuers constantly rerigged the tackle as the ship wallowed and was driven in closer.

They pulled in one man at a time until 2:30 in the afternoon when the last of the six, Captain Baines, put his foot on terra firma. One of the most dramatic rescues in the history of the Life-Saving Service was over.

Four more bodies were recovered that day, and all were "given Christian burial." During the weeks that followed, the bodies of men from the *Ariosto* continued to wash up at various places along the barrier islands. The Durants life-savers found one on December 27, and two more on January 12. Also on January 12 one body came ashore near the Ocracoke Station, and another at Creeds Hill. On January 22 the Portsmouth Station reported recovering "the body of a man in advanced stage of decomposition and buried it in the sand hills about 6 miles S. of the station."

These were seafaring men who had fared their last sea. The century turned without them.

After the storm subsided and salvage vessels reached the site the *Ariosto* was found to have withstood fairly well the pounding of the storm. Salvors lightered as much cargo as possible. By January 16 all 2,816 bales of cotton had been removed. Lloyd's reported that the "grain and cottonseed cake is being jettisoned," no doubt ruined by salt water. The last of the lumber was removed on January 23. Of a cargo valued at a million and a half dollars, half was saved.

An inspection proved that the vessel was still intact. Intermittant winter storms kept the Merritt Wrecking Company's salvage tugs from serious work. On February 1, the tug *Rescue* moved alongside and pumped out the flooded holds; at that point there was still hope that the hull could be salvaged. But the winds kept blowing, forcing temporary abandonment. By February 14 the ship had been driven so far up onto the beach that it became impossible to pull her off. The wrecking company then stripped the ship of everything of value.

On March 28, 1900 the *Ariosto* was sold at public auction. Prior to grounding she had been worth over a hundred thousand dollars. The wreck sold for $305.

Steve Lang says that the *Ariosto* is known as the Styron's Hill Wreck, and that it is completely broken up. The wreck is not a grave site, but it *is* a monument to the heroism that took place on one Christmas Eve when some men died and others lived to tell about it.

Skate.

ARROYO

Built: 1890   Sunk: February 20, 1910
Previous names: None   Depth: Unknown
Gross tonnage: 3,564   Dimensions: 340' × 43' × 26'
Type of vessel: Freighter   Power: Coal-fired steam
Builder: R. Stephenson & Company Ltd., Newcastle, England
Owner: Arroyo Steam Ship Company (Gow, Harrison & Co.)
Port of registry: Glasgow, Scotland
Cause of sinking: Ran aground
Location: Five miles south of the Portsmouth Life-Saving Station

A fog lay upon the coast like a pall. For three days Captain L.L. Lawrence, master of the *Arroyo*, had been unable to make navigational observations. He steered his ship by dead reckoning as he crept along the coast from Santiago de Cuba, bound for Philadelphia with a load of iron ore. The Gulf Stream must have carried him northward faster than he had calculated. He had not yet made the wide, sweeping turn to the east in order to round the Diamond Shoals when without warning the ship grounded hard. The time was 11:10 on the night of February 20, 1910. The tide was at flood high.

Because of the weight of her cargo the ship drew nearly her full draft. She stranded some 550 yards offshore. There was no panic on board, nor was the ship in imminent danger. As the hours passed and the tide receded, the *Arroyo* found herself inextricably stuck.

The ship was not visible from shore due to the thick fog. At 7:30 in the morning Captain Lawrence sounded his steam whistle. The deep throated howl traveled through the dense atmosphere with such speed that, although it immediately alerted the life-saving crew at the Portsmouth Station, none could tell from which direction it came—from the sea or the sound.

Surfman Homer Horris went out on horseback to inspect the beach. He rode south as far as ten miles, but due to the fog saw nothing untoward. On his way back, however, as the fog slowly lifted, he discovered the stranded steamer some five miles from the station. He wasted no time reporting her predicament to the station keeper.

Rescue operations commenced at once. The beach apparatus was hauled to a point opposite the ship, the Lyle gun was set up, and the anchor set deep in the sand. By this time it was afternoon. Wrote the keeper: "Made five unsuccessful shots and lost four projectiles by the powder burning the line from the shot after it was wet well in water before the line was made fast in the shank of the shot. I then saw that there was no chance of getting a line on board, so I sent the crew back to the house after the self bailing SurfBoat.''

Meanwhile, Captain Lawrence took matters into his own hands. The sea was calm, so there seemed no reason to waste the life-savers' time and energy. In an orderly manner the crew launched the *Arroyo's* lifeboats and rowed ashore, taking direction from the life-saving crew as to the best place to land. All thirty men arrived safely.

The *Arroyo's* crew were put up at the Portsmouth Life-Saving Station for the next week, being served in all "552 meals." During that time there was a constant flurry of activity regarding the ship. The life-saving crew made half a dozen trips through the surf in order to bring back the steamer crew's personal effects. Captain Albert Lewis, the underwriter's agent, inspected the vessel for insurance purposes. The wrecking tug *Alexander Jones* arrived from Southport to see what could be done about pulling the *Arroyo* off the bar. By February 23 the ship was reported "strained and leaking."

Ultimately, mother nature took control of the situation. Strong winds whipped up a seething sea that pounded interminably against the steel hull. The ship was forced broadside to the waves. On March 10 the underwriter reported, "Hull broken up in three sections, breaking up and settling, further salvage useless." Both ship (worth $126,360) and cargo (worth $316,870) were written off as a total loss.

The wreck of the *Arroyo* has not been identified. It lies in a shallow sandy grave off Portsmouth Island. Today, the town of Portsmouth is abandoned and the island is part of the Cape Lookout National Seashore. No one lives there.

ASHKHABAD

Built: 1917   Sunk: April 29, 1942
Previous names: *Dneprostroi, Kutais, Mistley Hall, Aldersgate, Milazzo,*
                War Hostage   Depth: 55 feet
Gross tonnage: 5,284   Dimensions: 400' × 52' × 28'
Type of vessel: Tanker   Power: Oil-fired steam
Builder: Harland & Wolff, Glasgow, Scotland
Owner: U.S.S.R.
Port of registry: Odessa, Russia
Cause of sinking: Torpedoed by *U-402* (Kapitanleutnant von Forstner)
Location: 27037.1   39617.6

Contrary to policy in the U.S. merchant marine, Soviet ships often had female crew members. The *Ashkhabad* was no exception. Among the forty-seven Russians aboard the tanker were three women who comprised the steward's department.

The *Ashkhabad* was originally built as a freighter, but had been converted for carrying fuel oil: a much needed commodity on the Russian front. "Leaving Vladivostock on September 23, 1941, the tanker sailed to Seattle, where two 3-inch guns were obtained which were later installed at New Orleans. In addition to this armament, the ship carried two .30-caliber Lewis machine guns on the bridge and two on the poop deck."

On April 26, 1942 she left New York for Matanzas, Cuba, "in ballast, with only 1000 tons of fuel oil in the deep tanks forward of the No. 4 hold. The night of April 29 was clear, the weather good, and a full moon permitted a visibility of six miles. The HMS *Lady Elsa* was acting as escort." She plied a zigzag course in accordance with U.S. Navy routing instructions.

This picture of the *Ashkhabad* was taken two days after the sinking. (Courtesy of the National Archives.)

At 9:50 p.m., the *Lady Elsa* spotted a U-boat some five hundred yards off the tanker's starboard beam. She fired a single round from her 4-inch gun and forced the enemy to submerge, but not before it got off its deadly fish. One minute later the *Ashkhabad* "was struck by one torpedo on the starboard side below the water line in the vicinity of No. 4 hold."

None of the *Ashkhabad's* nine men on watch ("two on the bridge, one on the forecastle, and six members of the naval gun crew on the poop deck") saw the U-boat prior to the attack. "The concussion of the explosion strewed the deck with wreckage; the No. 4 hold, the deep tank, and the engine room were flooded by water which entered through the shaft alley. The engines were stopped and, although the ship had no water-tight bulkheads, only the stern sank until the decks were awash up to the forward part of the bridge. The bow and forward part of the bridge remained afloat."

There was no panic aboard the half-sunk tanker. Since the stern gun was underwater, the gun crew rushed to the forward .30-caliber gun and "fired three quick rounds at the submarine which had partially surfaced about 500 yards off the starboard beam." They scored no hits.

An hour later Captain Alexy Pavlovitch, master, placed all confidential codes in a weighted box and sank them. Then, sadly, he gave the order to abandon ship. In an orderly manner the crew lowered two lifeboats and a raft, and awaited rescue by the *Lady Elsa*. The Russian crew was taken to Morehead City. There were no injuries.

At this point the *Ashkhabad* might have been salvaged were it not for a series of military snafus. (Snafu—situation normal, all fouled up.) "At 1000 the next morning, a boarding party from the HMS *Hertfordshire*, a British armed trawler, went aboard the crippled vessel and salvaged part of her equipment." "Pilfer" might be a more appropriate word, since what they took were valuable navigational instruments and considerable amounts of clothing.

Five hours later the *Ashkhabad's* captain (this time given as Yaskevitch on the same official document as the one that previously called him Pavlovitch), some of his crew, and a Fifth Naval District Intelligence Officer, returned to the ship and discovered the loss. The *Hertfordshire* had already absconded with the loot.

The next day the Russians returned again to their ship, this time catching the British in the act. The *Hertfordshire* was tied up to the tanker, and her men were relieving the Russian ship of all loose items. Apparently, they had not been told that the *Ashkhabad* was not a derelict, and that salvage tugs were on the way. They returned what they had previously taken.

The *Ashkhabad* rode easily on her anchor. Because her condition appeared to be stable there was every reason to believe that she could be refloated. But word still had not gotten out that she was awaiting salvage. On the evening of May 3 the U.S. destroyer *Semmes* (DD-189) fired three

The *Ashkhabad* on May 1, 1942. (Courtesy of the National Archives.)

rounds from her 3-inch gun "in accordance with standing orders to sink all wrecks which might be menaces to navigation." The midship superstructure caught fire.

Attracted to the flames like a moth to a light, the HMS *St. Zeno* proceeded toward the Russian ship. One wonders whether the next action was taken out of malice. "A shell was fired at the burning ship by the *St. Zeno*, after authorization had been received from the commanding officer of the *Hertfordshire*, who was in command of all British trawlers at Morehead City. The latter explained that he had authorized the firing in the belief that the *St. Zeno* might sink the *Ashkhabad* and extinguish the fire, which he considered a menace to a large convoy expected in that vicinity."

By the time the Navy salvage tug *Relief* arrived on the scene the vessel was a total loss. Siegfried von Forstner wound up with the tonnage credit, although perhaps it should be shared with the USS *Semmes*, the HMS *St. Zeno*, and the HMS *Hertfordshire*.

These pictures were taken after the *Ashkhabad* was shelled and caught fire. Both views show the nearly total destruction of the midship wheelhouse; only the bridgewings are left standing. Notice the depth charges in the racks of the vessel from which the pictures were taken. (Both courtesy of the National Archives.)

Because it presented a hazard to navigation, the wreck was marked by a quick flashing green buoy. In 1943 it was demolished by explosives, and again in 1944, "to a depth in excess of 40 feet."

The *Ashkhabad* lies on the finger of a shoal; the bottom is deeper on both sides. As would be expected after being blown up twice, the wreck is pretty well broken up; nevertheless, it makes for a picturesque dive. Tropical fish are prevalent among the coral, sponge, and sea fans.

The hull shows a distinct waist; upper hull plates were laid out flat and have sunk beneath the sand. There is no sign of the engine—it was probably blasted apart, and its remains lie under encrusted rubble. Two large boilers sit close to the stern. Fifty feet of open space and sand separate the boilers from the next discernible debris, where the cross ribbing becomes evident. The starboard waist disappears about one hundred feet short of the bow, while the port waist rises three feet off the bottom all the way to the anchor chain. The wreck has a tendancy to "come and go" due to shifting sand.

If the identity of the *Ashkhabad* had not been so well established there would have been considerable doubt about the wreck's name when Mike Sheen recovered the ship's bell, for inscribed in Cyrillic letters was the name *Chelyuskinets*. No one knows why.

Kapitanleutnant Siegfrieg von Forstner turned the *U-402* for home after sinking the *Ashkhabad*. On the way he chanced upon the USS *Cythera* (PY-26), a 215-foot patrol boat. Two torpedoes sent her to the bottom so quickly that only two crew members got away from the sinking vessel. Forstner surfaced his sub and rescued them both, then took them to Germany where they were interned for the duration of the war. This was a switch for the *Cythera*. On two separate occasions during the First World War she had picked up survivors from Allied merchant ships torpedoed by U-boats.

In October 1943, the *U-402* was depth-charged by a plane from the U.S. aircraft carrier *Card* (CVE-11). It went down with all hands.

The date on the original print was May 29, 1942: one month after the *Ashkhabad* was sunk. Although the smokestack is gone, two ventilators are still standing. The circle in the lower left corner is the bow gun tub. (Courtesy of the National Archives.)

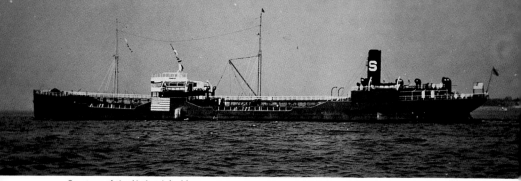

Courtesy of the National Archives.

ATLAS

Built: 1916
Previous names: *Sunoil*
Gross tonnage: 7,137
Type of vessel: Tanker

Sunk: April 9, 1942
Depth: 125 feet
Dimensions: 430' × 58' × 33'
Power: Oil-fired steam

Builder: William Cramp & Sons Ship & Engine Building Co., Philadelphia
Owner: Socony-Vacuum Oil Company
Port of registry: New York, NY
Cause of sinking: Torpedoed by *U-552* (Oberleutnant zur See Topp)
Location: 27023.6   39721.5

The night of April 8–9 was a fiery one off the eastern seaboard. As many as four U-boats were creating havoc among the merchant fleet, five ships were sunk, and thirty-three lives were lost. Off the northern Florida coast Hardegen in the *U-123* took out the *Esparta*; Lassen in the *U-160* sank the *Malchace* (q.v.); Mutzelberg in the *U-203* accounted for the *San Delfino*; and that ace among aces Erich Topp dispatched both the *Atlas* and the *Tamaulipas* (q.v.) within hours of each other.

Captain Hamilton Gray paced the decks of the *Atlas* in great consternation. Since he had begun this voyage he had received three sets of routing instructions, all different. U-boat activity approaching the Diamond Shoals was intense, and his ship was unarmed. The only protection he had was the darkness of night, and the hope that his blacked-out ship could blend in with the thin haze that hovered over the gentle ocean swells. He was responsible for his ship, his crew, and 83,000 barrels of gasoline bound from Houston, Texas to Seawarren, New Jersey. No other vessels were within sight.

Without warning, a torpedo struck the No. 6 tank on the starboard side amidships. "The Captain stopped the engines and at once ordered the lifeboats lowered. The men were calm. They had had frequent boat drills. Abandonment was completed by the entire crew of thirty-four in three lifeboats only seven or eight minutes after the attack."

It was good that Captain Gray wasted no time, for the men had just pulled away from the stricken tanker when they spotted a U-boat on the surface barely three hundred yards away. The men watched in horror as an eerie, irridescent wake sped toward their ship. The second torpedo exploded in almost the same spot as the first. Instantly the ship erupted in flames as gushing gasoline was ignited by the blast. As the gasoline spread outward, the sea became a fluid, fiery cauldron.

The men rowed furiously. One lifeboat was overtaken and surrounded by burning oil. "The eleven men in this lifeboat leaped overboard in an attempt to escape the flames. Several were badly burned and a little later, when the boat had drifted out of the danger zone and its flames had been extinguished, it was found that two men—the third mate and a seaman— had been lost. The other nine reboarded the lifeboat. No. 3 boat held nine men and No. 4 fourteen."

Due to an equipment failure after the first blast, no distress call had been sent. "The three lifeboats moved toward shore from the burning tanker and at 0700, when about six miles from the scene of the attack, all three boats were picked up by Coast Guard patrol boats," and taken to the Section Base at Morehead City, already swollen with the men from the *Tamaulipas*. "Five of the survivors were sent to the hospital, suffering from burns of varying degrees, some serious."

When last seen, "the *Atlas* was enveloped in flame from stem to stern, though still afloat." When she sank is unknown, but where was definitely established by the survey vessel *Anton Dohrn*, which located the wreck on June 9, "standing upright in 116' of water. 32–55' above ocean bed. Oil slick showing."

The wreck appears broken into three pieces, each within swimming distance from the adjacent piece but often, due to visibility less than fifty

The *Atlas* spurning great quantities of smoke into the atmosphere. (Courtesy of the National Archives.)

feet, not necessarily in sight. Because the sections are fairly well intact with the hull and bulkheads still standing, the decks climb to a depth of 90 feet.

Sand built up around the stern has buried the propeller. The upright rudder post looks like a support holding up the fantail. The interior compartments forward of here are exciting to explore because of the various deck levels accessible to the curious diver, and because of the proliferation of machinery and attendant brassware found in the rooms.

Part of the stern section rests against the engine, which is exposed under an overhang. From here it is possible to enter the machine shop and see lathes, anvils, cups of grease, and dies and taps. The depth at the top of the engine is 115 feet. Forward of the engine the deck juts up to 90 feet, then drops to the sand for a short distance, then, except for cracks and rust slits climbs back up to 90 feet all the way to the bow. The midship and forward sections consist mostly of big empty tanks with ladders visible inside the hatches. Part of the port side has collapsed inward. A debris field extends away from the wreck in the midship area, and is a good place to fan the sand for wheelhouse items.

During his seven day shooting spree in the Eastern Sea Frontier, Erich Topp sank six ships and was responsible for the deaths of fifty seamen. The woeful tales of the *Tamaulipas* and the *British Splendour* are covered elsewhere in this volume. For the *Lansing* and the *Byron D. Benson* see *Shipwrecks of North Carolina: from the Diamond Shoals North.* For the *David H. Atwater* see *Shipwrecks of Virginia.*

Topp and his boat survived the war.

This photograph of the sunken *Atlas* was taken by an underwater camera lowered and fired remotely from the survey vessel *Anton Dohrn*. The shiny object at right center is the back of the flash reflector. Note the lack of marine growth on the wreck. (Courtesy of Lamar Worzel.)

This view of a sister ship shows more detail than available photographs of the *Bedfordshire*. The *Bedfordshire* did not have the large trawl drum shown on the stern deck. (Courtesy of the National Archives.)

BEDFORDSHIRE

Built: 1935
Previous names: None
Gross tonnage: 443
Type of vessel: Converted armed trawler
Builder: Smith's Dock Company, South Bank, Middlesborough, England
Armament: One 4-inch gun, one machine gun, depth charges
Owner: British navy
Cause of sinking: Torpedoed by *U-558* (Kapitanleutnant Krech)
Location: 27048.6

Sunk: May 12, 1942
Depth: 105 feet
Dimensions: 162′ × 26′ × 14′
Power: Coal-fired steam

39562.1

Because England was thickly embroiled in the war against Germany and sorely needed every ship she could get in order to protect the home isles, the United States agreed to lend to England for the duration of hostilities fifty outdated, World-War-One-era destroyers and ten Lake class Coast Guard cutters in exchange for ninety-nine year leases on sites in the Bahamas, Antigua, Jamaica, St. Lucia, Trinidad, and British Guiana, for the establishment of U.S. military bases. This trade permitted the U.S. to aide the Allied war effort while maintaining a facade of quasi-neutrality. The "destroyer for military base deal" became known as Lend-Lease.

At that time the U.S. did not need an extensive fleet of naval ships because, although sentiment was with the Allies, her political stance did not permit her to openly engage the Axis powers. The situation changed dramatically when Japan bombed Pearl Harbor. The U.S. declared war against Japan and her allies, Germany and Italy, and overnight found herself without adequate floating defenses.

Within a month Germany sent its first barrage of U-boats to the U.S. east coast (Operation Drumbeat), and found a "happy hunting ground" serenely unprotected. During the first six months of 1942, German U-boats wreaked havoc along the eastern seaboard, sinking tankers and freighters on an almost daily basis. The Eastern Sea Frontier (ESF) was hard pressed to protect the merchant fleet because most Naval warships were needed to escort convoys and troop transports on the way to the British Isles.

To help alleviate the strain on American defenses, England sent to the States two dozen armed trawlers and their British crews. These were fishing trawlers that had their trawl gear replaced with depth-charge racks, and that were armed with deck guns and small arms; the refrigerated holds once filled with fish now became magazines.

The command structure for these armed British trawlers was somewhat nebulous. While each individual trawler was under British command, and was operated in accordance with British standards, the ships received their orders from U.S. Naval authorities. This double standard presents a nightmare for the historian and researcher because neither country maintained records on activities, each country deeming that it was the other's responsibility.

The *Bedfordshire* witnessed the reality of U-boat activity soon after her arrival on the U.S. east coast. On the morning of April 14 she provided protection for the USS *Roper* (DD-147), the destroyer that had just sunk the *U-85* off Nags Head, North Carolina, while the bodies of German sailors were recovered from the water. (For full particulars see *Shipwrecks of North Carolina: from the Diamond Shoals North*.)

Under the command of Lieutenant R.B. Davis, the *Bedfordshire* patrolled an area that stretched from Norfolk, Virginia to Cape Lookout, North Carolina. She escorted ships and convoys around the Diamond Shoals (a spot known at the time as Torpedo Alley because of the number of ships attacked in the vicinity by German U-boats) and conducted solo antisubmarine warfare patrols. During one of her stays in port at Morehead City the beginning of a strange coincidence occurred. The incident is related by L. Vanloan Naisawald in his book, *In Some Foreign Field*.

Aycock Brown was a civilian investigator for the Office of Naval Intelligence (ONI). His duties were to identify "personnel washed ashore or recovered at sea, as well as the collection and analysis of any intelligence gained from bodies and debris. He had recently had the task of identifying four bodies recovered from the surf above Nags Head as being from the British tanker *San Delfino*, torpedoed on 9 April." (See *Shipwrecks of North Carolina: from the Diamond Shoals North*.)

Since the bodies were to be interred in American soil, U.S. Naval authorities thought it would be appropriate to use British flags for the burial rites. Brown visited the *Bedfordshire*, asked for the officer of the deck, and was introduced to black-bearded Sub-Lieutenant Thomas Cunningham. Brown explained his mission. Cunningham acquiesced to Brown's sentiments and took him to the wardroom, where the flags were kept. There they also had a drink of rum (British tars were given a daily ration) and exchanged pleasantries. Afterward, Cunningham gave Brown not just the four Union Jacks he asked for, but two extras.

This view of the *Bedfordshire* prior to conversion shows her with a stern mast. (Courtesy of the Virginia Beach Life-Saving Station.)

The *Bedfordshire* pulled out that night to resume her coastal patrol. During the next several weeks she returned to Morehead City whenever she needed coal and supplies. Although the U-boat war was going hot and heavy the *Bedfordshire* managed to miss most of it. She was sitting comfortably in port on May 9 when the U.S. Coast Guard cutter *Icarus* sank the *U-352* (q.v.) only twenty miles away.

One engagement she did not miss, unfortunately, was with the *U-558*. On the night of May 12, Kapitanleutnant Gunther Krech was operating in the *Bedfordshire's* patrol zone. Krech had not had any successful kills in the ESF, the area from Maine to Georgia described at the time by German U-boatmen as "the great American turkey shoot." Otherwise, he may not have elected to expend a valuable torpedo intended for a fat freighter or heavily laden tanker on a lowly fishing trawler. But he did. The "eel" struck the *Bedfordshire* squarely amidships and caused such an explosion that the trawler was lifted right out of the sea; she came down like a pile of pick-up sticks and disappeared beneath the waves. The *U-558* submerged and slunk away to avoid possible retribution. It avoided retribution for more than a year, until July 20, 1943, when it was sunk in the Bay of Biscay by Allied bombers. Krech was badly wounded during the engagement, but he and four other men survived the sinking; they were captured by the Canadian destroyer *Athabascan*.

What of the men from the *Bedfordshire*? The explosion had been so sudden and so violent that no message of the disaster was transmitted. As far as anyone ashore knew, the trawler was still on patrol and maintaining radio silence. Not until two days later were suspicions aroused about her possible fate.

About seven o'clock on the morning of May 14, two Coast Guardsmen patrolling the Ocracoke beach by truck spotted a body in the surf. Arnold Tolson dashed into the water and dragged the dead man out. Tolson and his companion wrapped the body in canvas, placed it in the truck, and headed for the Ocracoke Coast Guard Station. On the way they were waved down by a local citizen and told that another body had come ashore. The Coast Guardsmen followed directions and, sure enough, found a body being tumbled around by the surf. Tolson again plunged into the sea to effect the recovery. Both bodies were taken to the station.

Because of the large number of merchant marines falling prey to stalking U-boats, bodies washing ashore were not that much of a rarity. Aycock Brown was duly called in his official capacity. He caught a plane to Ocracoke in order to perform the gruesome task of identification. As soon as he pulled back the tarpaulin, he exclaimed, "I know that man, from Morehead City. He's off the *Bedfordshire*!" It was Sub-Lieutenant Thomas Cunningham. Papers found in his pocket bore out the truth of Brown's exclamation.

According to papers found on the other body, it was that of Stanley Craig, Ordinary Telegraphist. If it was his job to broadcast the *Bedfordshire's* condition, his body was mute if grisly testimony of his last act of duty.

Brown spent a busy afternoon making funeral arrangements. He must have been an man of incredible resourcefulness, for by evening he had obtained two duck-hunter's boxes to be used as coffins, had acquired a private plot in which to bury the bodies, and found a willing church-goer to officiate the religious services. The ceremony was held that night. Uniformed Coast Guardsmen acted as pallbearers. As a final bit of irony, the makeshift caskets were draped with the two extra Union Jacks supplied by Cunningham himself only weeks before.

Then Brown called headquarters and made his report over the phone. At first the information was greeted with doubt. As far as anyone knew, the *Bedfordshire* was still out on patrol. A quick check revealed that she had not reported in since May 11. During the next several days a search was conducted by Naval and Coast Guard vessels, and aircraft were warned to be on the lookout for survivors in rafts or life jackets.

Arnold Tolson had the continued misfortune to be aboard Coast Guard picket boat #63-067 a week later when two more bodies were found floating in the sea. These bodies were never identified because they were too far decomposed, but since they were wearing the same dark blue turtleneck sweaters worn by other British tars, Brown assumed that they must have come from the *Bedfordshire*. They were subsequently buried in the same plot with Cunningham and Craig.

The remaining three officers and thirty ratings of Her Majesty's Trawler *Bedfordshire* were carried as "missing presumed killed." What horrors these men suffered, whether they died in the torpedo's explosion or struggled in the water for hours—or days—will never be known.

The wreck was discovered during the *Gentian* survey in 1944, but was mistaken for the *Ario* (q.v.). This hardly makes sense. The *Ario* was a 435-foot-long tanker grossing 6,952 tons: hardly comparable in size to the *Bedfordshire*.

George Purifoy found the *Bedfordshire* when he was dragging back from another wreck over what he thought was a rock. When he and Mike Sheen dived the hang they were surprised to find the battered down remains of a wreck. Although very little structure remained, the border was distinct. A small boiler provided the highest relief. Six depth charges were exposed in the stern. The steering stand with the British manufacturer's name was the clue that led to the wreck's identity.

The vehemence of the torpedo's explosion can be attested to by the spread of the wreckage. The bow lies some fifty feet off the port side of the hull, and steel plating can be found two to three hundred feet off the main wreck. The compass recovered by Purifoy had shrapnel holes through the top. The sand shifts constantly, sometimes covering and sometimes exposing the depth charges. There is no sign of the guns.

Today the flag still waves above the small cemetery maintained by the Coast Guard, in honor of the British allies who gave their lives for freedom that so many people take for granted.

Courtesy of the Peabody Museum of Salem.

BRITISH SPLENDOUR

Built: 1913
Previous names: None
Gross tonnage; 7,138
Type of vessel: Tanker
Builder: Palmers' Company, Ltd., Newcastle, England
Owner: British Tanker Company
Port of registry: London, England
Cause of sinking: Torpedoed by *U-552* (Oberleutnant zur See Topp)
Location: 26976.7

Sunk: April 7, 1942
Depth: 100 feet
Dimensions: 441' × 59' × 33'
Power: Two diesel engines

39957.4

According to the War Diary of the Fifth Naval District, the *British Splendour* "departed from Houston, Texas, on March 30 and was to meet an Atlantic convoy in the neighborhood of Halifax. John Hall, Master of the vessel, had received his routing instructions from Galveston and was to pass thirty miles off Cape Hatteras. But revised orders, radioed from Washington on April 2, caused him to proceed close East of Diamond Shoals Buoy "12 A". It had been his intention, after leaving Cape Lookout, to pass through this area in daylight."

The tanker was heavily laden with some 10,000 tons of gasoline desperately needed by the British for the defense of the home isles. The precious cargo was guarded by a 4-inch deck gun, a 12-pounder, one Bofors .40 mm, and four machine guns. "Seven lookouts were on watch, one man forward, two atop the bridge, the Captain and third mate on the bridge itself and two gunners aft." In addition, the British armed trawler HMS *St. Zeno* hugged the tanker in escort. Such protection and large number of observers would seem to have been more than adequate to repel a U-boat attack.

Yet, as the blacked out tanker motored along at a steady ten knots, Erich Topp, lying in wait for just such a target, ignored the firepower under British control and boldly launched his deadly torpedoes against the Allied vessel. Captain Hall heard a brief "buzz like an airplane motor," but shrugged it off. When the nighttime quiet resumed, Captain Hall studied the smooth sea under clear skies; "visibility was excellent for a late hour." It must have been a miss.

Ten minutes later, at 10:15 p.m., "an enemy torpedo crashed into the port side of the tanker, below the waterline and aft of the engine room. The ship's position at this moment was 35-07N; 75-19W, about two miles North of Diamond Shoals Buoy. The explosion caused heavy damage and the *British Splendour* tilted stern down and almost at once began to slide from view. All the aft superstructure had been virtually destroyed and the engine room skylight was blown off."

The lives of twelve duty personnel were snuffed out in the flicker of a candle.

As the radio operator tapped out a distress call on the wireless, the surviving members of the crew leaped for the lifeboats. It took only moments to launch three lifeboats and a raft; the remaining forty-one men (including Captain Hall and the radio operator) got away safely. After an unsuccessful search for the U-boat, the *St. Zeno* began rescue operations. "The first boat load of survivors was picked up forty-five minutes after the attack and within the next two hours all of the forty-one persons who had abandoned the ship were rescued."

Now comes a contradiction in the official documentation that so often plagues the diligent researcher. According to the War Diary, "when last seen, the *British Splendour* had not entirely vanished below the surface. A bit of the bridge, the bow and "perhaps six feet" of the funnel were still showing. On April 7, however, when a careful search of the area was made by U.S. aircraft, no trace of the stricken tanker was discovered." A mark was placed on the chart as the ship's final resting place. Anyone looking for the wreck would begin his search pattern north of the Diamond Shoals. But the hull of the *British Splendour* lies more than twenty miles southwest and nowhere near the Shoals. It is inconceivable that the huge tanker, with its stern resting on the bottom, dragged *over* the shallow water of the Shoals to reach the deeper position where it ultimately came to rest.

A confidential summary of the attack offers an explanation for the mystery. It discloses that it was Captain Hall's "intention after passing Cape Lookout Shoals to follow the eight fathom line to Diamond Shoal so as to make that position by daylight." If the good captain did not intend to reach the Diamond Shoals until dawn, he could not have been there already two hours before midnight. The wreck hunter should also note that attack positions do not necessarily agree with sinking positions.

Another inference from this confidential information is Erich Topp's

This underwater photograph was captioned *Proteus*, but the position given was that of the *British Splendour*. The obvious lack of marine encrustation seems more in keeping with a recently sunken ship. (Courtesy of Lamar Worzel.)

position at the time of the attack. Since the *British Splendour* was paralleling the coastline to port, the *U-552* was operating in even shallower water toward shore: a direction in which lookouts were likely to be less attentive. Furthermore, if Captain Hall actually followed the eight fathom curve, then Topp must have been patrolling in less than 48 feet of water, a position of jeopardy for a U-boat with no room to make a submerged retreat. Topp sank five other ships during this patrol: the *Atlas* and *Tamaulipas* recounted herein; the *Lansing* and *Byron D. Benson* (see *Shipwrecks of North Carolina: from the Diamond Shoals North*); and the *David H. Atwater* (see *Shipwrecks of Virginia*). Not only was Topp audacious, he was infamous for having torpedoed the U.S. destroyer *Reuben James* (DD-245) six weeks *before* Germany and the United States were at war. One hundred fifteen American sailors died because of Topp's premature aggression. On September 8, 1942 Topp was booted upstairs to landside duty. The *U-552* survived additional partrols under the command of Kapitanleutnant Klaus Popp. Popp, Topp, and the *U-552* outlasted the war, although the U-boat was scuttled by its crew upon Germany's capitulation.

One other condition of the *British Splendour* that went unobserved is that the ship capsized before plunging to the bottom: the wreck lies completely upside down at the location that the 1944 *Gentian* survey identified as the *Proteus*, despite photographic evidence of extremely little marine growth on the nearly undamaged hull. The *Proteus* is actually located where the *Gentian* thought she had found the *Malchace* (which turned out to be the *Manuela* (q.v.). Through this blizzard of misinformation the wreck researcher must trudge.

The hull of the *British Splendour* lies at a depth of 100 feet. Washouts as deep as ten feet are caused by strong currents siphoning through the wreck, making conical holes with the appearance of inverted ant hills and dipping down to 110 feet.

The bow is so intact that no large openings allow access. The chain locker is broken open on the starboard side, with the iron links falling out. The height above the bottom is about 15 feet. About seventy-five to one hundred feet aft of the stem the wreck is broken open; scattered wreckage and collapsed hull plates are so strewn about that it is not apparent that the wreck has turned turtle. Machinery such as pumps and valves, most of it brass, lies in tumult amid the skeletal framework of beams and steel plates, the latter mostly buried.

The stern section is the most interesting, rising above the sand nearly twenty feet. One can enter the hull through the partially destroyed transverse bulkhead, then swim the entire length of the stern: a distance of over one hundred feet. Each succeeding compartment has side entrances that shed a green glow, offering enough ambient light to see by. A dive light will illuminate valve wheels and gauges, some with the glass faces intact, in the engine room, although the coral growth obscures much of the artificial shape of individual instruments. Oddly, the coral appears to be much thicker insider; or, perhaps, that is because one can see recognizable shapes against which to gauge the thickness. Each side of the engine room is pierced by a large, cavernous hole that permits easy access or egress.

Outside the stern, the rounded fantail is easily recognizable, as is a huge crankshaft on the port side. there is no sign of the rudder or propeller.

The wreck lies on a soft sand bottom that stirs up easily, and which is kicked up by surface wave action. This often enshrouds the wreck with a nebulous white cloud that, while allowing sunlight to penetrate, limits visibility to a milky twenty or thirty feet. The hull is drab in color, the thin veneer of marine encrustation being predominantly dull brown with none of the many-hued corals seen farther south. This is especially true inside the extensive intact portions where sunlight never reaches.

Left: An example of the large brass works found on the wreck. This one weighs more than a ton. Right: A gong inside the engine room.

CARIBSEA

Built: 1919   Sunk: March 11, 1942
Previous names: *Buenaventura, Lake Flattery*   Depth: 80 feet
Gross tonnage: 2,609   Dimensions: 251' × 43' × 25'
Type of vessel: Freighter   Power: Oil-fired steam
Builder: McDougall Duluth Company, Duluth, Minnesota
Owner: Stockard Steam Ship Corp.
Port of registry: New York, NY
Cause of sinking: Torpedoed by *U-158* (Kapitanleutnant Erich Rostin)
Location: 27042.5   39741.0

    Captain Nicholas Manolis was perhaps the most prepared ship's master ever to ply the U-boat infested waters off the eastern seaboard. He had good reason to be. At the time he left Santiago, Cuba, on March 5, 1942, twenty-nine ships had been torpedoed and sunk in the previous six weeks in an area stretching from Maine to Georgia designated by the U.S. Navy as the Eastern Sea Frontier. He was charged with the safe delivery of 3,600 tons of managanese ore to the bustling port of Norfolk, Virginia, just inside the mouth of the Chesapeake Bay.

    The *Caribsea* was defenseless against enemy attack; she carried no guns. Neither the United States Consul nor the British authorities in Santiago were able to supply him with safe routing instructions: official orders that would tell him how best to avoid the chance of encountering deadly U-boats, or where to pick up an armed escort through "torpedo alley" (as the area off the Diamond Shoals was quickly becoming known.)

    Therefore, Captain Manolis took some rather unorthodox precautions. "The radio operator had been instructed to stand watch only at night. At the beginning of this watch at 2000, he was given a paper listing the expected position of the *Caribsea* for every two-hour period throughout the night, and was told to send an SOS the instant any explosion might be heard,

Courtesy of the U.S. Coast Guard.

without even awaiting orders from the bridge. He was then to give the approximate position of the ship from the list in his possession."

In addition, "the engine room had orders to put the vessel full astern the moment there was trouble, also without awaiting instructions from the bridge; and each lifeboat was equipped with a hatchet at every fall. The crew had been told to chop the boats loose instantly, in the event of a torpedoing, and not to attempt to lower them in the usual way. . . . Captain Manolis had also made sure that each lifeboat and life raft included in its equipment a mirror or some bright piece of metal which might attract attention to survivors, if disaster came."

Here was a captain who was taking no chances. Yet, in the event, even these strict safeguards were not protection enough for the twenty-eight men whose lives were not in the whimsical hands of fate, but in the cruel cogs of the German war machine.

Came March 10. Captain Manolis had received "coded instructions by radio to proceed so as to pass Cape Hatteras by daylight." The *Caribsea* slowed to five knots so she would not reach the cape before dawn. The ship was completely blacked out. The midnight watch came on duty. Atop the bridge a lookout scanned the horizon in visibility described as "fair." In the wheelhouse were the second mate, in charge of navigation, and the helmsman. All the rest of the crew including the captain were below deck; most were asleep in their bunks.

"The mate on watch reported to the captain that an unidentified tanker was in sight and that another ship, type undetermined, was off the bow."

Moments later, at 2 a.m. there came a titanic explosion on the starboard side at No. 2 hold. The *Caribsea* took an immediate severe list and began to settle by the head. Jarred to instant full awareness, the crew scrambled up the companionways onto a sharply tilted deck that was already slipping beneath the waves. In three minutes the *Caribsea* was gone.

Despite all the captain's precautions, the ship went down so fast that no SOS was transmitted and no lifeboats were launched. Those men who had managed to escape the sinking hull floated in the sea with nothing to support them but "bits of debris" and "pieces of lumber."

Ordinary seaman Gerald Thibodeau later testified before Congress, "I found myself in the water and I managed to reach a hatchboard to which I clung until a life raft came near and I got aboard that. There were five men hanging on to the hatchboard when the life raft came by. Since the life raft had no means of control or propulsion it was just a matter of luck that the wind drifted it near us so that the four of the five men were able to board the raft. One of the men on the board could not make it because the raft had begun to drift away at the time.

"There were altogether on the life raft seven men. . . . I later found out that the life raft had been thrown in the water by the force of the explosion and found by men swimming in the water." Perhaps in compensation for his forethought, the man who first climbed aboard the life raft was Captain Manolis.

Oiler Francisco Ribera stated that "two life rafts were seen in the water with no one aboard either." Nowhere else in the broad expanse of the sea were any other survivors to be seen. These seven wet, bedraggled men huddled together in the close confines of their providential raft. They were the only survivors, but they were not alone.

Descriptions vary as to what they saw—a yellowish light "25–30 feet off the water, rectangular in shape, about 12 × 16 inches, and having the appearance of a kerosene lamp;" or a mast "of steel, the center portion being squarish with flanges on either side. At the mast head, these flanges widened out forming sort of cross trees."

But the crew was in solid agreement on one account: that the light and mast rose above the conning tower of a submarine. A U-boat, perhaps, that had disguised itself to be mistaken for a merchant ship while it prepared its torpedoes for launching.

Said Captain Manolis, "The submarine remained in the vicinity with the light showing until 0600 or 0630 when it submerged."

With dawn came the hope of rescue. Frustrated hopes. "At about 0800 a convoy of 3 tankers escorted by a destroyer passed within 3 miles of the liferaft but evidently did not sight the survivors as no attempt was made to rescue them. About 0830 a seaplane headed South was sighted. About 1000 another seaplane headed North and then Eastward was sighted." Each time the men waved a yellow signal flag, and each time they were disappointed as ships and planes passed them by. Added Thibodeau about the planes, "One of them came about three miles of us, swooped low, and returned. Yet, there was no report given."

According to official records, "As the sun grew stronger, they made use of a small metal can which had been stowed among the raft's gear, employing it as a reflector. This brought help at last. Aboard the SS *Norlindo*, bound north for Baltimore, the tiny stab of light flashing on the empty expanse of sea registered through a lookout's glasses. The ship turned off its course to pick up the survivors. The time of rescue was approximately 1230, March 11.

"The crew of the *Norlindo* furnished the seven exhausted men with food and clothing and, early on the morning of March 12, they were transferred to a Coast Guard dispatch boat and taken to Little Creek Coast Guard Station. At Little Creek, Navy Intelligence officers met them and accompanied them to the Marine Hospital, Norfolk, Virginia. Three survivors had to be moved by ambulance because of injuries. The other four were suffering from exposure but were able to travel by Navy station wagon."

On March 23, 1942 an anti-submarine patrol plane mistook the mast of the *Caribsea* for the periscope, and delivered a depth-charge attack on it. Thereafter, the wreck was marked with a quick flashing red buoy. "During the spring of 1944 the wreck was demolished to a claimed clearance 'in excess of 40 feet' by the Navy Salvage Service."

The *Caribsea* is one of the better dives on the east side of Cape Lookout Shoals, and is often used for training and checkouts. The depth is a comfortable 80 feet with washouts that go to 90. Visibility averages sixty feet and can be much better. Big barracuda thrive on the great quantity of fish that have made the site their home. Colors abound among the tropicals that flit through magnificent coral heads. To describe the wreck as picturesque is an understatement.

The hull is contiguous and for the most part broken open. The bow stands upright some thirty feet above the sand, with winches in place and anchors in their chocks. The plating is beginning to slough off, a process that was accelerated by hurrican Hugo in 1989.

Abaft the bow a large debris field extends to the boilers and engine, all accessible since they are uncovered. Debris fields can be found amidships both to port and starboard. Ribbing in the stern is high enough to enable a diver to swim underneath it easily; minor penetrations can be made into a partially enclosed interior. The rudder has collapsed and lies loose on the sand.

The *U-158* also sank the *Ario* and the *John D. Gill*, both described elsewhere in this volume. Erich Rostin and his boat lived less than four months after these actions against the Allied merchant fleet. On June 30, 1942 the *U-158* was sunk by aerial attack in the Gulf of Mexico. It went down with all hands, unfortunately including two officers of the merchant marine previously taken aboard as prisoners.

African pompano.

CASSIMIR

Built: 1920

Previous names: None

Gross tonnage: 5,030

Type of vessel; Tanker

Sunk: February 26, 1942

Depth: 120 feet

Dimensions: 390' × 54' × 32'

Power: Oil-fired steam turbine

Builder: American International Ship Building Corporation, Hog Island, Pennsylvania; converted in 1921 by Curtis Bay Copper & Iron Works, Curtis Bay, Maryland

Owner: Cuba Distilling Company, Baltimore, Maryland

Port of registry: Baltimore, Maryland

Cause of sinking: Collision with SS *Lara*

Location: 27128.6   39250.1

Under ordinary circumstances the collision between two vessels that resulted in the sinking of one of the vessels and attendant loss of life would have created banner headlines, with newspaper reporters stampeding over each other to glean the gory details. But February 1942 was a time of war off the eastern seaboard. U-boats were sending merchant ships to the bottom on practically a daily basis. The same day that the *Cassimir* was lost by collision, the tanker *R.P. Resor* was burning in flames and creating a furor with its great number of fatalities as well as with a smoke plume that rose thousands of feet into the air. It was the U-boat war that captured the interest of the public, not an oceanic fender bender. (See *Shipwrecks of New Jersey* for details on the *R.P. Resor*.)

Despite the vicissitudes of war, however, and the consequent lack of coverage, the unfortunate collision proved just as fatal to seven innocent seamen as if they had been killed by the blast of the German torpedo they were trying to avoid. The *Cassimir* was bound for Baltimore with a cargo of molasses onloaded in Santiago, Cuba only days before. As she steamed through an early morning fog off Frying Pan Shoals, the bow of the steamship *Lara* coalesced alongside and drove at full speed into the *Cassimir's* starboard side, splitting her hull at the engine room like an overripe melon. Duty personnel were either crushed at their posts, or drowned in the flood that poured in as the *Lara* backed off.

Captain Bodman had no choice but to order abandon ship. The crew launched two lifeboats and a raft, taking with them their dead and injured. Fortunately, the *Lara* was able to effect a prompt rescue. When the final toll was made, two men were missing, four bodies were recovered, and thirty-two men of the merchant marine were saved; First Mate E. Heyliger, however, died of his injuries shortly thereafter.

Today, the wreck of the *Cassimir* is visually spectacular, effulgent in the profusion of colorful marine encrustation. Soft corals abound to such thickness that they almost completely obscure the substratum that is hardly recognizable as rusting hull plates. Nudibranchs and gaily-hued tropical fish in dazzling array inhabit every niche offered by overlapping girders.

The hull is upright and largely contiguous. About forty feet of the bow is separated from the main structure by a short stretch of sand; it is intact and points at an angle toward the sky. The overgrown anchors are pulled tight into their hawse pipes.

Abaft the bow is a section of vertical beams that appear like Roman columns because the hull plates have fallen off. Just abaft the windlass is a high flat deck that once supported the navitional bridge. The wheelhouse lies some fifty feet off the port side, upside down; apparently, it slid off the superstructure as the ship rolled over in its final plunge. Only the lower level protrudes above the sand; the rooms are open and easy to enter. In one room a toilet appears to hang from the overhead, festooned by long, snakelike tubeworms. The wheelhouse, and the bridge equipment that accompanies it, is buried.

Back on the main hull, abaft the bridge area the wreck is pretty well flattened; collapsed decks, twisted beams, and bent hull plates provide continuity until the machinery spaces are reached. This area is fairly intact, held up in part by the boilers and engine inside. The engine room can be entered and explored. Valves and piping are exposed, but much of the steam turbine is covered with sand. Recovered gauges have been stamped with the name of the ship building company.

The highest relief is found on the stern, which settled so far over on its side that the port railing lies almost against the sand. The top towers twenty-five feet above the bottom. Two doors lead into the after steerage, and to a corridor lined with portholes that permits access to rooms along the side.

The *Cassimir* is a wreck you just have to see.

CIBAO

Built: 1911
Previous names: None
Gross tonnage: 1,185
Type of vessel: Freighter

Sunk: December 4, 1927
Salvaged: December 24, 1927
Dimensions: 225' × 33' × 20'
Power: Coal-fired steam

Builder: Act. Sorlandets Skibsbyg, Arendal, Norway
Owner: A/S Frugtfart (L. Harboe-Jensen & Co., Mgrs.)
Port of registry: Oslo, Norway
Cause of sinking: Ran aground/later salvaged
Location: Hatteras Inlet

A terrific northeaster struck the North Carolina coast in early December 1927, bringing with it winds up to seventy miles per hour that tore up towns and ripped down communication cables. Into this tempest steamed the *Cibao*, bound from Port Antonio, Jamaica to Baltimore with 16,906 stems of bananas and a small consignment of liquor. Sorely strained by the awful seas, Captain Magnus Mylander was steering the small freighter for shelter in Hatteras Inlet when she ran hard aground.

A Coast Guard patrolman saw the ship coming in, and burned Coston flares to warn her away from the shoals, but his signals went unheeded. At 6:10 a.m. the *Cibao* bottomed out.

As soon as the patrolman's report was received, Boatswain Charles Peel, the officer in charge of the station, mustered his crew to action and sent out a call for help. Peel and his men launched a power lifeboat, and raced out the inlet and down to where the wreck had struck in the surf. The pounding waves prevented them from approaching close enough to aid the stricken sailors. The boat was forced to return to the station.

By that time all the officers and crews from the Cape Hatteras, Creeds

Hard aground. (Courtesy of William Quinn.)

Hill, and Ocracoke stations had gathered at the Hatteras Inlet Station, and reported for duty. Peel took command of the power surfboat and, along with a hand-picked crew of volunteers from all the stations, charged into the foam-flecked sea. "The surfboat was swamped several times in an endeavor to get through the line of heavy breakers, which almost washed the men out of the boat." Soaking wet and cold, the rescuers "succeeded in reaching a position about 150 yards from the bow of the stranded vessel."

No closer could they get without fear of dashing their boat to pieces against the stout steel hull. The ocean was whipped to a froth, the wind howled like a horde of banshees. Peel could not even make himself heard to the men aboard the *Cibao*.

Finally, "the crew of the *Cibao* was signaled to drift a line through the breakers to the surfboat, whereupon a smaller line was drifted down to the surfboat, to which a life preserver was made fast and sent on board the wreck ... upon signal from the surfboat, each man of the *Cibao*, twenty-four in number, with line bent around him, jumped overboard and was hauled through the breakers from the ship to the surfboat ... after heroic efforts in the rough seas, the rescued men were transferred from the surfboat to the lifeboat, which took them ashore."

Said Seventh Coast Guard District Commander O.A. Littlefield of the operation, "It was nothing but a miracle that they managed it. In the usual shipwreck, the crew of the lifeboat goes out into open water with a crowd on shore ready to help if accident happens. But these fellows were two miles from shore and they were in imminent danger without the possibility of rescue if anything went wrong. It was as fine a piece of work as I ever heard of and if ever man deserved praise, these men do."

The storm went unabated throughout the day. The next afternoon Coast Guard officers boarded the wreck—but not for the purpose of ascertaining the possibility of salvage. This was the era of prohibition, and they were looking for contraband. The cargo manifest openly acknowledged twenty-one cases of rum intended for the Bolivian Legation in Washington, DC. This was not illegal trade because embassies were technically foreign soil. Nevertheless, the alcoholic portion of the cargo, along with six quarts of whiskey that were part of the sea stores, was duly offloaded and locked up in the Hatteras Inlet Station.

On the sixth a more thorough inspection was made. "The ship having a full cargo of bananas made it impossible to search beneath the cargo but all hold and cargo spaces were thoroughly examined. ... The only contraband found was eleven (11) pint bottles of rum hidden among the clothing in the crews quarters."

The twenty-one cases of legal liquor were delivered unopened to the Collector of Customs in Wilmington, North Carolina. W.H. Munter, commanding officer of the Coast Guard cutter *Modoc*, which handled transportation, stated that "the six (6) quarts of whiskey and eleven (11) bottles of rum taken from the *Cibao* were destroyed in my presence and in the presence of Prohibition Agent A.M. Beck and Assistant Collector of Customs S.F. Highsmith, at the request of the Prohibition Agent.'' Oddly, no mention is made as to whether the rum was forwarded to the Bolivian Legation—undoubtedly only an oversight.

The position of the stranded freighter was given with considerable variance, especially for a wreck that was so highly visible. One Coast Guard document puts the wreck one and a half miles southeast of the Hatteras Inlet Station. Commander Littlefield said two miles from shore. A Treasury Department memorandum states ''The *Cibao* . . . now lies in an average of seven feet of water at low tide about ¾ of a mile 100° from Hatteras Inlet station and is at least one mile from the four fathom line.'' The wreck researcher should keep this in mind when using official documents to locate sunken hulks, since the possession of either one of these reports without awareness of the others might lead one to accept the available information as gospel.

Furthermore, the wreck hunter conducting only secondary research might look hopelessly today for the *Cibao's* rusting steel ribs, and should know the following information. The wrecking tug *Relief* arrived on the sixth with the hopes of kedging the fruiter—as banana boats were called in those days—off the shoal. Adverse weather conditions prevented a hasty salvage, but on December 28 the *New York Maritime Register* was able to report that the *Cibao* ''was refloated on the morning of Dec. 24 and was towed to New York.'' The *Cibao* continued in operation and was listed in the Lloyd's Register until well into the 1930's.

Notwithstanding the above, books and tourist charts continue to mark the *Cibao's* stranding position as if she were still there.

The salvage report did not go into detail about how the operation was conducted, or if the cargo was lightered. If I let my imagination run wild I can picture the contents of the fruiter being dumped overboard in order to lighten the load and refloat the vessel. If so, Hatteras Inlet must hold the distinction as the site of the world's largest banana split.

Nudibranch.

Courtesy of the Mariners Museum, Newport News, Virginia.

CITY OF HOUSTON

Built: 1871   Sunk: October 23, 1878
Previous names: None   Depth: 95 feet
Gross tonnage (1871): 1,253   Dimensions (1871): 240′ × 33′ × 20′
Groos tonnage (1875): 1,515   Dimensions (1875): 290′ × 33′ × 20′
Type of vessel: Passenger-freighter
Power: Coal-fired direct acting steam engine
Builder: Reany, Son & Archbold, Chester, Pennsylvania
Owner: Charles H. Mallory & Company
Port of registry: New York, NY
Cause of sinking: Foundered
Location: 45170.6   59281.6

    With the end of the Civil War came renewed vigor directed toward the expansion of the West. As the awful trauma of "brother fighting against brother" slowly faded from the public consciousness, pioneers came into vogue. Wagon trains more than a mile long rolled toward the land of the setting sun. Conestoga's pulled by oxen became a sight that Indians abhorred, for they brought settlers who gradually and incessantly confiscated their ancestral land.

    The 1870's was a time of homesteading, cattle ranches, Indian massacres, cavalry charges, outlaws, gunslingers, and the Iron Horse. In the midst of this was Galveston, Texas, very much a frontier town and the jumping off point for teamsters transporting goods and staples to the more remote communities popping up across the range land.

    To service this growing western population the C.H. Mallory Company authorized the construction of the propeller ship *City of Houston*, the first iron-hulled vessel in its fleet. As was common in steamships of the day, she was fitted out with two masts and auxiliary sails that were, in this case, barkentine rigged. Her primary route was New York to Galveston via Key West, Florida. She carried passengers in spaceous accomodations, and much-needed supplies in her ample cargo holds. Fast steamer service was more desirable than the bouncy, dusty, weeks-long travel sufferable by stagecoach.

But the passengers who sailed on her maiden voyage could not have been convinced of that. The trip that began with such a promising outlook on August 12, 1871 nearly came to disaster in the Straits of Florida, where the *City of Houston* encountered a fierce cyclone. Circular winds of phenomenal speed lashed her rigging hard enough to bring down her foremast. Storm-whipped waves tossed the steamer about like a toy boat in a river rapid. Her boilers were shifted off their bedplates, rupturing feed pipes and steam lines. The ship was temporarily disabled and Captain Partridge, master, must have been chagrined.

The difficulties that ensued can be interpreted from Secretary of the Navy George Robeson's praise for six seamen (Edward Norton, Charles Williams, Thomas Perry, W. Welsh, Angel Daniels, and Edward Hopkins) and landsman Charles Miller, who helped save the day: "These persons, forming a part of draft of men which had taken passage in the vessel, worked unceasingly during three days and four nights, and received special mention from their commanding officer for energy and zeal." The *City of Houston* was forced to turn back and put in at Fernandina, Florida for repairs. The steamship arrived at her ultimate destination not in brand new condition, as expected, but strained and weather worn and already seasoned.

The *City of Houston* was a fast ship for her time. In 1872 she reportedly ran from New York to Key West, a distance of 1,145 miles, in four days seven hours thirty-six minutes, thence to Galveston, another 850 miles, in three days one hour ten minutes. Total time from port to port: seven days eight hours forty-six minutes.

According to the Steamboat Inspection records, the *City of Houston* was involved in another calamity on May 13, 1874. "While descending the Mississippi River, collided in the vicinity of Point a la Bache, 45 miles below New Orleans with the tugboat *Tillie C. Jewett* ascending, where by the tug was sunk almost immediately and two of her crew were drowned. John T. Davis, master and pilot of the tug and on watch was fined $50, license suspended for 15 days; A suspension of the license of C.H. Andrews, pilot of the steamship for 15 days."

In March 1875 the *City of Houston* returned to the shipyard of her birth for overhaul, improvement, and an additional fifty feet in length. When she resumed her regular route from New York to Galveston her tonnage had increased by two hundred fifty-seven. This enabled her to carry more cargo for the city folk in Galveston and for the cowboys "home on the range."

When the *City of Houston* left New York on October 20, 1878 her departure was like any other. Her holds were loaded with a cargo of general merchandise from dozens of east coast suppliers. Thirty-four passengers eagerly looked forward to landing in Galveston a week later. Captain Stevens, master, looked upon his ship with pride; already that season she had endured the wrath of two great storms and withstood them well. She seemed to be staunch and seaworthy.

Two days from port she ran head-on into a gale moving north along the coast. The storm quickly increased in intensity until the *City of Houston* was engulfed by mountainous waves that slapped her hull with rivet-loosening violence. It was maiden voyage deja vu, only this time the bilge pumps could not stem the rising tide. The boiler fires were soon damped, the engine coughed its last, and the ship was driven broadside to the sea where she wallowed sickeningly in the troughs. By this time it was two in the morning of October 23.

Captain Stevens had the passengers roused from their staterooms. He explained the situation as he passed out life preservers, and told them to stand by and be ready to abandon ship. The outlook was bleak. The lifeboats were prepared, but it seemed sheer madness to put people into the wave-tossed sea, especially women and children, and expect them to row to shore in the dark during a tempest. They were abreast of Frying Pan Shoals, and off an area nearly as desolate as the plains of Texas. There seemed little chance for survival.

"Signals were burned from the pilot house, but it was intensely dark and raining heavily, so that no vessel saw them." The ship was settling by the stern, where the water had risen to a depth of ten feet. "A little brig was seen 10 miles to leeward at daybreak, but owing to the wind she could not reach them. The steamer was now beginning to sink, and the boats were about to be lowered when" a savior arrived in the form of the steamship *Margaret*, New York to Fernandina, Florida.

The *Margaret* hove to as the *City of Houston* launched lifeboats. With

tantalizing lack of detail it was reported that "an hour later the passengers and crew were all safely transferred to the *Margaret*, although there was a heavy sea running at the time. The boats were admirably managed, and the passengers seemed thoroughly satisfied with the conduct of Capt. Stevens and his crew." All the people were landed at Fernandina, Florida.

The *City of Houston* was gone. The only thing left to mark her existance was "a quantity of wreck stuff, consisting of furniture and a number of boxes, one of which was marked 'Galveston.'" For a short time her masts stuck up out of the water. She was valued at $200,000, her cargo at $150,000.

The passengers lost all their personal belongings: an awful tragedy for most because for them this was not just a vacation cruise or a business trip, but emigration. The call of the wild, wild west was what enticed these people to take passage. Now, all their worldy possessions were packed in trunks sitting on the ocean floor, irretrievable—

Until 1987, when Wayne Strickland strapped a scuba tank on his back and dived down to a wreck whose position had been given to him by a fishing boat captain. He did not know it at the time, but he had just found the remains of the *City of Houston*. More than just a deteriorated iron hull, he found what he calls a "frontier time capsule," for much of the miscellaneous cargo that the ship had been transporting to the Lone Star state was still packed away in crates and boxes and trunks. And, because it had been covered with sand and therefore protected from the destructive elements of the sea, much of it existed in an excellent state of preservation despite more than a century submerged.

Here is a brief list of artifacts rescued by Strickland and others: tooth brushes, brass rings, china bird whistles, miniature china dog figures, assorted sleigh bells, harmonicas, lady's kid and men's leather boots, Singer sewing machines, railroad wheels, vases, snuff bottles, lamp parts, wooden croquet mallets and balls, coach springs, iron kettles, lead shot, rope, wire, shoe brushes, millstone grinding wheels, braziers, cruets, clothes pins, door knobs and locks and keys, solder bars, bolts of cloth, felt hats, straight pins, thread spools, pencils and slates, patent medicines, hardware tools, bottled foodstuffs, sulphide marbles, Charles Field Haviland china dinnerware, silverware, silver serving pieces, coins, and china dolls.

Many of these items are not necessities, but, Strickland believes, Christmas toys for frontier children. The dolls in particular have no survival value for town dwellers, homesteaders, or cowboys driving cattle over the vast western range lands. In fact, these dolls were of European manufacture: a common import item for a country still largely colonial in nature and not yet fully developed as an industrial nation.

The dolls were made of either porcelain or bisque (pottery that has been fired once but not glazed.) Afterward, the hair and the eyes were painted by hand. Some dolls were complete human forms called Frozen Charlottes. Others consisted of busts, arms, and legs sewn to a fabric body

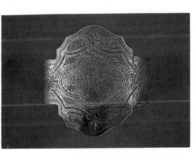

packed with sawdust. Of the latter variety only the disconnected hard parts remain. As fascinating as these finds are today because of the insights offered about the playtime activities of borderland children at the time the West was being opened to settlers, such merchandise was cheap at the time and considered strictly middle class: what we might expect to find today in K Mart.

Other recovered items originally intended for children are bisque animal figures, lead soldiers on horseback, red rubber balls (the rubber is remarkably well preserved), wooden farm animals, alphabet and number squares, building blocks, toy tops, miniature tea sets, teething rings, and baby rattles.

More remains of the cargo of the *City of Houston* than of the wreck itself. The iron hull is sadly deteriorated by more than a century of salt water immersion and dynamic destruction. The hull has long since fallen flat, splayed out amidships like a disarticulated framework, with very little recognizable as a ship other than beams and structural support members. The single-cylinder engine dominates the scene; the broad base and converging frame gives it the appearance of a miniature Eiffel Tower. It rises some twenty-five feet off the bottom. There is no sign of the boilers that supplied steam, only a donkey boiler to port.

Both the bow and stern are partially intact; both lie over on their port sides. Two anchors grace the bow. The tip of one propeller blade is visible at the stern. The propeller shaft and tunnel are partly obscured by wreckage, but can be discerned to within twenty-five feet of the engine. Machinery and ship's appurtenances such as bollards, cleats, and mooring bitts largely overgrown with marine encrustation lay scattered about in junkyard fashion.

The value of the *City of Houston* lies not in its exploratory potential, but in its recoverable contents. Strickland has saved thousands of items that might otherwise have been lost forever. He was witness to the destruction caused by Hurricane Hugo in 1989 when deep ocean swells and storm generated currents washed away tons of sand, taking with it whatever cargo samples it contained and spreading it out across the vast unreachable bottomlands.

To better preserve these historical treasures of a bygone age, Strickland has helped establish the Southport Maritime Museum, to which he has donated a large representative display of artifacts rescued from the *City of Houston*. Duplicate items have been put up for sale, the money to be reinvested into further recovery efforts. He hopes these ventures will increase the cultural consciousness of marine antiquities while returning to the stream of commerce the products once intended for the children of our sagebrush ancestors.

In these ways, what Strickland calls "the Christmas that wasn't" in 1878 will become the presents for modern collectors: those people who more than anyone appreciate the value of the memorabilia of the past.

From *Harper's Weekly*.

CITY OF NEW YORK

Built: 1851
Previous names: None
Gross tonnage: 574

Sunk: January 15, 1862
Depth: 24 feet
Dimensions: 166' × 27' × 18'

Type of vessel: Wooden-hulled screw steamer
Power: Coal-fired two-cylinder vertical direct-acting engine, built by Hogg
    & Delamater, New York, NY
Builder: Capes & Allison, Hoboken, New Jersey
Owner: Boston & Philadelphia SS Company (William P. Williams, Mngr.)
Port of registry: New York, NY
Cause of sinking : Foundered
Location: Hatteras Inlet

    The *City of New York's* career got off to a slow start. Her original owners, Mailler & Lord, used the ship only once. She left for Chagres, Panama in February 1851, returned in April, then was laid up for the rest of the year. In January 1852 she sailed for the Independent Line owned by wealthy financier Cornelius Vanderbilt, again running to Chagres and back, whereupon she was once more laid up. Later that year she was purchased by the newly formed Boston & Philadelphia Steam Ship Company which, as its name implies, shuttled freight and passengers between those two ports. The *City of New York* settled into this comfortable route and maintained regular passage for the next decade. During this time she was "furnished with new boilers at a cost of nearly $30,000."

    At the outbreak of the War of Secession the U.S. War Department began chartering ships in order to transport men and materiel around the Mason-Dixon line, and to establish blockades outside Confederate ports. June 8, 1861 found the *City of New York* in federal employ at the rate of $10,000 a month. Because her anticipated itinerary would keep her for long periods in the warm waters of the south, it was decided in August to have her hull plated with copper: a procedure intended to keep wood boring mollusks from eating away wooden hull planking, and to help cut down the amount of fouling marine organisms (such as barnacles) that clung to ship's hulls and slowed their speed.

Because the *City of New York* was not in constant use the charter rate was renegotiated so that as of November 1 the owners were paid $4,500 per job: the fare paid for delivery of goods and return to port of origin. The rate of pay was changed again on December 30, this time to $300 per day, because the government foresaw long-term employment.

Already in the works was a bold plan proposed by Colonel Ambrose Burnside of the United States Army. He was perhaps one of the few men in history promoted to general just because his ideas found favor with his superior officers. So exciting was his proposal that he was given an audience with President Lincoln. At this meeting, under the stern eyes of Secretary of State William Seward, General George McClellan, and Admiral Louis Goldsborough, Burnside elaborated on his plan of campaign to organize "a division of from 12,000 to 15,000 men, mainly from States bordering on the Northern sea-coast, many of whom would be familiar with the coasting trade . . . and to fit out a fleet of light-draught steamers, sailing vessels, and barges . . . with a view to establishing lodgments on the Southern coast."

The *City of New York* was attached to the fleet being formed under Army auspices, and known officially as the Burnside Expedition. Burnside, now a general, described how he put his "motley fleet" together: "North River barges and propellers had been strengthened from deck to keelson by heavy oak planks, and water-tight compartments had been built in them; they were so arranged that parapets of sand-bags or bales of hay could be built upon their decks, and each one carried from four to six guns. Sailing vessels, formerly belonging to the coasting trade, had been fitted up in the same manner. Several large passenger steamers, which were guaranteed to draw less than eight feet of water, together with tug and ferry boats, served to make up the fleet."

The *City of New York* was under the command of Captain J.W. Nye, and operated by a crew of eighteen men. She had on board seven passengers, "mechanics who were on their way to join the expedition." As arms and ammunition she carried "7 battery carriages, 352 barrels powder, 800 shells, 111 hand grenades, 10 boxes muskets, 45 boxes guns, 3 boxes fuse."

According to her cargo manifest she was laden with "1 forge, 1 anchor and chains, 1 package deck lines, 3 bales duck, 2 coils rigging, 631 cot bottoms, 240 frames, 31 bundles bedding, 30 bales bagging, 90 mattresses,

61 life-preservers, 3 cases boots, 1 case crockery, 1 lot furniture, 4 boxes furniture, 7 chairs, 1 copying-press, 134 cases merchandise, 4 cases merchandise for Capt. Biggs, 165 bales hay, 97 boxes bread, 9 barrels beef, 12 barrels pork, 9 barrels beans, 7 barrels flour, 3 boxes soap, 3 boxes candles, 5½ barrels rice, 4 barrels vinegar, 1 barrel coffee, 1 barrel salt, half barrel syrup, 4 barrels sugar, 2 barrels hams, 1 chest tea, 1 chest commissary stores.''

The total value of stores and munitions was over $200,000.

On January 9, 1862 Burnside left Annapolis with more than eighty jury-rigged gunboats and federal transports. The ships pooled at the mouth of the Chesapeake Bay. Since Norfolk was in Confederate hands it was widely surmised that that city was the object of the maneuver. No one, not even the ship's captains, knew for sure whither they were bound. Spies were everywhere. However, on the night of January 11 the fleet was ordered to sea. Sealed orders were not permitted to be opened until after passing Cape Henry. Then it was learned that Burnside's objective was Roanoke Island. To get there meant rounding the Diamond Shoals and entering Pamlico Sound through Hatteras Inlet.

Several ships backed out of the expedition because their captain's considered their vessels unseaworthy. Others, such as the floating batteries that were nothing more than converted canal boats, struggled along under tow and shipped quite a bit of water because of their low freeboard. As the weather thickened and the seas grew fierce, some had to be let go. When the *Grapeshot* parted her tow line in mounting seas, the men leaped overboard and were rescued by ropes thrown from the towing vessel *New Brunswick*. The *Grapeshot* was "thrown ashore to the northward of Hatteras." There was no loss of life, only the hay and oats with which the canal boat was heaped.

The fleet forged ahead despite this calamity. Upon approaching the dreaded Diamond Shoals the expedition encountered a heavy northeast gale that scattered the ships like leaves in an autumn breeze. Leading the charge was the *City of New York*, forging ahead because of her powerful engine and new boilers. When she arrived off Hatteras, Captain Nye dropped anchor outside the outer bar and waited patiently for the seas to moderate. The ship rode the waves for twenty hours. Then:

"He had a signal flying for a pilot four hours, but as it was not answered, the pilot who was taken on board at New York attempted to get the vessel over the bar, and while so doing she grounded. The tugboat *Ceres* then came up and took the hawser of the *City of New York*, and while endeavoring to bring her round, the hawser slipped or parted, and the tugboat refused to render further aid. She made a circuit round the vessel twice, but would not take the line a second time. The pilot told Capt. Nye that his vessel was in four fathoms of water, and he could get her over himself, although she was then fast aground. Shortly after the *Ceres* steamed away and left the vessel to her fate."

Thus was the condition of the *City of New York* on the afternoon of the thirteenth. "During the night she drifted up into the breakers, and on Tuesday morning the waves began to tell with terrible effect upon her deck, cabins and joiner's work. The masts were cut away, and a battery carriage, forge and other heavy articles were thrown overboard to lighten her. During that night and a portion of the next day the men were obliged to cling to the rigging for fear of being washed overboard. The vessel was filled with water, and was rapidly going to pieces. The men were chilled and nearly exhausted, but combatted manfully with the elements, cherishing a hope that they would soon be relieved from their perilous situation by means of boats from the fleet, which was about a mile distant.

"At about 10 o'clock Wednesday morning, in the midst of a frightful sea, Capt. Wells, of the gunboat *Seymour*, sent a boat to their assistance, and took off the Captain and five others. This was the only naval boat that went to them, and Capt. Wells said he took the responsibility of the act upon himself, as the rules of the navy prohibit the sending away of a boat without permission from the Flag-Officer. One other boat from a schooner went off, and took off the remainder of the crew. Before these two boats came to their relief, several boats from the fleet were seen hovering round the wrecked vessel within hailing distance, picking up trunks and other personal property which had been washed away, but made no effort to save the lives of those on board. By Wednesday night the vessel had become a total wreck, and in a short time nothing could be seen of her but fragments."

Captain Nye complained that had the *Ceres* passed another line the *City of New York* "might have been saved, as she was only twice her length from being over the bar. . . . The engines worked continually till the vessel was given up for lost." The next day "her bulwarks and after-house were gone; she was heeled hard off shore, and was fast settling into the sand. Her cargo is a total loss to the Government."

The terrible storm continued to take its toll of Burnsides' fleet. On January 17 the gunboat *Zouave* was lost in Hatteras Inlet "caused by overrunning her anchor during the storm, which knocked a hole in her bottom." She was registered at 170 tons, her dimensions were 106′ × 21′ × 8′, and she carried four guns: one 30-pounder Parrott, two 12-pound Wiard rifle guns, and one 12-pounder boat howitzer. All hands were saved, and the guns were reported recovered.

On January 18 the *Pocahontas* (see *Shipwrecks of North Carolina: from the Diamond Shoals North*) went ashore some twenty miles north of Cape Hatteras. Nearly a hundred horses of the Rhode Island Fourth Infantry were drowned; some were driven overboard ten miles at sea, others died in the surf after the ship drifted onto the beach. Nineteen horses swam through crashing waves and reached land alive; they survived on hay and oats washed ashore from the *Zouave*. The crew and teamsters abandoned both vessel and horses long before grounding, and were all saved.

The gale washed several other ships and boats aground, including the steamers *New Brunswick* and *Louisiana*, all of which were gotten off without loss of life. The only casualties occurred when twelve men were returning by boat to their ship, the *Ann E. Thompson*, which was riding out the storm several miles from the inlet. The boat overturned in the surf, drowning Colonel Joseph Allen, Surgeon S.F. Weller, and Second Mate William Taylor. Thus the Burnside Expedition suffered only three fatalities due to marine casualty, a number that was considered "marvelously small" under the circumstances.

In another respect the gale actually helped Burnside's fleet. The abnormally high tides permitted some deep-draft ships to cross the shallow bar, instead of anchoring outside the inlet and being lightered. The Burnside Expedition succeeded in its goal to conquer Roanoke. On February 8 the Confederate defenders were driven out of their fort; over two thousand were captured.

There is no record of the *City of New York's* cargo being recovered. In addition to that monetary loss, the government was forced to pay $40,000 for the vessel.

What of the wreck today? The position given at the time of her destruction was "at the entrance to the harbor." What this means in relation to the present position of Hatteras Inlet is difficult to say. Where was the "outer bar" that the ships had to cross? Was it what is known today as the Outer Diamond Shoals, or another bar immediately outside Hatteras Inlet? That ships were able to pass completely around the *City of New York* implies that there was deep water on all sides. For now, the answers to these questions lie hidden by the shifting sands of time. ·

It has been suggested that the wreck known locally as the Unis, or the Urn Wreck, is the remains of the *City of New York*. However, that wreck has been positively identified as the *Nevada* (q.v.), and, even had it not, even a cursory examination of the machinery reveals that the Unis has a single-cylinder engine, not a two-cylinder. Furthermore, the Unis lies in sixty feet of water some nine miles offshore, whereas the deepest depth given at any time for the grounded *City of New York* was four fathoms, or twenty-four feet, and in the surf zone. Since all accounts describe the *City of New York* as bilging in shallow water, that is where she must still lie; the weight of her machinery would prevent her flooded, wooden hull from drifting.

Lest there be any confusion, another vessel named *City of New York* was sunk about a hundred miles southeast of the Diamond Shoals on March 29, 1942. She was torpedoed by the *U-160* (Oberleutnant zur See Georg Lassen).

Somewhere, beyond Hatteras Inlet, a cargo of Civil War munitions and provisions lies waiting to be discovered.

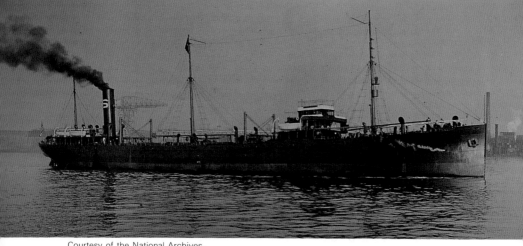

Courtesy of the National Archives.

DIXIE ARROW

Built: 1921

Previous name: None

Gross tonnage: 8,046

Type of vessel: Tanker

Sunk: March 26, 1942

Depth: 90 feet

Dimensions: 468' × 62' × 32'

Power: Oil-fired steam

Builder: New York Ship Building Corp., Camden, New Jersey

Owner: Socony-Vacuum Oil Company

Port of registry: New York, NY

Cause of sinking: Torpedoed by *U–71* (Kapitanleutnant Flachsenberg)

Location: 26949.7   40038.3

Along with three other vessels, the *Dixie Arrow* and the *F.W. Abrams* (q.v.) were constructed as near-sister ships. The *Dixie Arrow* was nine inches longer than the *F.W. Abrams*, and fifteen inches less abeam; the internal configuration was slightly different; there were differences in the number and placement of winches, booms, and kingposts; and, although the engines were the same, those of the *Dixie Arrow* produced ten percent more nominal horsepower. Furthermore, due to modifications made during their careers, although they shared essentially the same displacement tonnage, deadweight tonnage, and net tonnage, the amount of gross registered tonnage differed drastically between the two vessels. It is a coincidence, then, that two ships built in the same yard barely a year apart came to grief only a few miles away from each other.

March 19, 1942 found the *Dixie Arrow* approaching the Diamond Shoals on a zigzag course with tacks of forty-five degrees made at irregular intervals between six and nine minutes. She was on route to Paulsboro, New Jersey with 96,000 barrels of Texas crude from the storage facility at Texas City; unarmed, but with a cautious master in charge. Captain A.H.

Johanson was "very particular about observing all precautions, including absolute blackouts at night and all anti-smoke regulations."

During the heyday of U-boat activity along the eastern seaboard, routing instructions issued by the Navy were subject to change. Captain Johanson first received instructions to follow the 40-fathom curve, then told to skirt the mine field off Cape Hatteras, and also warned about the dense concentration of shipping rounding the Diamond Shoals. Revised orders called for a course close to shore, but far enough off to skirt the friendly mine field off Cape Hatteras. All attempts to clarify how far to sea the mines had been sown came to grief; either the patrol boats he hailed did not have the information or did not respond. Bewildered by confusing and contradictory advice, he decided to stick to the 40-fathom curve and keep a sharp lookout for both Allied ships and marauding U-boats. He posted a watch on the forecastle head. The sea was calm, the breeze was light, and visibility was "excellent." At nine a.m. Captain Johanson saw one ship ten miles astern and another ahead; there was comfort in numbers if not safety.

Without warning a torpedo detonated against the starboard side of the ship, "just below the deck house, setting fire to it." According to one report, "eight men were believed instantly killed when trapped below deck in the dining room." Within sixty seconds two more torpedoes hit the *Dixie Arrow* abaft the first, "causing the vessel to buckle amidships."

The wheelhouse was soon engulfed in flames. Oil spurting from ruptured cargo tanks quickly spread out over the sea. Once ignited, it created a huge burning slick spouting hot tongues of flame that licked the sky, and created billowing clouds of smoke thousands of feet high. The *Dixie Arrow* was a charnel house of German design.

The holocaust racing from the bridge to the forecastle placed some of the crew in desperate straits. They had no way to escape the flames except to leap overboard into a sea of boiling oil. Able-Bodied Seaman Oscar Chappell came to their rescue. According to survivor Paul Myers, "he was at the wheel. Fire was shooting up all about him. He saw several men trapped by flames that the wind was blowing toward them. He turned the ship hard right which took the flames off the men on the bow but threw them directly upon himself. He lasted only a few minutes after that. He died at the helm."

Courtesy of the National Archives.

Courtesy of the Outer Banks History Center.

The successive torpedo blasts knocked out the lights in the engine room, plunging the crowded machinery spaces into virtual darkness. Communication with the bridge was severed. The engine room crew poured onto deck into a torrent of flames. Already, two of the ship's four lifeboats had been destroyed in the blaze. "An attempt to lower number 3 boat did not succeed as the lines fouled and the boat caught fire and apparently fell, killing one man and throwing its other occupants into the sea." At the same time, "another died when his life raft drifted into a pool of burning oil and still another was killed when the explosion hurled him against a davit."

Blood surrounded the *Dixie Arrow* thicker than oil.

No distress call was transmitted because the radio operator, as well as every one of the deck officers including Captain Johanson, had been killed by the first blast. Fortunately, the U.S. destroyer *Tarbell* (DD-142) was on patrol in the area and spotted "vast columns of smoke that blackened the sky." she steamed toward the blighted hulk at high speed and arrived thirty minutes after the attack. "Two empty life rafts and much debris floated nearby. Two boats were drifting on the water, one full of men, the other afire, and a number of men were swimming about to escape the burning oil which ate hungrily along the surface."

The *Tarbell* lowered lifeboats to go after the beleaguered seamen, then circled the wreck and dropped a barrage of depth charges "with the object of insuring safety while the rescue job was in progress." Perhaps the *Tarbell* was a bit overeager in its protective measures. According to survivors still in the water at the time, the exploding depth charges felt "like blows in the stomach." Others reported that they were "almost thrown clean out of the water."

The death toll reigned in at eleven. Fourteen men were plucked from the sea and eight more were taken from the *Dixie Arrow's* lifeboat. They were landed at Morehead City. Said survivor Victor Hoffman after he was safely put ashore, "I had my hat on when I jumped overboard, and here it still is, right on my head. I'm going to put it in the parlor in a glass case, the way some folks put out their best silver."

The *Dixie Arrow* remained afloat throughout the day, filling the sky with black inky clouds of smoke and soot that were visible for miles around. Official reports state that her actual sinking went unobserved. In fact, the burned out hulk drifted right into the Hatteras minefield. She may even have detonated a friendly mine before coming to rest on an even keel in 90 feet of water.

On March 30 a Coast Guard plane reported sighting three masts showing above the surface; the buoy tender *Orchid* was dispatched to the scene, where she established a red nun buoy. For the next year, training planes operating from the Marine Corps Air Station at Cherry Point used the *Dixie Arrow's* masts for target practice. By 1943 the masts had been bombed away.

In 1944 Navy divers were put down on the wreck. Although it was previously thought to be the *Ario*, the true identity was confirmed when the divers recovered the ship's bell. The wreck was then demolished with explosives and wire-dragged to a least depth of 43 feet.

Today the hull is contiguous from bow to stern although completely gutted in the middle with no sign of where the wheelhouse may one time have been. The bow rises nearly twenty-five feet off the bottom, and viewed from the front appears to be sitting in dry dock. No decks remain in the forepeak so a diver can drop right through to the keel. The chain locker is exposed, with two great heaps of linked anchor chain piled in their compartments; the chains rise up through both overhead hawser pipes. The forward hatch cover frame is held in place by crisscrossing beams, but all the decking has rusted completely through leaving a skeletonlike

Some of the *Dixie Arrow's* survivors. (Courtesy of the National Archives.)

appearance to the interior. The upper structure has peeled off on the port side, and lies in the sand adjacent to the wreck.

About seventy-five feet abaft the bow the high relief drops off suddenly to ten feet or less. The hull plates have peeled off both sides and most of them lie buried under the sand. Jumbled wreckage consisting of twisted angle iron and bent hull plates extend all the way to the boilers, with no identifiable bridge or superstructure visible.

Three boilers lie side by side with a six-foot passage on either side. Immediately abaft is the huge engine, which towers twenty-five feet above the level of the sand, and which is so open that a diver can swim through the cylinders. A deteriorating auxiliary boiler rests off the port side of the engine. All around the machinery spaces lie brass pipes, valves, and tubing.

At the extreme stern of the wreck one blade of the bronze propeller protrudes from the sand, while behind it the rudder stands straight up, although nothing is above it. The stern superstructure has fallen off and lies mostly on the port side, apparently upside down.

A large monofilament gill net that is still catching fish is wrapped partially around the engine. Other nets are snagged on various sections of the midship section and bow. Fish bones lie scattered over the bottom as the remains of dead fish fall out of the netting after the flesh has been devoured by scavangers.

The wreck lies on a hard sand bottom that does not stir up easily. It offers high reflection and little loose particulate matter so visibility is usually fifty feet or better. The *Dixie Arrow* is not a colorful wreck, being covered largely with a thin veneer of encrustation of predominantly brown hues. Iron rust shows through everywhere.

Both Walter Flachsenberg and the *U–71* survived the war. The crew scuttled the U-boat at Wilhelmshaven when Germany capitulated.

The graceful stern of the *Dixie Arrow* shown at left (courtesy of the National Archives) exists now as only the upstanding rudder, the propeller, and, in the distance, the engine.

EA

Built: 1893
Previous names: *Cambay*
Gross tonnage: 2,632
Type of vessel: Freighter
Builder: J. Readhead & Sons, South Shields, England
Owner: Sota y Aznar
Port of registry: Bilbao, Spain
Cause of sinking: Ran aground
Location: 27063.2

Sunk: March 15, 1902
Depth: 30 feet
Dimensions: 298′ × 40′ × 20′
Power: Coal-fired steam

39623.1

March 15, 1902 found the Spanish steamer *Ea* at the midpoint of a voyage from Fernandina, Florida to New York with phosphate rock and resin. According to Captain W.V. Garry, master, "Everything went well until the morning of Saturday, the 15th, when in trying to feel our way through a thick fog we grounded on a sand bar off Cape Lookout Lighthouse. The sea was smooth at the time, and I immediately ordered full speed astern, but it was no use, and the *Ea* did not budge. At high tide we tried to get off again, but the attempt as in the first case was of no avail, and the *Ea* remained hard and fast."

The ship was not sighted from land until that afternoon, and then was only dimly seen through the mist. she was on the outer shoal some six miles from the nearest point of land. The crew of the Cape Lookout Life-Saving Station wasted no time launching a surfboat and braving the mounting seas. The fog persisted, so when the life-savers reached the vicinity of the shoal they could find no sign of the stranded steamer. Captain Gaskill, keeper of the Cape Lookout station, kept the men at the oars until after midnight. They searched and searched, but finally gave it up and returned to the station, exhausted from the hard work and frustrated at their lack of successful rescue.

In response to telegraphic instructions, the revenue cutter *Algonquin* and the wrecking tugs *Alexander Jones* and *I.J. Merritt* arrived after dawn on the sixteenth. Said Captain Garry, "Sunday morning the sea became rough and as the ship started to pound she began to break in twain." The men aboard the *Ea* were in desperate straits.

According to the life-saving records, "The stranded steamer was surrounded for several hundred yards by high and dangerous breakers that rendered it impossible for any boat to reach her, and the steamers and life-savers stood by through the night waiting for a chance to rescue the imperiled crew."

Captain Garry: "Monday the gale was still raging with unabashed fury. On this day our water tanks burst and we were without any drinking water. The *Alexander* and *Algonquin* were still trying to get to us, but found the feat impossible owing to the rough sea and our perilous position."

The life-saving crew was not standing idly by. Despite the frightful weather they launched a surfboat and headed for the shoals in case by some miracle they could slip up close to the *Ea* and effect the rescue of the crew. In order to save their strength, the *Alexander Jones* towed the surfboat as near as possible to the stranded steamer, then stayed there turning slow revolutions to keep abreast of the wreck. "Council was held on board the tug and it was decided that no boat could live in the breakers."

By late afternoon on the seventeenth, when the *Ea* had been aground for more than two days, the only refuge for the crew was the top of the bridge. The hull had split completely apart, and all the lifeboats but one had been dashed to pieces by the pounding surf. Water continually rolled across the decks, washing off all loose gear and slowly flooding the ship through loosened hatch covers. Each wave caused the ship to shake and shudder as if she were made of sheet metal instead of thick steel. The men had no choice but to hang on for another night.

By daybreak on the eighteenth the wind had shifted from the north. The sea was still running high, but the *Ea* formed a slight lee that made it seem as if a boat could survive long enough to get away from the shoal without swamping, and to reach the relatively calm water beyond. Captain Garry ordered the men to lower the last remaining lifeboat over the side. He put either fourteen or seventeen men aboard (the exact number differs according to accounts), then prayed for them as they pulled on the oars. They made it into the clear.

Meanwhile, the *Algonquin* lowered a boat and sent it for the rest of the *Ea's* crew. "It being impossible to breast the wind and sea from leeward, the lifeboat was towed to windward and pulled through the weather breakers to the wreck. . . . At the first trial the lifeboat missed the wreck, but a second attempt was made, and the remainder of the ship's company . . . was brought safely through the breakers, thus completing the rescue of all hands, twenty-seven in number."

The *Algonquin* then took the men to Morehead City. The *Ea* soon fell apart, a $96,000 loss for the underwriters. Also lost were 2,500 barrels of resin, 2,500 tons of phosphate rock, and the ship's dog Tiger.

Very little remains of the *Ea*. The wreck is in two distinct parts. The pointed bow sits upright with a huge anchor tight in its hawse pipe. It is separated from the stern by a long stretch of sand. On the stern section the engine rises spectacularly twenty-five feet from the bottom; it is surrounded by rusted crossmembers and a narrow debris field. The propeller shaft is visible, as are two blades of the iron propeller.

The *Ea* is known locally as the Old Smokestack Wreck. It was identified by historic interpretation of its location. Winter storms can move as much as ten feet of sand, thus exposing portions of the wreck not previously visible. Pieces of resin still remain.

E.M. CLARK

Built: 1921
Previous names: *Victolite*
Gross tonnage: 9,647
Type of vessel: Tanker
Builder: Federal Ship Building Company, Kearny, New Jersey
Owner: Standard Oil Company of New Jersey
Port of registry: Wilmington, Delaware
Cause of sinking: Torpedoed by *U-124* (Kapitanleutnant Mohr)
Location: 26905.3

Sunk: March 18, 1942
Depth: 240 feet
Dimensions: 499' × 68' × 30'
Power: Oil-fired steam

40062.2

The *E.M. Clark* was a twin-screw tanker that ran for Imperial Oil, Ltd. before joining the Esso fleet. She carried mostly crude oil from the fields to refinery towns, concentrating on the runs between the Gulf of Mexico and the Caribbean to U.S. east coast ports. After the outset of war in Europe she completed forty-two voyages and delivered 4,812,472 barrels of cargo.

Her first contact with U-boat activity came when she picked up the distress call from the *Venore* (see *Shipwrecks of North Carolina: from the Diamond Shoals North.*) when that ship was torpedoed off Cape Hatteras on January 24, 1942. It is understandable then that Captain Hubert Hassell, master of the *E.M. Clark*, kept his crew alert to the dangers of enemy torpedoes—especially in the vicinity of the Diamond Shoals, and especially after dark on March 17, when the airwaves were jammed with distress calls from two of Johann Mohr's victims: the *Acme*, which did not sink, and the *Kassandra Louloudis* which did. (see *Shipwrecks of North Carolina: from the Diamond Shoals North.*)

Into this battlefield steamed the *E.M. Clark* at a steady ten knots. Sloshing in her tanks were 118,725 barrels of heating oil pumped aboard at

Courtesy of the National Archives.

Baton Rouge, Louisiana: destination New York. She was traveling independently along a track prescribed by the Naval Routing Officer at New Orleans. The ship was completely blacked out: all her ports were closed and her navigation lights were switched off. She was unarmed.

The lookout in the forecastle head was exposed to nature's nasty elements. Rain fell steadily, squalls whipped the sea to a froth, and jagged bolts of lightning split the broad hemisphere of the sky. Claps of thunder rang out like rifle shots.

Not until after midnight did Captain Hassell retire to his stateroom for a few minutes rest. Suddenly there came a tremendous explosion. In a flash the captain was back on the bridge. He ordered the engines full astern, then stopped. He snatched the latest fix from the plotting board and raced to the radio room.

Radio Operator Earle Schlarb was off duty and asleep in his room. An automatic alarm bell rigged to the radio room rang him out of his bunk. "I hurried into my clothes and snatched up a flashlight. As I opened my door I breathed in the sharp, acrid odor of burnt powder in the companionway. Rushing up to the radio room, I turned on my flashlight and found the whole place in chaos. Parts of the apparatus, the filing cabinet, spare-parts locker, table, and racks were in a tangled heap on the floor. The typewriter had been flung across the operating chair and table and had crashed into the receiver-battery charger. The door leading to the boat deck had been blown off and part of the bulkhead was gone." He turned off the alarm bell.

Captain Hassell charged into the room right behind him. "Sparks, get on the air!"

Schlarb's account is vivid: "There was no ship voltage, as the power lines were broken; that was why the alarm bells rang. A battery started them when the line voltage fell below normal. Immediately I threw in the battery switch for the emergency transmitter power supply. It worked! Then I connected the antenna transfer and telegraph key switches and 'sat on the key', sending and repeating SSSS-SOS. But there was no radiation on the dial. Had the main antenna been broken?

"Going outside to the boat deck, I stumbled in the darkness over more wreckage. A flash of lightning showed the damage done by the torpedo; the lifeboat was a blasted heap of torn and twisted metal and splinters; a jagged hole yawned in the sagging deck. Awning and stanchion bars were smashed off or hanging loosely.

"When the lightning passed, inky blackness shut in tightly. I could not see whether the mainmast was still standing. Feeling my way by flashlight, I crossed to the starboard side and bumped into the first assistant engineer, who was coming up from aft. I asked him if the mainmast was down. 'Damned if I know,' he said, 'but the deck is full of wires. Your antenna must be broken!'

"Another flash of lightning revealed the starboard lifeboat being prepared for launching. Some of the men were in it, others on deck. I returned to the radio room, put on my life jacket, and grabbed the coil of spare antenna, tangled by the explosion, but intact.''

Schlarb unrolled the coil of wire as he made his way along the deck looking for someplace to attach the emergency antenna. "Suddenly, off the port side of the ship, distant about 300 yards, a submarine's yellow searchlight was turned on and played about the *E.M. Clark*, apparently to inspect the damage caused by the torpedo.''

Schlarb ignored the inquisitive enemy and concentrated on the task at hand. Captain Hassell and Second Mate Richard Ludden located him by shouting, then untangled the wire while the radio operator scaled a bulkhead to the bridgewing. "Part of the awning bar was still up. To get the spare antenna as far out from the ship's house as possible, I inched along in the murky dark, holding the rail with one hand, the wire with the other. As if by instinct, I halted where I found the railing gone. At the same instant a bolt of lightning showed that the outer wing of the bridge had been torn off. Black water and wreckage gleamed up from far below.''

The connections were all completed and Schlarb was back on deck when, according to Captain Hassell, "a second torpedo hit the ship, portside, between No. 1 and dry cargo holds. This second explosion caused the ship to settle by the head rapidly.''

Schlarb: "The ship's whistle jammed and sent forth a steady roar. Broken steam lines hissed loudly. ... I thought it had started to rain but what I felt on my face was not water: the 'rain drops' were oil! Cargo heating oil had been blown high and was falling in a fine spray! It seemed a miracle that the ship had not caught fire. The explosion had ripped down the spare antenna.''

Barely audible above the uproar, Luddel shouted, "Captain, she's going down fast.''

Captain Hassell transfixed the radio man with bulging eyes. "How long will it take to repair this and send an SOS?''

With the insulators broken and the wire still unraveled, Schlarb estimated, "At least fifteen minutes, maybe more.''

Captain Hassell surveyed his shattered, sinking ship. "I doubt if we have fifteen minutes.'' He gave the order to launch the boats. Then, "I went to my office and collected the ship's documents and secret wartime codes. I took the former along with me, but threw the codes overboard in a weighted canvas bag provided for the purpose.''

Schlarb: "Captain Hassell, believing all hands were accounted for, was the last man to enter the lifeboat. Although we were on the windward side, the boat was safely launched, but once it was in the water the trouble started, as the wind and waves slammed us against the ship's side with great force. All hands worked hard trying to shove off, using the heavy oars and boat hooks. Finally we got the boat clear and all the oars in the water. Rowing was difficult because of the choppy waves and the rolling of the lifeboat.

"Suddenly a seaman yelled and pointed to a man standing at the ship's rail. Captain Hassell directed us to pull back part way, and shouted to the man to jump. His orders were muffled by the din of the ship's whistle. The man on the deck, Wiper Glen Barnhart, slid down a boat fall and dropped into the sea. He wore a life jacket but weighed about 240 pounds and floated low in the water. A wave picked him up and tossed him within a few yards of the lifeboat. He was soon hauled aboard and covered with a blanket.

"The captain told us to row around the stern of the vessel to see if anyone else could be picked up. We had just started when the loom of a light showed, creeping around the ship's stern. 'It's the sub!' someone called out. 'Let's get the hell of of here!' The captain gave orders to pull away and wait until the enemy U-boat submerged. We saw the submarine heading for the stern of the ship as its yellow light silhouetted the torpedoed tanker in the darkness.

"The E.M. Clark was then deep down by the head and filling rapidly. The sea was covered with oil, which kept the waves from breaking over our lifeboat, but the fumes were sickening. Several of the men—I was one of them—became violently ill.

"The ship's stern began to lift high as she plunged forward and down. Just before the smokestack disappeared under the surface, the whistle, which had been blowing steadily since the second explosion, stopped for about 10 seconds, then started again. A great bubbling noise was heard as the E.M. Clark slid smoothly beneath the waves."

The lifeboat circled the field of debris. "A black shape now came alongside. It was one of the life rafts, which Chief Mate Andrew Kadek had released between torpedo hits, at the risk of his life. A shark, possibly killed by the concussion, floated by, white belly up.

Captain Hassell's lifeboat held fourteen men; another lifeboat got away with twenty-six. Thomas Larkin, a utilityman, was missing and presumed dead, "killed by the first explosion while asleep in the hospital room, about where the torpedo struck."

The two boats could not find each other in the dark. Said Schlarp, "We rowed until the lifeboat was out of the oil slick. The waves were now six to eight feet high and all hands were busy with the oars, keeping the boat's head into the wind. ... The submarine's course could be followed by its light, which kept swinging back and forth over the place where the ship had sunk. Now and then the searching beam passed over our boat, but each time this happened we were hidden by wave crests. About two hours later the sub disappeared."

Thunderstorms were still sweeping through the area. A sea anchor was dropped "to keep the boat from broadsiding to the seas and shipping water." The men huddled together for what warmth they could generate. Each and every one was soaked; the cold air bit through their clothing; the wind whistled through their hair and sprayed them with spume.

Added to their discomfort was the sure knowledge that no one knew they were out there. They were completely on their own.

Schlarb: "Our lifeboat drifted till just before dawn, when the compass was broken out to determine the direction of the nearest land. As the wind was blowing toward shore, a sail was hoisted and we moved along at a good clip before a stiff breeze. . . . At about 7 a.m. a destroyer appeared over the horizon. We shot two red flares and she changed course. A few minutes later another flare was fired and before long the destroyer neared us, maneuvered to windward, and carefully came alongside."

The captain and his men were soon ensconced aboard the USS *Dickerson* (DD-157). At about the same time the men in the other lifeboat were picked up by the Venezuelan tanker *Catatumbo*.

Interviews with the crew elicited several interesting sidelights. James Miller, wiper: "there were great bright flashes of lightning and you could see for miles. I think the sub would have missed us if it hadn't had this light to aim by." Harold Rew, an oiler, told how the attack broke up a poker game in which he was ahead; he "didn't even have time to pick up the money." Able Seaman James Stafford didn't know "but what the ship would burst into flames any minute. She didn't burn and that's all that saved us."

Exclusive of cargo, hull insurance on the *E.M. Clark* was $1,202,250; settlement in full was made on April 16, 1942.

The *U-124* was lost with all hands west of Gibraltar on April 2–3, 1943; it was sunk by the HMS *Stonecrop* and the HMS *Black Swan*. See elsewhere in this volume for its depredations against the *Esso Nashville*, *Naeco*, *Papoose*, and *W.E. Hutton*.

According to Roger Huffman the current on the wreck of the *E.M. Clark* is unpredictable except when the Gulf Stream has been pushed out as by a northeaster and the so-called "green" water is in. Otherwise, the current can pick up fast without warning, end the same way, and change several times during the course of a day—all of which makes it extremely difficult for divers forced by the depth of the dive to make long decompression stops in the water. He once lost a buoy with one hundred pounds of flotation when it was pulled under the surface and never came back up. Another time his boat, the *Quiet Waters*, drifted over five miles in one hour.

I have experienced this current on the *E.M. Clark*, and can vouch for Huffman's cautionary notes. One time the current was so strong that after I pulled the hook, the dive boat drifted broadside *into* a 25-knot wind with such speed that the anchor line hung practically horizontal, resulting in what I call a water-ski decompression. The wind blowing against the current makes for sloppy conditions and short, choppy waves.

The wreck lies on its port side with the keel facing the prevailing current. Because of the constant high speed of the water much of the hull is scoured clean by sandblasting. The resultant lack of marine growth is the reason no fish are caught there. With visibility averaging a hundred feet or better, the wreck is visually spectacular and awesomely impressive. The average depth on the lee, or superstructure, side is 240 feet, with sand built up higher on the hull side. Washouts at either end go as deep as 255 feet. The hull looms up as high as 197 feet. The wreck is totally intact, but pockmarked by growing rust holes.

The huge starboard anchor can be seen tight in its hawse pipe. Nearly all the superstructure has collapsed into the sand. A narrow lip exists where the bridge once stood, while the wheelhouse lies on the bottom like a pile of pickup sticks. All along the main deck are walkways, or the stanchions that supported them, as well as bollards and cleats. The deck planking is loose and rips out if pulled too hard. What appears to be the stack lies flattened on the sand.

Most of the stern structure is gone except for the central core. Portholes and china from the starboard rooms and corridor have fallen against the large room in the middle, and more have fallen all the way down to the sand. The engine room skylight is wide open: twenty feet high and wide. Catwalks descend horizontally into a dark maw that swallows the brightest dive light as if it were a candle.

The extreme stern structure is missing, including the twin helms of the auxiliary steering station, but the steering quadrant is still there—its gear teeth clearly recognizable. Perhaps the most majestic sight is that of the giant rudder straddled by two large bronze propellers. The three blades of the starboard propeller are free and clear of the bottom. The weight of the rudder has made it fall hard aport. Below it the upper blade and hub of the port propeller stand above the deep washout.

The wreck has vast potential for future exploration.

ESSO NASHVILLE

Built: 1940

Previous names: None

Gross tonnage; 7,943

Type of vessel: Tanker

Sunk: March 21, 1942

Depth: 120 feet

Dimensions: 445' × 64' × 34'

Power: Two oil-fired steam turbines

Builder: Bethlehem Steel Co. Ship Building Division, Sparrows Point, MD

Owner: Standard Oil Company of New Jersey

Port of registry: Wilmington, Delaware

Cause of sinking: Torpedoed by *U-124* (Kapitanleutnant Mohr)

Location: 27156.3   39163.8

The career of the *Esso Nashville* is as strange an odyssey as one is likely to find in the annals of the sea. She was a ship thought sunk, brought back by a captain believed dead. She led a double life, both of them charmed, carrying petroleum products in two different hulls under the same name. Sound mysterious? In truth, it is. But never fear; there is a logical explanation for everything.

From the time of her birth in 1940 to that fateful day in March 1942, the *Esso Nashville* completed thirty-eight coastwise voyages and success-fully delivered nearly four million barrels of oil. There was a war on, and Germany was doing its best to see that tankers carrying precious fluids for the Allied campaign did not reach their destinationss. U-boats sent to the American coast were assigned the specific task of sinking these tankers in order to paralyze the shipment of men and materiel to the beleaguered British Isles. By the time the *Esso Nashville* steamed into sight of a submerged periscope with such disastrous results, the U-boat arm had already taken an effective punch at the merchant marine. In just two months, twenty-one tankers had been sent to Davy Jones's locker in an area from Maine to Florida designated as the Eastern Sea Frontier. Numerous freighters, liners, and warships were also sunk during that time, accounting for the loss of over a thousand lives.

With these hardboiled statistics in mind, the Standard Oil Company spared no expense for the lives of its tanker crews. Company vessels were equipped with the latest life-saving apparatus, all lifeboats were properly maintained, and all crew members were supplied with lifesaving suits. The U.S. Government had not yet gotten around to arming the merchant fleet, or supplying Naval gunners, so the *Esso Nashville* went unarmed. She plied a zigzag course during the day, and ran blacked out at night. In addition to the bridge watch, two extra lookouts kept vigil: one atop the wheelhouse, another on the forecastle head. The lifeboats were carried swung out, ready to be launched at a moment's notice, and frequent evacuation drills were held. It was Captain Edward Peters' way of increasing the odds of survival.

Traveling independently, the *Esso Nashville* passed Frying Pan Shoals around 11 p.m. on the twentieth. It was not a pretty night; a moderate sea splashed against the hull, a southwesterly wind whistled through the bridgeworks, and a cold rain fell. The lookouts shivered in their drenched southwesters. The ship's tanks were filled with 78,000 barrels of fuel oil bound from Port Arthur, Texas to New Haven, Connecticut.

Captain Peters remembered the fateful moment. "At 12:20 a.m., as I was resting in my room, I heard a thud against the ship's hull as if it had brushed against a buoy or some wreckage. I immediately got up and went to the bridge to inquire about the cause of the shock. As I reached the bridge, a terrific crash occurred on the starboard side abaft the midship house, raising the vessel up bodily and throwing her to starboard and then keeling her to port so violently that I feared she was going to turn over. The entire ship was flooded with oil which spouted as high as the foremast; dense smoke and sparks emanated from the explosion of the torpedo. All communications with the engineroom were disrupted at once, but in accordance with previous instructions the engine was stopped."

The blast knocked out all the ship's lights. Radio Operator Thomas Rhiel was thrown from his bunk. Third Assistant Engineer Henry Garig was knocked off a ladder. Chief Mate Christian Hansen, asleep at the time, "felt the deck rising under my feet. My room filled with smoke and what seemed to me to be a gas which made me cough and drew tears to my eyes." Third Mate John Kerves actually spotted the torpedo's wake: "I saw a streak in the water coming toward us rapidly. When I realized it was a torpedo I turned around and started to go inside, but it hit before I managed this. It struck within three seconds. Flames shot in the air and oil was thrown everywhere. Some of the hot oil was blown in my face."

Rhiel: "The door to my room burst open and flames shot into the room. I went to the wireless room to send an SOS, but I couldn't because the shack was so full of smoke and gas."

The turbine was shut down. Garig "found many of the crew in the outside passageway, standing in water and oil up to their knees. I held my flashlight to assist them and they all followed me to my room and waited while I put on my rubber suit."

Captain Peters: "Second Mate Boje sounded the general alarm, all hands rushed to their station, and the lifeboats were made ready for launching. Both the ship's bow and stern were raised high out of the water and as she was settling amidships where the torpedo struck, I gave the order to abandon ship.'' The captain tried ''to fetch the ship's secret documents and papers, but I was unable to reach my room because of the smoke and gas.''

Second Mate Johannes Boje added that the sagging midship made ''a sort of scoop of her, which acted as a brake,'' causing ''the ship to lose headway much quicker than she would have done if the engines had been stopped.''

Kerves became violently sick from the fumes of the explosion. ''I was covered with oil and my eyes were full of it.''

Garig: ''Electrician Christie and I got into the boat and I held the light so that the other men could slide down the falls. We cast the falls loose, but as we were on the windward side the waves were banging the boat against the side of the ship. With 21 of us in the lifeboat the men at the oars had too little space to row. I therefore called for the six other men wearing life suits to follow me into the water. They all responded and we hung on to the gunwales. We were then able to clear the ship.''

The average man needed a lifesuit in order to survive. Not so Oiler Leonard Mills. At the age of fifty-six, Mills, a retired fireman with a comfortable pension, volunteered out of pure patriotism for service in the merchant marine. Said Garig: ''When the men were getting into No. 4 boat, Mills appeared in a life jacket but on that cold night with the drenching rain he was clad only in his trunks. When one of the younger men standing nearby yelled for a life preserver, Mills took his off and gave it to him. I at once told Mills to take his life jacket back, but he told me he could swim better than the younger man. Later, when I asked the men wearing rubber suits to get into the water, Mills jumped in before we did and he stayed with us, hanging on in the cold water for 3 or 4 hours. When we got back into the boat he was suffering from the cold and I offered him my rubber suit. Refusing it, he wrapped himself in a blanket and took one of the oars.''

No. 1 boat was having its own problems. Kerves: ''I started cutting the lashings holding the lifeboat to get it ready for lowering. All this time the bow of the ship was going up and it had a bad list. When I succeeded in cutting the boat free it was getting difficult to stand up because of the oily deck and plight of the vessel, and I slid toward the after davit. ... We started to lower the lifeboat away, but everything was so oily we couldn't properly lower the boat; the lines slipped through our hands and the boat fell into the sea.'' Working the after falls, Rhiels fell overboard and slid down the line like a fireman down a fire pole. He hands were severely blistered.''

By the time Captain Peters got back to the stations the boats were in the water. As he climbed down to No. 2 lifeboat his foot slipped on the pilot's ladder. Hansen described the incident: ''The sea was choppy and carried the boat away from the ship. The captain fell into the water between the ship and the boat. The captain was a good swimmer but the sea was covered with heavy fuel oil. You can't swim in that. It paralyzes you. We never saw him again. We heard him holler 'Here I am' and we yelled 'we are coming.' But by the time we could row back toward the ship there was no sign of the captain."

The lifeboats got separated in the dark, nighttime drizzle. For hours they drifted aimlessly about, unaware of the location or the condition of the others, and not knowing who was dead or alive. Dawn found them each in different quadrants.

Only two men had gotten away on lifeboat No. 1: Kerves and Rhiel. Said Kerves: "About dawn we rigged the mast and sail and passed within approximately one-quarter of a mile of the *Esso Nashville*, but saw no one either in the water or on the ship, nor did we see any of the other lifeboats about. As we passed the ship we could see that the after end of the midship boat deck was level with the sea."

Garig, in lifeboat No. 4, had a different view: "At daybreak we could see the *Esso Nashville* about half a mile away. She was so low in the water amidships and her bow and stern so high that her two masts had almost come together."

According to Pumpman James Dix, "No. 3 boat sent up flares about 6 or 7 a.m. About a mile off from the lifeboat we saw the conning tower of a submarine."

What might have happened next is anyone's guess had it not been for the fortuitous arrival of three U.S. warships. Coming to the rescue like the United States Cavalry to the sound of trumpets were the Coast Guard cutters *Agassiz* and *Tallapoosa*, and the flush-deck destroyer *McKean* (DD-90). Against this awesome array of firepower and decks full of depth charges and hedgehogs, the U-boat quietly withdrew. The *Agassiz* picked up the men from Lifeboat No. 3, the *Tallapoosa* recovered those from No. 4, and the *McKean* saved those aboard Nos. 1 and 2. Only Captain Peters was unaccounted for.

Imagine the rejoicing when a signal was spotted on the fantail of the buckled tanker. The *Agassiz* drew close for inspection. Although suffering from a fractured leg, crushed between the ship's side and the lifeboat's gunwale when he had fallen overboard, Captain Peters was very much alive. He had tried to swim after the lifeboat, but:

"After three-quarters of an hour of hopeless efforts, I decided to swim back to the ship, which was still afloat and where it seemed I would stand a better chance of being rescued. I boarded her quite easily forward of the mainmast, where her deck was awash, and after considerable effort I got aft to the engineer's quarters. After resting in the second assistant's room and bandaging my leg which had badly swollen, I fastened a white sheet to the rail on the windward side and ran up the ship's ensign upside down on the flag pole on the poop deck. I also tried to put on one of the lifesaving suits, but could not manage to fasten it around my neck and gave it up.

"At daybreak I sighted three U.S. Navy vessels about three miles off the bow, which were apparently picking up the crew from the lifeboats. One of them came off the stern of the *Esso Nashville* as I tried to swim to it and then launched a lifeboat from which a line was thrown to me and I was rescued."

On May 3, 1943 U.S. Coast Guard Rear Admiral Stanley Parker presented Captain Peters with the American Legion Medal for his outstanding heroism. The citation read, in part: "Without regard to his personal safety, Captain Peters, in ordering away the boat, undoubtedly prevented the loss of the lives of many of his shipmates. His act of courage and bravery above and beyond the call of duty will be an inspiration to the men of the U.S. Merchant Marine."

On a sad note, Leonard Mills, the volunteer oiler who gave up the retired life to go to sea for his country, who gave his life jacket to a younger man, and who was the first to plunge into the frigid, oil-covered water in order to save an overcrowded lifeboat from foundering, lost his life less than four months after his acts of heroism. He went down with the *R.W. Gallagher*, and claimed a permanent grave in the sea. Because of men like him and Captain Peters, the American merchant marine earned a place of the highest regard among the freedom fighters of the world.

According to an official memorandum the *Esso Nashville* split apart, "being held together for several hours by deck plating and pipe lines. ... The forward end turned over with bow above water." Usually in such cases the stern sinks due to the weight of the machinery; sometimes the separated forward section of a tanker remains afloat because it consists essentially of connected airtight tanks with sufficient reserve buoyancy despite the weight of the cargo. In this case, however, the five tanks making up the forward section sank, while the stern, with two tanks intact and a third breeched, was set adrift. The U.S. Naval tug *Umpqua* (No. 25) was able to tow the after section into Morehead City.

"This difficult task was accomplished without mishap and the success of the operation was largely due to William S. Lawson of the *Umpqua*, who had an intimate knowledge of the channel, and to Pilot Charles Piner, of Morehead City, on the salvage tug SS *Relief*, which assisted the *Umpqua* through the channel. When the 'half-ship' was towed to Morehead City it was listing about 40° to port; the starboard bilge keel at the forward end was above water and the port side of the main deck at the break of the poop was about 3 feet above water level."

Eventually, the engine room was pumped dry, the transverse bulkheads were reinforced, and other temporary repairs were effected. The truncated ship was then returned to the yard that had built her, where a 300-foot-long forward section was fabricated and welded on. The job took a year and cost a million and a half dollars. After a second launching ceremony the *Esso Nashville* "was again ready to join the large fleet of tankers engaged in the transportation of vital cargoes to the fighting forces of the United

Nations," and ready "to make repeated successful voyages delivering war supplies, for the invasions, to the British Isles and the Mediterranean." Between rebirth and the end of the war she carried an additional two million barrels of much need petroleum products, including motor fuel, diesel oil, butyl alcohol, and alkylate blending agent. She certainly did her part for the war effort.

That part of the *Esso Nashville* that the Germans sent to the bottom is still largely intact. It rests upside down in 120 feet of water and rises to a depth of 90 feet. The anchors can be seen on either side dangling in the sand. It is easy to swim under the deck between the bow and the wheelhouse and ascend into tanks so huge they resemble caverns with ribbed ceilings. Ladders are mute reminders of the men who once climbed down into the tanks to perform inspections. Plenty of light enters from the sides at the level of the sand, but the hull overhead is a dark canopy.

Working aft along the white sandy bottom one begins to see the beginnings of debris fields that spread out on both sides of the wreck. Large scale items such as pumps and machinery are mixed in with pipes, valves, and brass fittings. Most of the debris is found at the after end where the hull separated, as if the ship had spilled its guts after being torn apart and flipped over.

Today the tanker is a haven for large lobster and grouper—a fisherperson's paradise because it is far enough offshore to keep it from being dived on a regular basis. The hull is covered with thick marine encrustation and colorful tropical fish. Nature has concealed the ugly iron oxide with a special blend of hues from the palette of life.

The *Esso Nashville* remains a silent testimonial to a time when political aggression ruled the world, when men followed blindly the crazed leaders in power, when might—not right—was the watchword of human civilization.

See elsewhere in this volume for Kapitanleutnant Johann Mohr's other depradations: *E.M. Clark, Naeco, Papoose,* and *W.E. Hutton.* During the dark hours of April 2 and 3, 1943, the British warships *Stonecrop* and *Black Swan* sank the *U-124.* There were no survivors.

A trigger fish guarding the nest.

Courtesy of the National Archives.

F.W. ABRAMS

Built: 1920
Previous names: *Nora*
Gross tonnage: 9,310
Type of vessel: Tanker
Builder: New York Ship Building Corp., Camden, New Jersey
Owner: Standard Oil Company of New Jersey
Port of registry: Wilmington, Delaware
Cause of sinking: Allied mines
Location: 26967.3

Sunk: June 11, 1942
Depth: 90 feet
Dimensions: 467′ × 62′ × 31′
Power: Oil-fired steam

40073.6

The *F.W. Abrams* began life as the *Nora*, built for the W.R. Grace Company, and was a near-sister ship of the *Dixie Arrow* (q.v.). With a pumping rate of 3,000 barrels per hour she could disgorge a full cargo of oil in thirty-four hours. During the time between the outbreak of the war in Europe and her eventual sinking she completed forty voyages from Gulf of Mexico and Caribbean loading ports to various refineries and distribution points in the Americas: an east coast tramp carrying mostly crude oil, "with occasional loadings of fuel oil, Diesel oil, and distillates."

On June 2, 1942, she took on 90,294 barrels of fuel oil from the holding tanks on Aruba, and proceeded through U-boat infested waters toward the port of New York. The tanker was armed only with Captain Anthony Coumelis's knowledge that enemy activity was intense along the prescribed route. According to U.S. Naval operating procedures, ships were permitted to round the Diamond Shoals only in daytime: not because of their age-old treacherousness due to storms and uncertain seas, but because the Germans preyed upon the concentration of shipping that passed through the area.

Near noon on June 10 the *F.W. Abrams* passed Cape Lookout. She reached Ocracoke six hours later, and was directed by a Coast Guard patrol boat (*CGC 484*) to anchor for the night. Because protective mine fields had been placed around Ocracoke and Hatteras inlets, the *CGC 484* stood by in order to escort the tanker to the open sea, "from the Mine Field south to Hatteras Mine Field Buoy 8," then east for thirty miles from where she could proceed on her own course. This surprised Captain Coumelis because he knew nothing about American mine fields; he had been out of the country under charter to the British since the previous December. Nevertheless, he followed instructions.

"The early morning of June 11 found extremely inclement conditions, and although the sea was moderate, the weather was squally, with a heavy fog alternating with rain. The wind was south southeast, force 3–4, and visibility in general was limited to one-quarter of a mile."

Under these conditions the *CGC 484* lighted a white lantern on her stern, and directed Captain Coumelis to follow closely behind. Ship traffic does not move bumper to bumper like automobile traffic; there needs to be room to maneuver because vessels bucking the sea cannot turn with the spin of the wheel. Because of the distance between them (three ship's lengths) the Coast Guard cutter kept fading in and out of view to those straining their eyes from the tanker's bridge, and to the lookout on the forecastle.

They had temporarily lost sight of their escort when, in Captain Coumelis's words, "Junior Mate saw the torpedo wake. I saw something that could possibly resemble a wake, and due to the fact it was raining very heavy, I'm not quite sure it was a torpedo wake or rain water hitting the surface of the sea. This was on the starboard side, on the starboard bow, I should say, right under the windlass, which apparently damaged all the dry hold and the fore peak." The lookout was injured by the blast. The time was 6:40 a.m.

Captain Coumelis telephoned the engine room and ordered full astern. Boatswain Arthur Smith opened the control valve that opened the steam-smothering line, to prevent fire. Radio Operator Eldon McCarthy tapped out an SOS and gave the ship's name and position. The *F. W. Abrams* soon lost way and came to a stop. A quick examination divulged that the ship was ten feet down by the head, but not in immediate danger of sinking.

Then the crew began caterwauling that a U-boat had surfaced abaft the beam. With the enemy bearing down upon them and the Coast Guard cutter nowhere to be seen, it was time for action. The captain called for full speed ahead.

Coumelis: "The vessel at that time had about three feet freeboard on the bow, and the blade of the wheel was half-way out of the water. That, of course, caused us not to be able to manage the ship so well. At that time we could get slow speed ahead in the engine room, as we had trouble in the boilers keeping the water up." (Due to the ship's downward tilt the combustion chamber tops were not covered with water.)

"About 7:17 another explosion occurred at about No. 5 main tanks, which is almost amidships, and this buckled all the plates from the starboard side in, of the deck, and almost it came out on the port side. The plates on the port side was buckled out. The vessel then sank to the water's edge, and the forward main deck was awash."

The *F. W. Abrams* was half sunk and unarmed, adrift in a battering rain storm, a sitting duck for another attack. Captain Coumelis stood by his ship, but gave "orders to lower No. 2 boat, with the injured man aboard, and to stand-by close to the ship, that in case of fire and someone should jump overboard, to pick them up, in charge of A.B., second in command. This A.B.—McGowan was his name—and somebody else, they launched the boat. About a few minutes after they launched the boat they started hollering "Submarine on the port quarter." They were on the port side; I was at the time on the starboard wing of the bridge, as the ship was taking a little list then, a list to starboard, and I had taken soundings. I instructed the Second Mate to take soundings, and I found out there was 17 fathoms of water, and I knew we weren't in danger so far yet. I never saw the submarine. I turned around to see it, but I didn't see it. Between the time I heard the people yelling "submarine" and the third explosion was about a minute or two. At this time it apparently hit us on the port side, a glancing blow, at No. 4 main tank, and it came out somewheres on the bow. This was the third torpedo.

" . . . The third one was a more bigger explosion than the other two, more powerful hit. Well, then the ship automatically started sinking fast, very rapidly then. At 7:40 we abandoned the ship, and before we cleared the ship's side, the ship's pilot house was under water; nearly 45-degree angle the ship was at that time, and water close to the fidley deck, the edge of the dry deck and close to the fidley deck.

"The Chief Officer was at the time in my boat, and then I put him in charge of his boat, No. 2, which already had been launched, and we waited about five minutes to see the result of the ship, and I came to the conclusion it would be better to go ashore and get some help, as we were only 9–10 miles from the beach. We landed, all safely, except the injured man who was given first-aid at the Coast Guard station and was removed to the Navy Base.'' The captain neglected to mention that it took them five hours to row ashore. All thirty-six men survived the ordeal.

This is how the incidents appeared to the men of the *F.W. Abrams.* From their perspective an aggressive U-boat captain had pursued their ship relentlessly, firing torpedo after torpedo until the tanker took the final plunge. In actuality, after losing sight of the escort vessel, the *F. W. Abrams* wandered off course and blundered into the Hatteras mine field. When the *CGC 484* turned around in response to the tanker's SOS, her low hull was mistaken for that of a U-boat. In order to evade further attack, and in order to ground his ship to prevent it from sinking altogether, Captain Coumelis steered for the nearest shoal water shown on his charts—the Diamond Shoals—thus heading directly into the thickest part of the Hatteras mine field, where the *F.W. Abrams* set off two more mines.

It developed later that a crew member in one of the lifeboats "observed a hemispherical object with three horns approximately three inches long and one inch thick protruding from the top, floating in the water and as this object came in contact with the ship, the third explosion resulted.''

According to Standard Oil Company records, "Captain Coumelis and Chief Engineer Larsen stood by for the purpose of determining whether or not the *F. W. Abrams* could be salvaged. When the lifeboats left the tanker, her stern was still above water and even three days later, on the 14th, when Captain Coumelis went out with Navy authorities to inspect the ship, she was partly visible. Subsequently, however, heavy seas battered her until she was completely submerged and there was no hope of salvage.''

The tanker suffered further ignominy at the hands of Allied explosives. Because both masts protruded above the surface, the wreck became a handy target for training planes operating from the Marine Corps Air Station at Cherry Point. "On several occasions reports of periscope sightings were traced to the mast of this wreck, and on one occasion depth charges were dropped on it by a patrol plane.'' After the masts were blown off the Navy Salvage Service, in 1944, demolished the wreck to a clearance "in excess of 40 feet.''

The wreck of the *F.W. Abrams* lies on a soft, silty bottom that stirs up easily; visibility is sometimes reduced to a milky white by fine particulate matter. Steel hull plates are overgrown with a thin veneer of marine encrustation that is essentially colorless, with a pervading sense of brown as the predominant hue. Occasional fan corals with a deep purple tint reach a diameter of eighteen inches; some yellow corals extend to two feet.

The wreck is essentially contiguous, although a forty-foot gap separates one half from the other. The highest relief is in the stern, where the exposed low pressure cylinder of the triple expansion engine rises some twenty feet off the bottom. Abaft of that, the wreckage is flattened for about forty feet to the stern post. The rudder, propeller, and shaft are buried.

Forward of the engine, three boilers lie touching side by side like eggs in a nest, stretching the breadth of the wreck. Along the engine and boilers, to port, the upper hull plates lie out in the sand. From here to about midships, where the break occurs, relief is less than eight feet, and the wreckage is jumbled.

Forward of the break the wreck sticks up some fifteen feet sheer. Valves, pumps, and piping are all about. From here to the bow the wreck is reduced to an eight-foot relief of scattered, broken down and indiscernable wreckage. Steel ladders lie everywhere, bow and stern. The bow itself is broken, with huge links of anchor chain visible all over. Relief rises to ten feet. Very little shiplike structure is recognizable anywhere, and no obvious signs of the bridge are identifiable.

Courtesy of the National Archives.

GEORGE WEEMS

Built: 1874
Previous names: *George S. Blake*
Gross tonnage: 234
Type of vessel: Oak-hulled freighter
Builder: Baltimore, Maryland
Owner: Mason L. Weems Williams (Baltimore & Carolina Steam Ship Co.)
Port of registry: Baltimore, Maryland
Cause of sinking: Fire
Location: 45216.5

Sunk: May 20, 1908
Depth: 40 feet
Dimensions: 148′ × 26′ × 10′
Power: Coal-fired steam

59190.9

  In 1874 the U.S. Coast and Geodetic Survey commissioned the newly constructed vessel *George S. Blake*, and outfitted her with the most up-to-date equipment then available for conducting deep-sea survey work. She was the first survey vessel equipped with piano-forte wire for sounding purposes, and the first to use wire rope for dredging. She carried the latest appliances and state-of-the-art instrumentation necessary for taking hydrographic measurements.

  For the first five years of her career she worked in the Gulf of Mexico. Thousands of depth soundings taken during that time helped to make a bathymetric map of the bottom of the Gulf, but her work did not stop there. The ship worked round the clock when at sea, recording temperatures, densities, and the strength and direction of the current. She also collected bottom soil samples, and took surface, bottom, and intermedial specimens.

This rather full work schedule was performed by a hydrographic team that consisted of Naval officers and men assigned to the *George S. Blake* for the purpose. At that time, the U.S. Navy often detached its men for non-military assignments such as exploration and survey work. Many of the Arctic and Antarctic expeditions were sponsored by the Navy. For example, in 1879, Lieutenant George Washington De Long commanded the *Jeannette* in an attempt to reach the North Pole via the Bering Sea. In 1881, Lieutenant Adolphus Washington Greely led the Lady Franklin Bay Expedition, during which he established the "farthest north." In the twentieth century, Richard Evelyn Byrd (who wound up an admiral) flew Navy planes over both the North and South Poles, and established a Naval base in Antarctica. Today, the Navy still maintains bases in these cold, nether regions.

A description of the *George S. Blake* can be found in *Deep-Sea Sounding and Dredging* (1880), by Charles D. Sigsbee. "The *Blake* was built for the special work on which she is employed. She is of three hundred and fifty tons O.M., one hundred and forty feet in length on the load line, twenty-six feet six inches beam, and has a deep draught of eleven feet. Her engine, which is compound, of about seventy nominal and two hundred and seventy actual horse-power, gives her a speed of eight knots, under ordinary circumstances, for an expenditure of four tons of coal in twenty-four hours; and she may be pushed to nine knots under steam alone. Under both sail and steam she has been known to maintain a speed of ten and a half knots. Her bunkers will accomodate coal for thirty-eight days steaming, at a daily expenditure of four tons. The rig is that of a fore-and-aft schooner, and consists of foresail, mainsail, jib, fore-stay sail, and fore and main gaff-topsails. Aft on the main-deck are spacious and well ventilated quarters for the officers. Forward of the wardroom, on the same deck, is a continuous line of midship houses, reaching nearly to the foremast and forming the engine-room, boiler-room, galley, pantry, draughting-room, lamp-room, and mechanics' sleeping-room. The arrangement of the main-deck houses leaves, on either side, a wide gangway, ventilated and lighted along its whole length through square ports which can be kept open at sea in any ordinary weather. Beneath a sufficiently large berth-deck is a good-sized hold with tanks for holding 2,500 gallons of fresh water, while under the cabin and wardroom, and accessible only from those apartments, are large store-rooms. The upper deck is flush, and gives ample room for the reception of all the necessary machinery and gear."

The disparity in tonnage and dimensions between Sigsbee's description and those given in the Lloyd's Register (in the statistics sidebar) can be ascribed to different measurement standards. It is interesting to note that Sigsbee was the captain of the U.S. battleship *Maine* when she was sunk in

Havana Harbor in 1898; the incident fueled growing unrest that culminated in the Spanish-American War.

For the next twenty-five years her hydrographic responsibilities carried the *George S. Blake* along the entire east coast, from Maine to the Caribbean. For three decades she was a busy and peripatetic little ship. But progress marches on, and after a long and venerable career the *George S. Blake* was replaced by newer and larger vessels. The final entry in her deck log was written on January 25, 1905; it reads, "accounts of this vessel closed."

On August 1, 1905 the ex-survey ship was sold to Mason L. Weems Williams, president of the Baltimore and Carolina Steamship Company. According to her certificate of enrollment she was altered and remeasured for the coasting trade. Under the name *George Weems* she plied the freight lanes between Baltimore and Charleston for the next three years, without incident.

The year 1908 was a trying one for the crew of the *George Weems*, and a disastrous one for the ship. First, on April 7, as the ship rode her anchors off Cape Lookout, four of her crew sailed her boat toward shore. As the boat rounded Wreck Point it capsized, plunging the men into the water. Fortunately, the alert life-saving crew at the Cape Lookout station observed the accident and came to the rescue. The life-savers launched their surfboat, picked up the men "and brought them ashore, then towed the boat in, righted it, and bailed it out."

A month later came the end of the *George Weems*. At five minutes past noon on May 20, as she was steaming from Charleston and Georgetown for Baltimore, fire broke out on the after bulkhead of the engine room. Captain L.G. Hudgins, master, gave the alarm for all hands on deck. The crew manned the fire hoses and within ten or fifteen seconds had three streams of water directed at the blaze. They battled the flames valiantly for the next hour and a half but, once ignited, the timbers burned without abandon.

By 1:30 Captain Hudgins realized that the fire could not be controlled. Rather than risk loss of life he ordered abandon ship. "After seeing all hands safely in the lifeboat, the captain left the ship and laid his course for Frying Pan light-vessel."

The pilot boat *Elma Brooks* happened upon the burning ship that afternoon. She noticed that distress signals were set, but upon close inspection found that the lifeboats were gone and the ship was deserted. The *George Weems* sank around eight o'clock that night.

It was a sad end for a ship that had served science so well.

Captain Hudgins and his crew were taken off the lightship by the steamer *Chatham* at two o'clock the next morning, and went with her to New York.

The wreck was first dived by Wayne Strickland when he was checking out numbers given to him by a fishing boat captain. Lying as she was in shallow water, the hull had been pummeled ignominiously throughout the years by storms and pounding waves. The engine had been knocked over on its starboard side, the two boilers had rolled off their bedplates to either side, and the rest of the wreck lay nearly flattened on the bottom. But in the debris field lay some cherished treasures.

First the capstan cover then the ship's bell were recovered; each offered positive identification. Lloyd's Register lists the original name of the *George Weems* as *G.S. Blake*; in Sigsee's book he commonly refers to her simply as the *Blake*. Later captains wrote *Geo. S. Blake* in the log. But the name engraved in bronze was *George S. Blake*.

Strickland says that the wreck constantly sands and unsands, and reports that of the ship's twenty-four portholes only two have been recovered. With normally clear water and a profusion of colorful marine growth, he considers the *George Weems* to be "one of the prettiest wrecks off Southport."

These pictures of the *George Weems* as the USGS survey vessel *George S. Blake* were taken from Charles Sigsbee's book, *Deep-Sea Sounding and Dredging*. Notice the ship's bell.

From *Steamboat Disasters and Railroad Accidents in the United States.*

HOME

Built: 1837
Previous names: None
Gross tonnage: 550

Sunk: October 9, 1837
Depth: 10 feet under the sand
Dimensions: 198' × 22' × 12'

Type of vessel: Wooden-hulled side-wheel steamer
Power: Square vertical engine
Builder: Brown & Bell, New York, NY
Owner: Southern Steam Packet Company (James P. Allaire)
Port of registry: New York
Cause of sinking: Disabled engine, then run ashore
Location: Six and a half miles northeast of Ocracoke lighthouse

The *Home* was built at a time when confidence in steamboats was on shaky ground at best. In the early days of industrialization people maintained an unreasoned distrust for all things mechanical. Where ships and trains were concerned, however, sometimes such fears were well founded. Locomotive and ship boilers had a nasty habit of exploding if the pressure got too high; steam vessel expansion and metal stress engineering was in its infancy.

Yet the *Home* was a staunchly built paddlewheeler that received praise from contemporary mariners. Her machinery was designed by the respected James Allaire, and constructed at his Iron Works in New York City. Brown & Bell added their expertise to hull configuration. Said engineer W.C. Redfield in 1842, "The *Home* had, of course, been condemned in advance by certain nautical prophets, as has been common in all early attempts at ocean steam navigation, and on the completion of her first voyage was greatly traduced, through the ignorant misapprehensions of passengers and others, many of whom had mistaken the arched form which had been given to her deck for its greater strength, and which was most strikingly visible at two points, forward and aft of the centre, which, viewed in connection with the usual depression of the wheel guards at midships, was taken as a conclusive evidence of that injurious strain which is designated by the term *hogged*. Another effective scarecrow had also been found in a single set of bearing braces above the gunwale, on each side, which were intended to distribute more extensively a part of the weight of the engine and boilers. These braces, however, being placed at a very low angle, broke loose from their shoe or socket on the deck at their forward ends, by the elastic movement of the vessel in a heavy sea, as might reasonably have been expected, causing a slight dislocation in some light work above the deck which had been attached to these braces and which formed the enclosure of an upper stateroom on the guards, occupied by a passenger. This trivial accident on her first voyage caused considerable fright among timid persons, and the laying of a foot-mat over the end of the dislocated brace, while in Charleston, was construed into an act of desperate treachery to the lives of the traveling public."

In fact, other than the loose hogging brace, the *Home* was well constructed. The wooden hull was launched on April 16, 1836. It was then towed to Delancy Street in New York City where the machinery was installed and fitting out was completed. She was supposedly finished in January 1837 but laid up until April. A contemporary account stated that "she was calculated to accommodate one hundred and twenty persons with berths or state rooms. In her appointments and finish, she ranked with the 'floating palaces' for which our American waters are famed, and in speed, another characteristic of American ship building, she was unsurpassed."

That summer found the *Home* on passenger service between New York and Charleston. (Remember that this was a time when the only other mode of commercial transportation was stagecoach.) Her builders must have been satisfied with the performance of her engine; on her second voyage the *Home* steamed from New York to Charleston in sixty-four hours (or sixty-eight hours), "a shorter passage than was ever made before by any vessel."

Unfortunately, it is the third voyage for which the *Home* is remembered: a voyage that began inauspiciously, proceeded badly, and ended disastrously. She left her wharf at the foot of Market Street at 4:00 p.m., October 7, 1837. On board were approximately ninety passengers and some forty-five crew; last minute arrivals add uncertainty to the exact numbers. Between thirty and forty of these people were women, and several were children.

Although Captain Carleton White was the master of the vessel, it was pilot E.C. Price who, from the steamboat *Isis*, led the *Home* through Buttermilk Channel. After passing Governor's Island the *Isis* peeled off. Captain White put an experienced helmsman in charge of the wheel while he went about other duties. An ebbing tide and a westerly wind gently pushed the *Home* off course so that she grounded hard on Romer Shoal only an hour and a quarter out of port.

Backing the engine proved ineffectual. Captain White was forced to wait for high tide. The passengers had their tea and evening meal unencumbered by the swaying motion of the sea. The flood tide arrived at 10:30. Under both steam and sail Captain White managed to work the *Home* free. The possibility of breaking her own speed record vanished.

After noon the next day the wind picked up and the seas grew heavy—nothing that the *Home* could not handle. The roll of the ship was little more than a mild discomfort for the passengers.

Around 7:30 that evening Chief Engineer Hunt reported that "the feeder-pipe of the forward boiler had opened at the joint, so that it forced more of the water into the hold than into the boiler, consequently, there was not a supply for that boiler." Captain White steered the *Home* before the wind on one boiler and the squaresail, and angled toward the Chesapeake Bay as a possible refuge, while Hunt effected repairs. This was accomplished by midnight. With a full head of steam under both boilers the *Home* continued south-southeast, "this being the course along the land." By heaving the lead, Captain White kept well informed of the depth of water under his keel.

The sails were reefed as the weather worsened. The morning of the ninth found the *Home* steaming into a gale off Hatteras Island. At 9:00 a.m. a leak was found in the machinery spaces. Some later said that the ship's hull was strained when she ran aground on Romer Shoal, and that the sea squeezed in between warped timbers, but Captain White stated that the feeder-pipe had broken again.

With only one boiler providing steam for the engine, the *Home* began to wallow at the whim of the waves. A goodly spread of canvas soon got her under control. Captain White spotted Wimble Shoals in the distance and, fearing that the ship would founder, steered for the beach. Again the engineer "woulded" the pipe, as the captain put it. With full steam restored the *Home* was turned for deeper water.

Because of the proximity of Wimble Shoals, waves of monstrous proportions assailed the ship. "In passing these shoals we received the shock of three heavy rollers on our larboard beam, which stove in our after gangway, several of the larboard state-room windows, and one of the dining-room windows." Yet the *Home* survived the onslaught of the sea, and continued away from shore.

By now some of the passengers were offering advice and helping in any way they could. Captain John Salter and Captain Alfred Hill knocked away the forward bulwarks "that the sea might have a fair breach over her" because they were afraid that the *Home* "might ship some of those seas and fill the deck and cabin." Mr. Lovegreen prepared the lifeboats for launching.

By two o'clock in the afternoon the ship was in serious trouble. Whether the hull had sprung was not explicitly stated. The engineer was quoted as saying only that "the boat had commenced leaking badly." When Captian White asked him if the engine pumps could expel the water, Hunt said, "You had better send men to the hand pumps, and perhaps we may then keep her free."

Captain White complied. All hands were called out to save not just the ship, but their very lives. Under urging from Captains Salter and Hill, Captain White went looking for leaks in the hull. "I then went down into the forward cabin with the said captains, took up the floor scuttles, went down into the hold, found no water over the platform, broke some holes in the platform with the marlinspike, and then found no water."

But water was coming into the after hold. Because the crew was busy bailing the engine room, it was a work party of passengers and waiters who pulled up the scuttles in the after hold and begin passing out the coal that was stored inside, so they could commence bailing.

The *Home* passed around the Diamond Shoals and took a more westerly tack. Now there was several inches of water sloshing across the deck in front of the furnaces, soaking the coal and washing it back and forth as the ship rolled with the seas. The firemen stoked the furnaces with wood. The engine pumps became clogged with coal dust and shavings; only the hand pumps remained free and uobstructed. The men worked in rotation.

At first the pumps were adequate for the task, but all too quickly the leak increased to the point that, according to Captain White, "it gained very fast on us." Men and women worked side by side with buckets, pails, pans, and kettles: anything that held water. To no avail. At 8:00 p.m. the furnace fires were doused by the incoming flood, and "we were obliged to run under sails only."

The wind whistled through the rigging with thunderous fury. With land in sight Captain White steered the ship for shore. The sailors who clambored up the ratlines must have had ice for blood and steel for nerves. The masts swayed sickeningly in the face of the gale. No sooner had the men set the squaresail than it split "from head to foot," and they were forced to take it back down.

Passenger John Roland later contended that the ship's hull "bent like a read. The bows would work up and down three or four feet, and those best acquainted with her expected that she would break in two every moment."

Captain White was then accosted by Captain Salter, who accused him of being drunk and who tried to relieve him of command of the ship. An argument ensued. At the end of it Captain Salter stalked off the bridge muttering under his breath. Captain White then checked on the passengers bailing the after hold and prepared them for what was to come. He was truthful, and told them that there was little chance that the ship would survive. "I soon returned to go forward, and in passing the dining room ... door, saw the ladies and many of the gentlemen sitting in there, apparently in great distress and anxiety."

The sea moderated somewhat in the lee of the Hatteras Shoals. The *Home* moved sluggishly because of the weight of water in her holds. Even though the sails were torn and tattered, Captain White had them raised once again in order to keep the ship's head toward the beach. There was a heavy surf running. It was going to be a difficult landing.

Captain Salter, still trying to take command of the situation, said to the mate, "Mr. Mathews, you had better look out for a smooth place for beaching." Mathews made no comment. Then, someone dashed up on the bridge and said that the water was over the cabin floors. "Bail away," yelled Captain Salter. "Bail away, boys."

"The boats are all ready," said Mr. Mathews to Captain White. "Off the starboard bow it looks like a good place."

Captain Salter paced the wheelhouse with Captain White. "That's as good a place as any."

Captain White ordered the helm put to port.

In his anxiety Captain Salter kept shouting, "Port! Port!"

Said Captain White calmly to the helmsman, "Mind yourself, stand clear of that wheel when she strikes, or she will be breaking your bones."

According to Captain White, because the *Home* sat so low in the water she "immediately struck on the outer reef, slewed her head to the northward, the square sail caught aback, she heeled off shore, exposing the deck and upper houses to the full force of the sea. The squaresail halyards were let go, but the sail would not come down, as it was hard aback against the mast and rigging; it had previously been split, and was now blown to ribbons."

The *Home* grounded to a halt a hundred yards from shore. The beach was only dimly lit by the nighttime sky; it must have seemed a million miles away.

Captain Salter was still trying to take command. He shouted, "The ladies had all better come forward." He went to join them along the inshore side of the ship, where the upper deck offered some protection from the crashing waves.

The sea was a bedlam of wind, wild water, and splitting timber.

From *Steamboat Disasters and Railroad Accidents in the United States*.

Captain White gave no order to abandon ship because he thought there was no possibility of anyone making land alive in the lifeboat. One boat was already stove in, and another filled with water. But he told Mr. Mathews to muster the crew and get the remaining boat launched, and to help aboard all those who wanted to take their chances in it. The captain elected to remain with his ship.

The crew managed to pull the boat alongside in the lee provided by the hull. In moments it was loaded with frightened passengers and crew men. It got no father than thirty feet from the *Home* when it capsized, plunging the people into the surf.

Already, the *Home* was coming apart. Each mountainous wave tore off pieces of the wooden superstructure, and parted planks and timbers. The mainmast snapped like a toothpick; down came the spars, tattered canvas, and a massive web of rigging. The noise was deafening.

A giant comber brought down one of the smokestacks, which crushed a mother with an infant in her arms; another stove in the starboard staterooms, yet another dashed the dining cabin to pieces. The upper deck separated from the hull. People were swept off the ship into the sea like bugs being washed down a drain. The screams of the women were pitiful.

Captain White jumped down from the bridge deck and worked his way forward over the collapsed rigging. He misstepped and fell into the hatch, but was saved by a shred of canvas. He used the remnants of the sails for handholds and managed to gain the relative protection of the forecastle, where he found several people hanging onto ropes. One of them was Captain Salter.

"Captain White, my dear fellow, I am glad to see you here," said Captain Salter. "Come forward here, take the other end of this rope, it is long enough for both of us. I picked out this place for myself, long before the boat went ashore."

The *Home's* captain gratefully took the proffered rope and lashed himself to a stanchion. Then, thinking better of it, said, "I don't like this being tied fast to stanchions, for if the bow falls over on to us we have no means to clear us from being crushed by it." Captain Salter agreed. Subsequently, he was twice knocked off his perch by nearly solid walls of water; both times, by superhuman effort, he made it back to the ship.

Meanwhile, people were drowning one by one.

A scant twenty-five minutes after stranding, the *Home* went to pieces. The forecastle deck broke loose and floated towards shore along with an odd-lot collection of timbers and scantling. Through the raging surf went the makeshift raft. One man jumped off when it grounded, and gained the beach. The rest followed. Captain White crawled up onto the sand wearing only a shirt, pantaloons, stockings, and hat. The other six people with him on the forecastle all survived the last few feet, including the sometimes irascible Captain Salter.

This ragtag lot saw no one else around, so they headed towards the only sign of human habitation in sight: the glow of Ocracoke light. It was six or seven miles away. They had not gone far when they came upon several passengers who had miraculously survived the swim through the surf. Andrew Lovegreen threw his arms around Captain White, happy that they were both alive. Captain Hill "was very much exhausted and asked for assistance to help him along, as he could not proceed without." He and his wife had clung to a spar, but when they reached the last wave hitting the beach it tumbled them over and tore loose his wife's grip, so that she drowned.

The party split up, some continuing on toward the lighthouse for relief, others, including Captain White, searching the shore for survivors in need of help. Those who remained pulled bodies out of the surf, and dragged up onto high ground any flotsam that might prove of value. Captain White found "Mrs. Schroeder, Mr. Cohen and Mr. Johnson, under the lee of a sandhill, suffering much from wet and cold, and Mr. Cohen badly hurt."

Mr. B.B. Hussey floated in on a spar. Mrs. Lacoste was practically insensate, and not certain how she made it to shore, but believes she was lashed to a settee that rode the waves to the beach. She was nearly seventy years of age, and described as "very fleshy, and almost helpless," and as "quite large. ... When on shore she walks about with considerable difficulty."

Due to the crosswise current some people came ashore as far as a mile and a half from the wreck. The survivors were "nearly naked, and famished and exhausted." The only child to live through the ordeal was a twelve year old lad. The body of one infant was recovered.

The wreck itself was scattered by the surf, with the keel and keelson washing up a mile from where the engine and boilers marked the site of the grounding. "The shore, for some miles to the southward, was covered with fragments." One passenger, Mr. H. Vanderzee, claimed that "the hull of the boat broke into three pieces, and the shore was completely strewed with portions of the wreck, baggage, etc. for four or six miles in extent."

Among the dead was James B. Allaire, nephew of the owner. The Honorable George Prince, formerly a senator from Georgia, his wife, and their servants, all died in the catastrophe. Others who left this mortal coil represented a cross section of society: some rich, some poor, some young, some old, some well known, some with bright futures prematurely dimmed. All were human beings, all had souls. When the final toll was taken there were forty who had lived through the ordeal (twenty passengers and twenty crew) and ninety-five who had perished.

Throughout the night those who were able catered to those who needed sustenance. Apples and pears that had washed up from the wreck were the only source of food and drink. When the relief party reached Ocracoke the town's folk were called into action. Soon a group of rescuers took off on horseback for the wreck site to care for the survivors. They took cloaks and blankets and what foodstuff was available.

The sun rose that day above a scene of horrible tragedy, for everywhere along the beach were littered the remains of the *Home* and the bodies of the dead. The living were cared for at once, and were carried back to town where the few residents put them up in their houses. There were no hotels on Ocracoke in 1837. Boats eventually came to take the survivors back to civilization. Captain White stayed on in order to oversee "burying the dead and taking care of the property of the passengers, crew, owners, and underwriters." He was there until November 22.

Meanwhile, Captain Salter published "calumnious charges" against Captain White, accusing him of intoxication and otherwise impugning his character, and stating that he—Salter—was forced to take command of the *Home* prior to her loss. Several other passengers added their opinions against the captain of the *Home*, as did the ship's barber, Hiram Force. This is unfortunately a common response to situations of stress in which people have lost friends, relatives, loved ones, and physical possessions. It is the desire to lash out, to blame someone—anyone—for circumstances beyond an individual's control; to sooth the traumatic sting resulting from a person's perceived sense of helplessness and victimization. Today, this overreactive emotional response forms the basis for many lawsuits involving injury and the death of family members that can best be described as "an act of God." But God does not pay big awards or punitive damages, so it is the bystanders who are made to suffer for the grief of the survivors.

In order to defend himself, Captain White solicited affidavits from those surviving crew members in agreement with his cause, as well as residents of Ocracoke with whom he worked during the aftermath of the wreck, including two Justices of the Peace. These people refuted the allegations of Captain Salter and his followers. Investigation revealed that some of Captain Salter's allies merely signed petitions written by Salter. Others made their allegations upon hearsay—that is, they heard from someone else that the captain was drunk—and upon more intelligent reflection retracted their derogatory statements.

One of the men who laid charges against Captain White was the ship's barber. In his story to the newspapers he concocted the deceit that he was a passenger who had boarded the *Home* at the last moment, going to Charleston "on a kind of an excursion." During the interview he forgot to mention that he had been arrested by Captain White and Captain Pike, the Commissioner of Wrecks, "for robbing the dead body of a lady of a gold watch, and for riflin a trunk of its contents, a suit of clothes having been found upon and taken from him." He subsequently denied the statements he had made against the good captain.

Captain White's reputation was eventually saved, but at great cost to his peace of mind. If he felt in his heart the calamity of the *Home's* final moments, he must have known intellectually that those who died were in reality victims of the sea.

The *Home* holds the dubious distinction of being the first major steamship to wreck off the coast of North Carolina. Her wooden beams may be scattered today, or may not even exist, but with the aid of a magnetometer Alan Riebe found her iron machinery buried under ten feet of sand on a lonely Ocracoke beach. The remains are still there.

Shovel-nose lobster, also known as a slipper lobster, and Spanish lobster.

ISLE OF IONA

Built: 1905
Previous names: *Haverstoe*
Gross tonnage: 3,789
Type of vessel: Freighter
Builder: Furness, Withy & Company, West Hartlepool, England
Owner: Isles Steam Shipping Co. (Dixon, Robson & Company, Mgrs.)
Port of registry: Newcastle, England
Cause of sinking: Ran aground
Location: Two miles southwest of Hatteras Inlet Life-Saving Station

Sunk: December 13, 1914
Depth: 20 feet
Dimensions: 340' × 47' × 20'
Power: Coal-fired steam

Captain G.W. Quack, master of the *Isle of Iona*, undoubtedly had a difficult childhood. Like the character in Johnny Cash's song, "A Boy Named Sue," growing up with a name that can so obviously be made the butt of jokes must have gotten him into fisticuffs with his schoolmates on more than one occasion; and it must have been much worse as a sailor on the main. Despite such a background, young Quack accelerated through the ranks of common seamen to become an officer, and eventually reached the rank of captain with his own ship to command.

All his experience with navigation, however, was not enough to save his ship from the capricious nature of the sea. The route from Cuba to Baltimore was one that passed by the mariners nightmare: the Diamond Shoals. Special care had to be taken during the northward journey because the Gulf Stream propelled a ship along at a clip faster than normal. Ground speed could exceed a vessel's cruising speed by several knots. When a dense fog closed in on the *Isle of Iona*, obscuring the sun and the stars whose observation is mandatory in order to fix a ship's position, Captain Quack's only recourse for approximating his location was dead reckoning: a "guestimate" calculated by multiplying engine revolutions by wind speed and direction and predicted drift.

Thus, as darkness fell on December 13, 1914, the *Isle of Iona* was moving north faster than Captain Quack reckoned. Instead of calling for a turn to starboard in order to round the dreaded shoals, he plowed straight ahead into the breakers on the south shore of Hatteras Island. All agree that the sea state was rough, but, according to different reports, the tide was either low or flood. The time was approximately 10:40 p.m. Coston flares informed those aboard the freighter that their plight was known to those on shore.

Within minutes both the Hatteras Inlet and the Durants life-saving stations were galvanized for action. Together the crews dragged the beach apparatus to a point opposite the stranded steamer. This was difficult work as the men had to pull on the traces like huskies, and the wheels of the carriage bit deep into the loose sand. By the time the Lyle gun was loaded and the messenger line was ready in the faking box, nearly four hours had passed. Five shots were fired, first with a six-ounce powder charge and a number seven line, then with eight-ounce charges and a thinner line, number four. All fell short. The distance to the wreck was estimated at 850 to 900 yeards.

Under the conditions prevalent at the time, the life-saving crews could do nothing more till daylight. At 6:00 a.m. they launched the power lifeboat through the breakers and, with a Jersey surf boat in tow, braved the high waves. They anchored the power boat close by the wreck, and used the surf boat as a shuttle. By this means they transferred the entire crew of the freighter—twenty-seven men—to the power boat and thence to shore. By 10:00 a.m. the rescue was complete.

The work of the life-savers was not yet done. One had to go to Hatteras in the power skiff and bring back a doctor, for one of the crew of the *Isle of Iona* had broken his thigh at the time of grounding; he was suffering badly. The doctor had to set the bone on site. The other members of the life-saving crew exerted all their energy in comforting the distressed sailors: brewing hot tea, cooking meals, providing clothes and bedding, and arranging transportation to civilization. The next day, December 15, the life-savers returned to the stranded ship and collected the personal effects of the erstwhile crew.

The *Isle of Iona* never again sailed the seven seas. She eventually broke up where she lay, and her cargo of iron ore became a total loss. Steve Lang once saw the wreck completely exposed, but more often than not has found all vestige of the hull covered with sand.

Assuredly, if they were alive today the captain's boyhood pundits would jeer with sarcasm that the *Isle of Iona* had "Quacked" up.

The horse conch on the left is slowly extruding a large mass of white eggs.

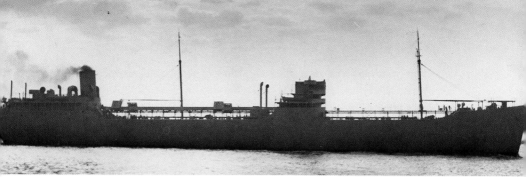

JOHN D. GILL

Built: 1941
Previous names: None
Gross tonnage: 11,641
Type of vessel: Tanker
Power: Oil-Fired steam turbine connected to electric motor and shaft
Builder: Sun Ship Building & Dry Dock Company, Chester, Pennsylvania
Owner: Atlantic Refining Company
Port of registry: Philadelphia, Pennsylvania
Cause of sinking: Torpedoed by *U-158* (Kapitanleutnant Erich Rostin)
Location: 27198.5

Sunk: March 12, 1942
Depth: 90 feet
Dimensions: 528' × 70' × 39'

39085.3

Although fresh from the shipyard on her maiden voyage, the *John D. Gill* was no stranger to the U-boat war plaguing east coast shipping. On February 27, 1942, on her way south from Philadelphia, she came across two lifeboats full of survivors from the torpedoed ore carrier *Marore* (see *Shipwrecks of North Carolina: from the Diamond Shoals North*). The twenty-five sea-soaked men who clambered aboard the tanker were grateful for her fortuitous arrival. They much admired the deck guns mounted fore and aft; if the *Marore* had had such protection she may very well have been able to even the score with the U-boat that had shot up their ship with shell fire.

The *John D. Gill* made Atreco, Texas without further incident. She onloaded her first cargo (gasoline and oil), then proceeded across the Gulf of Mexico on the first leg of her return voyage. She rounded the Dry Tortugas, hugged the Florida coast, and drove northward at fourteen knots into the thick of a battle still being waged. As a precaution, the tanker plied a zigzag course during the day and ran without navigation lights after dark. She stopped over for a day in Charleston, South Carolina before running the gauntlet past the Diamond Shoals, an area dubbed "torpedo alley." The night of March 12 found her off Wilmington.

The weather was described as "hazy; sea, calm; wind light from southeast; visibility, poor, one mile maximum." Of the forty-nine-man crew, eleven were on watch: the captain, one officer, two seamen, and all seven of the gun crew. Despite these precautions a torpedo struck the ship "amidships on starboard side at position of mainmast and #7 tank, below the water line. The plates on the side of the *John D. Gill* were knocked inward and a hole was knocked in the deck above the opening in the hull. ... The ship began to list to starboard but not heavily."

Oil gushed out of the ruptured tank and spread across the ocean in a huge slick that streamed aft as the ship's momentum carried her forward. Ensign Robert Hutchins, the commander of the Naval armed guard, had gone to his room and was reading in his bunk when the torpedo struck. "There was a terrific blast, and I ran from my room to join my gun crew. Everything was dark at first and I ran along the catwalk. When I got to the gun we looked for the sub, but nothing could be seen or heard."

Said Seaman Herbert Gardner, "We were calm at first, but it wasn't long before everybody got excited." Escaping oil ignited with a blast. Instantly the sea was aflame; sparks flying through the air touched off fires on the deck, and very quickly the tanker became a floating, fiery cauldron. "I guess we couldn't help it with that kind of death staring us in the face."

One lifeboat got away, another capsized. Gardner and a mess boy climbed down the falls to try to right the overturned lifeboat; the mess boy was never seen again. Gardner fell into the water when his strength gave out. "I saw a buddy of mine about fifty feet away and I began moving over toward him, intending to let him hang on to me if he didn't have a life jacket. He told me to stay away. I guess he thought I was after his jacket, and I don't blame him."

The gun crew was faring no better. They stayed at their post until "the flames got on top of us, and we jumped over the side," said Hutchins. "I saw two of my boys go into those flames and I heard them scream as they died." Two others succumbed, as well.

The hero of the night was Quartermaster Edwin Chaney, a man with a "booming bass voice." He scrambled onto a raft, "then began looking for his comrades in the burning sea. Whenever he saw men struggling, he used his voice to good advantage, yelling to them to swim over to the raft and keeping up the directions until they found it." Said one survivor, "We could hear that voice of his above the roaring of the fire."

Another seaman reported watching "two of his comrades ground to pieces by the propeller of the ship as they tried to escape the flames."

Gardner found himself surrounded by burning oil that was quickly closing in on him; the only way to escape was to duck underneath it and swim away. When he reached the surface his hair caught fire and he had to slap it out. When he finally made it to the raft he could hardly believe the smoking apparitions he found on board. The men's bodies were coated with thick black oil that got in their eyes and burned, and that seered their lungs when its fumes were inhaled. Their faces were blistered from fire. Not a man escaped unscorched.

Then it was discovered that although the raft had oars, it had no oarlocks. In order to row effectively some men had to hold the oars against their bodies while the others pulled at the shafts. For injured men in charred clothing this was no easy task.

By this time rescue craft were on the way. The sound of the initial explosion had reached shore, and the flames were visible for miles around. The Coast Guard cutter *Agassiz* and the *CGC 186* searched for survivors and kept a lookout for enemy U-boats. Coast Guard motor lifeboat *4405* put out from Oak Island; at dawn it spotted a flare, and soon took on board the eleven men from the life raft. These men were transferred to the *CGC 186*, which rushed them to Southport for medical attention. During the remainder of the day and well into the night, the *Agassiz*, the *4405*, and the Navy tug *Umpqua* (No. 25) kept up the search. They found no survivors but recovered fifteen bodies.

It was not until later that day that the *Robert H. Colley* came upon the one lifeboat that had gotten away from the burning tanker. It contained fifteen men. These were the only additional survivors found.

From his hospital bed Herbert Gardner reflected on the ordeal. He vowed to return to sea as soon as he was well, but was hoping to join the Navy and engage in the fighting from the deck of a warship. "I'm going to do the hunting, not be hunted."

The tables were turned on Erich Rostin and the *U-158* less then four months later, when the U-boat became the hunted instead of the hunter. It was sunk with all hands on June 30, 1942 after an aerial attack in the Gulf of Mexico. Sadly, two captured merchant marine officers went down with the U-boat. See elsewhere in this volume for the *U-158's* attacks against the *Ario* and the *Caribsea*.

Because the huge tanker sank in such shallow water it was necessary to demolish enough of the *John D. Gill* so she presented no hazard to navigation. The superstructure was razed down to the main deck. Still, for some of its length the wreck presents a vertical profile that rises some thirty feet off the bottom: an impressive sight that is augmented by the addition of large coral heads, sea fans, and tropical fish.

Although the midship section has been blown practically flat, the wreck is contiguous: held together by keel plates beneath the sand. On days of poor visibility (less than thirty feet) one might think that the wreck is separated into two parts.

The tip of the bow no longer shows a sharp point; it has collapsed outward, probably in part due to salvage operations in which explosives were used to free the bronze blades of the spare propeller. Lying upside down off the starboard side is the bow gun tub. The winch dominates the forward deck, which is as broad and as level as an interstate highway for a distance of about a hundred feet. Many pipes and fittings are still connected to the deck. The forward tank compartment can be penetrated either by dropping down through a hatch in the deck, or by entering through a breakdown area.

The wreck then drops precipitately nearly to the sand. This low area extends aft thirty or forty feet to where the hull again rises high, although, because the deck has separated from the starboard side and is falling down, the hull on both sides is bent outward. This portion of the wreck appears badly distorted, like a breadbox would if it were partially crushed. A small debris field on the port side appears to contain the remains of the wheelhouse.

Abaft of this is a long section of low and barely perceptible debris that eventually leads to the machinery spaces of the stern. By picking one's way from piece to piece one can reach the stern proper after a swim of about seventy-five feet. The after section is large but ill defined due to the nature of collapse: the superstructure and decks have rusted and fallen down but are supported by the engine underneath. The *John D. Gill* was propelled by a geared steam turbine, whose profile is squat when compared to that of a triple expansion steam engine: thus the relatively low relief of the area (about ten feet.) The engine is exposed, and much of the associated machinery is visible. Valves, piping, and flanges lie everywhere.

The fantail lies over on its starboard side. It has compartments that can be entered and explored. At this point the stern climbs some twenty-five feet off the bottom. In the adjacent sand the gun mount can been seen lying upside down.

Because the *John D. Gill* is designated by Wreck Buoy #4, the wreck is often referred to as the WR-4.

Grouper.

The *Keshena* pushing a barge. Note that the upper white superstructure to the left is part of the barge. Courtesy of The Mariners Museum, Newport News, Virginia.)

KESHENA

Built: 1939
Previous names: *Raymond Card, General*
Gross tonnage: 132
Type of vessel: Tug
Builder: Gulfport Boiler & Welding Works
Owner: U.S. government (Navy Department)
Cause of sinking: Struck friendly mine
Location: 26959.8

Sunk: July 19, 1942
Depth: 90 feet
Dimensions: 87′ × 22′ × 10′
Power: Oil engine; electric motor

40085.2

The sinking of the *Keshena* is incidental to the torpedoing of the *Chilore*, the *J.A. mowinckel*, and the *Bluefields*, an action covered in detail in *Shipwrecks of Virginia*. In summary, after firing a spread of torpedoes at a southbound convoy consisting of nineteen merchant ships escorted by seven warships, a Navy blimp, and several patrol bombers, the *U-576* was sunk with all hands, including Kapitanleutnant Hans-Dieter Heinicke. The reported position of the sinking was 34-51N/75-22W, in deep water off the Diamond Shoals.

The *Bluefields* sank at once. The *Chilore* and the *J.A. Mowinckel*, sorely wounded, made it to shoal water on their own steam. Unfortunately, due to a navigational error, they drove straight through the Hatteras mine field. Both detonated mines intended for encroaching U-boats. The ships had to be left at anchor until a channel could be swept to them through the floating mines.

The tugs *Keshena* and *J.P. Martin* were assigned to beach the *J.A. Mowinckel* so that temporary repairs could be made to her hull. With the *J.P. Martin* conducting the tow and the *Keshena* acting as rudder, the delicate operation got under way. As the three blind mice swung with the current the *Keshena* slipped too far to the side. There was a titanic explosion that killed two men and sent the tug to the bottom.

The *J.A. Mowinckel* was eventually put back into service, but the *Chilore* sank in the approaches to the Chesapeake Bay.

Until 1943, planes from the Marine Corps Air Station used the *Keshena's* mast as a practice bombing target, eventually blowing it off.

The wreck of the *Keshena* lies in an area of soft silt that stirs easily and obscures visibility. The bow rises nearly vertically, with a slight tilt to starboard, to a height of twenty feet. The anchors lie atop the pointed deck, with the chains running off through the hawse pipes. About twenty-five feet abaft the bow the hull is split open. The port side, with empty portholes visible, overhangs, giving a cavelike effect. The starboard hull is broken down and lies buried under the sand.

From this point aft, except for two auxiliary boilers and the engine, the relief barely rises more than five feet. However, the sides are prominent so that one always knows where the perimeter of the wreck lies. Behind the engine, one blade of the iron propeller stands upright out of the sand; the rest of the propeller is buried. The rudder is visible, and behind it the fantail is discernible although it has collapsed backward and is tilted to starboard. The steering quadrant is highlighted by a coating of yellow encrustation. The rest of the wreck is bland in color, almost completely brown except for spots of yellow coral.

Identification was made positive when Gene Peterson recovered the letters from both sides of the bow.

The steering quadrant is plainly visible in this view of the stern section of the *Keshena*. (Photo by Uwe Lovas.)

Notice the deck cargo of storage tanks. (Courtesy of the National Archives.)

MALCHACE

Built: 1920
Previous names: *Chicamauga*
Gross tonnage: 3,516
Type of vessel: Freighter

Sunk: April 9, 1942
Depth: 206 feet
Dimensions: 333′ × 48′ × 24′
Power: Oil-fired steam

Builder: Merrill Stevens Ship Building Corp., Jacksonville, Florida
Owner: Solvay Process Company, Solvay, New Jersey
Port of registry: Wilmington, Delaware
Cause of sinking: Torpedoed by *U-160* (Oberleutnant zur See Lassen)
Location: 26941.1   39881.4

The *Malchace* left Baton Rouge, Louisiana on April 1, 1942 with Captain Arnt Magunusbal in charge. The freighter's holds were crammed with 3,628 tons of soda ash, while on her deck sat six tanks filled with caustic soda. The *Malchace* docked at Fernandina, Florida on April 8 only long enough to discharge her deck cargo. Then she cleared for Hopewell, New Jersey.

Throughout the perilous journey north, through U-boat infested waters, the crew kept a sharp watch for anything unusual. Since the night was slightly overcast the blacked out ship blended in well with the dark horizon. However, the *U-160* blended in even better. No one spotted the low profile of the U-boat lurking in the shipping lanes. Lassen fired a torpedo that sped toward its target with unerring accuracy.

This picture was taken on February 13, 1942, barely two months before the *Malchace* was tropedoed and sunk. (Courtesy of the National Archives.)

The first anyone aboard the *Malchace* knew that they were being stalked was when the torpedo exploded against the ship's port side amidships. The shock of the blast was muffled by the cargo, but it was loud enough to startle the crew. Within moments all hands clambered on deck, to see great clouds of steam and soda ash flying through the air. "A small blaze started on the after boat deck."

One fireman panicked, jumped overboard, and was drowned.

Captain Magunusbal immediately ordered abandon ship. "The No. 2 lifeboat on the port side had been demolished by the explosion but the starboard lifeboat was lowered successfully and within five minutes after the attack, all members of the crew, except the Captain, the chief mate, Sawyer, and the luckless firemen, cast off from the side of the listing freighter in the lifeboat."

Meanwhile, the U-boat appeared a hundred yards off the stern. Running half submerged it slowly circled the ship. Said Second Mate Sawyer, "It wasn't more than 50 feet from the ship. Why, I could have dropped baseballs on it."

"The three officers then calmly launched a life raft from the forward starboard side and the abandonment of the ship was complete. ... Sawyer had slid down a line directly to the lifeboat, which then took in tow the life raft on which the Captain and chief mate had escaped."

The twenty-eight seamen had not gone far when "a second torpedo hit the ship again on the port side just below the waterline aft of number three hatch and blew a hole in the plates of the vessel flooding the engine room and wrecking the number one lifeboat." Then "the ship began to slowly settle by the stern and there was a bad list to port." Moments later the freighter disappeared beneath the surface of the sea. The U-boat was seen no more.

Captain Magunusbal and the chief mate then transferred to the lifeboat already crowded with twenty-six crew men. Because the initial explosion had destroyed the radio antenna, no distress call had gone out. The lifeboat bobbed on the lonely Atlantic swells. Early in the morning they heard a thunderous explosion, "and then saw a tanker well ablaze ten miles to the west." This was the *Atlas* (q.v.), which had just been torpedoed by the *U-552*.

About 8:30 that morning "they sighted smoke on the horizon to the south, heralding the approach of what turned out to be the Mexican tanker *Fajo de Oro*, which approached the men in the lifeboat very cautiously, carefully looking them over before launching a heavy line by which the lifeboat finally got alongside." By this time in the war merchant marine crews were taking no chances. U-boats had been flashing lights in order to disguise themselves as navigational buoys, and no one knew what other tricks they had up their German cuffs. The *Fajo de Oro* had left Tampico, Mexico about the same time as the *Tamaulipas* (q.v.), which had been sunk that very night only a few miles away.

"Stopping at the guard boat just inside of Cape Henry, the tanker transferred the twenty-eight survivors to a sub-chaser before continuing on to Baltimore, but the survivors were subsequently landed at the Naval Operating Base, Norfolk," Virginia.

Georg Lassen also sank the *Equipoise* (see *Shipwrecks of North Carolina: from the Diamond Shoals North*) and, far offshore, the *Ulysses*, *Rio Blanco*, and the *City of New York*. Lassen left the *U-160* in June 1943. A month later it was lost with all hands in the Central Atlantic, after being depth-charged by planes from the U.S. aircraft carrier *Santee* (CVE-29).

The wreck of the *Malchace* lies so far over on its port side that it is practically upside down. The hull is completely intact with the port bilge keel uppermost, rising to a depth of 180 feet. The bridge and superstructure wreckage is spread out flat over the sand to a distance of about fifty feet from the hull; relief here is less than ten feet. The remains of the wheelhouse are not recognizable as such; rather, it is discernible by the number of portholes lying about, and the navigational equipment (such as the engine order telegraph and compass binnacle found in the sand.) Because of its depth the wreck has gone relatively unexplored, but has great potential for the advanced wreck diver.

The wreck in the listed position was originally called the *Manuela* (q.v.), while the *Manuela* was called the *Malchace*, an erroneous switch in names that is still written in books and on charts. However, a cursory examination of both wrecks shows that only one of them has a deck gun and that therefore that is the one that has to be the *Manuela*. The *Malchace* was unarmed.

Whatever doubt there was on this score was settled unequivocably when the author found the *Manuela's* bell with the name clearly etched in bronze.

Above: *Malchace*. Clockwise from upper left: the bilge keel at the shallowest part of the wreck; the anchor on the bottom; the bridge telegraph in the wheelhouse debris; a porthole.

Below: *Manuela*. Clockwise from upper left: dinnerware found on the wreck has the Bull Line crest; a telescopic sight on the deck gun, after some of the coral has been cleaned off; the bronze propeller; a porthole with glass intact.

MANUELA

Built: 1934
Previous names: None
Gross tonnage: 4,772
Type of vessel: Freighter
Builder: Newport News Ship Building and Dry Dock Company
Owner: A.H. Bull Steamship Company
Port of registry: New York, NY
Cause of sinking: Torpedoed by *U-404* (Kapitanleutnant von Bulow)
Location: 26945.2

Sunk: June 25, 1942
Depth: 155 feet
Dimensions: 393' × 55' × 28'
Power: Two oil-fired steam turbines

39916.8

Otto von Bulow made two war cruises to the Eastern Sea Frontier during the heyday of the 1942 turkey shoot. In March he sank the *Tolten* and the *Lemuel Burrows* (for accounts of both see *Shipwrecks of New Jersey*); and the *San Demetrio*, offshore. Then he returned to Germany for refueling and resupply. Because it took nearly a month to make the Atlantic crossing, he did not get back to the east coast "happy hunting grounds" until June 1. He immediately encountered the *West Notus*, and blasted her apart with accurate fire from his deck gun; he was saving his torpedoes for later. What might have seemed like the beginning of a streak endured through three weeks of the doldrums. Von Bulow roamed along the coast searching for targets that were ever elusive, and hiding from anti-submarine warfare units that appeared in ever-growing numbers.

Not until June 24 did he prosecute another successful attack on Allied merchant shipping; then he sank three ships in one day. At three o'clock in the morning he drove three torpedoes into the *Ljubica Matkovic* that broke the ship in two. Forced to lie on the bottom during the daylight hours, when he was powerless against patrolling naval forces, von Bulow rose in the evening like a vampire rising from its grave, his tubes still bloody from the previous night's assaults and thirsting for more.

What to his wondrous eyes did appear but an eleven-ship convoy accompanied by seven escort vessels, all plowing northward with the speed of an ox-drawn share. Against a seven-knot target he had no difficulty plotting a course for his deadly torpedoes. He fired a spread that carved through the three overlapping columns with thunderous effect. First hit was the *Nordal*, a Panamanian freighter in the starboard column. The sound of the blast signaled the convoy to disperse. Ships veered left and right in a frantic effort to evade the unseen enemy.

Moments later a torpedo struck the second ship in the center column, the *Manuela*. Although none of the ship's five lookouts had seen an approaching wake, Captain Conrad Nilsen had already ordered full speed ahead, and followed it with a sharp right then a sharp left turn. But three minutes after the *Nordal* was struck, the bulkhead between the *Manuela's* engine room and boiler room was blown in. Three duty personnel were killed instantly, and the engines were put out of commission by the blast. The explosion sent "a spout of water and oil at least 100 feet in the air. Many of the crew were drenched as the oil and debris came showering down on them." The ship heeled over rapidly as the sea poured into the gaping wound.

Captain Nilsen ordered abandon ship. The *Manuela's* two lifeboats were carried in a swung out condition for just such an emergency. According to the captain, "The starboard lifeboat was blown up. You couldn't see anything left of it." The surviving crew men got away in the port lifeboat and three rafts. Captain Nilsen: "She listed so bad over to starboard, that at the time we got off, the water was up to the bottom of the hatch coaming." The six men of the armed guard never had a chance to fire the gun, nor did they see the offending U-boat.

Likewise, the *Nordal* acquired a heavy starboard list and settled by the stern. The entire crew managed to escape in lifeboats before the ship disappeared in deep water. A half hour later they were rescued by the British armed trawler HMS *Norwich City*. There were no casualties.

The *Norwich City* then picked up the twenty-two men who had gotten away in the *Manuela's* lifeboat, including Captain Nilsen. The fifteen survivors spread out among the life rafts were rescued by a Coast Guard cutter, the *CGC 483*. Four men were missing.

The *Manuela* did not sink. In her awkward position she hovered in near death, refusing to give up the ghost. The convoy regrouped and continued the voyage to Norfolk, but a Coast Guard cutter remained by the stricken freighter's side. If the U-boat returned to finish a job only half done, the Coast Guard was prepared to defend its charge.

To everyone's surprise, "Antonio Figuerosa, fireman, was found seriously injured on the deck of the ship the next afternoon. Figuerosa had been rendered unconscious by the explosion and after reviving himself to find the ship abandoned but still afloat, he had, eight hours later, dragged himself to the deck where he was found the next day by members of the crew from the *CGC 252*. Removed to the hospital at the Morehead City Section Base, Figuerosa was found to be suffering from compound fractures of the right leg and left arm, and from shock."

Still the *Manuela* did not sink. The salvage tug *P.F. Martin* attached a tow line to the freighter's bow and struggled to reach shoal water at Lookout Bight. They moved slowly toward shore, the tug's engine straining against the dead weight of the partially flooded and much larger ship. It was a valiant struggle, but one that ended in defeat. As Captain Nilsen later testified about the sad fate of his ship, "She remained afloat about 24 hours before she sank." It was "the first time he had lost a ship in forty-five years at sea."

The *Manuela* was valued at $1,500,000 and was fully insured at the time of her loss. Her cargo was listed as "general," weighed in at 6,401 tons, and was valued at $704,000. She had left San Juan, Puerto Rico on June 13, bound for New York.

Von Bulow fired his parting shot on the twenty-seventh. He sank the Norwegian freighter *Moldanger* on his way back across the Atlantic. The survivors suffered more perhaps than almost any other men in the merchant marine. Nine famished and dehydrated sailors lived through *forty-eight* days adrift on two six-by-nine-foot life rafts until they were rescued by a passing steamship. Von Bulow left the *U-404* for landside duty in July 1943. The following month, under the command of Oberleutnant zur See Schonberg, the U-boat was lost with all hands in the Bay of Biscay.

On August 12, 1942 Navy aircraft dropped four depth charges on a suspicious target, then called for reinforcements. The *CGC 473* and the HMS *Norwich City* continued the attack, blasting away with vigor at the suspected enemy U-boat. Not until the action was over and the position plotted was it determined that the sonar trace might be that of the sunken *Manuela*. Quite a few merchantmen suffered secondary destruction at the racks of Allied depth charges. But then, the Navy's wise motto in U-boat infested waters was "attack first."

Whether it was the hulk of the *Manuela* or that of the *Malchace* (q.v.) that the Navy depth-charged that day is not known. Somewhere along the line the positions of the two wrecks were interchanged. Books and charts place the *Manuela* where the *Malchace* is sunk, and vice versa, a fact that went unknown until this author recovered the ship's bell and found the name *Manuela* engraved in bronze. Previous to that, the only intimation that the wreck lying in 155 feet of water could not be the *Malchace* was the presence of a deck gun, which the *Manuela* had but the *Malchace* had not.

The wreck is visually impressive. The hull lies disjointed in three separate sections, looking like a cam shaft that has been pulled slightly apart. All three pieces lie on their starboard side, and each rises some twenty-five feet above the bottom. The forward forty feet of the bow section is completely intact; the giant windlass and winch drums are solidly attached to the vertical wall of the deck. Fallen plates and large rust holes permit entry into the upper rooms.

Ten feet away lies the huge center section that contains the forward cargo holds, the boiler rooms, and the engine rooms. The boilers are dislodged from their bedplates, and spill partway out of the hull. From the top you can follow the turn of the bilge right down to the sand; the bottom plates are in place and well preserved, offering no entry into the machinery spaces from below the water line.

The superstructure is spread out across an extensive debris field that extends more than seventy-five feet from the center section of the hull. This area is littered with twisted I-beams and miscellaneous wreckage. The midship wheelhouse is upside down. The navigational level that was at one time uppermost is buried under the sand to a depth of more than ten feet, unfortunately covering the steering station and related bridge equipment. The second level is exposed; access is unobstructed through skeletal bulkheads from which the steel panels have either fallen off or rusted through. Here are sinks and toilets either hanging from the overhead or lying in the sand. After entering this room, a diver can head away from the hull into a corridor that then turns right and goes aft. This corridor is lined with portholes, most with the glass, and comes out about thirty feet from

This is how much of the bell was exposed when I first found it. It looks like a flange.

the turn; because of the build-up of sand, the ceiling height is about four feet.

· If you look down at this section from above you'll see the tiled ceiling. The galley wreckage lies at the after end of the debris field. It is here that you can find china embossed with the shipping line crest.

The midship section is separated from the stern section by about thirty feet. Since visibility usually exceeds fifty feet, and because there is interconnecting wreckage stretching aft, you can easily swim to the partially intact stern and go right inside. The expanse is large, but empty. Passing around the fantail you can see three blades of the huge bronze propeller. Although the *Manuela* had two steam turbines, they were both geared to a single shaft.

When I first dived the *Manuela* the deck gun stood out prominently with its barrel pointed down. Just forward of it was the stern steering station: a large brass stand topped with a gear housing and a double helm whose wooden spokes had long since become teredo food; only the two brass hubs remained. Then one summer I saw that the gun had fallen from its mount. Apparently, when the gun mount collapsed, the downward pointing barrel hit the sand, pivoted forward, smashed the gear box and knocked it off; then, the gun fell on top of the hub assembly. What was once a majestic sight now appears like little more than a pipe (the gun barrel) and part of the breech. It is quickly being swallowed up by the sand. Unfortunately, there is no way to halt this collapse. A wreck begins disintegrating from the moment is sinks. All we can do is note how it existed during that brief moment in time, for in the next moment it is gone like a puff of smoke in an autumn breeze.

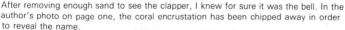

After removing enough sand to see the clapper, I knew for sure it was the bell. In the author's photo on page one, the coral encrustation has been chipped away in order to reveal the name.

Courtesy of William Quinn.

MIGET

Built: 1920   Sunk: February 4, 1952
Previous names: *Pinta, Falmouth, Lake Floravista*   Depth: 30 feet
Gross tonnage: 2,606   Dimensions: 251′ × 43′ × 25′
Type of vessel: Freighter   Power: Oil-fired steam
Builder: McDougall Duluth Company, Duluth, Minnesota
Owner: Cia. de Nav. Las. Crucess S.A.
Port of registry: Panama
Cause of sinking: Disabled engine, then driven ashore
Location: Portsmouth Island, two miles south of Ocracoke Inlet

The *Miget* was in the trade of transporting wheat from Baltimore to Brazil when she ran afoul the forces of nature on February 3, 1952. At first the brewing storm did not present a hazard to the staunch little freighter; but the farther south she steamed the deeper she became enveloped in the northward moving front. Even then, Captain Rudolf von Tangen had no presentiment of danger as his ship chugged effortlessly past the most hazardous part of the entire east coast: the dreaded Diamond Shoals.

Somehow, though, sea water insidiously invaded the fuel tanks and was sucked up into the fuel lines that fed the steam generating boilers. As the steam pressure dropped, the engine lost revolutions. The ship ran slower and slower, became unmanageable against the mounting sea, lost headway, and, when the engine conked out altogether, went adrift. Without power the *Miget* wallowed sickly in the troughs of thirty-five foot waves driven by gale-force winds.

It was ten o'clock at night when Captain von Tangen radioed for help. His intention then was to abandon ship, and that is what he told the Coast Guard. But he thought better of it after a while. The crew readied the lifeboats, then stood by until the captain gave the word.

A surfboat from the Ocracoke Island Coast Guard Station set out to render assistance, but was forced to turn back in the inlet due to high seas. The Coast Guard then dispatched two large cutters from Norfolk, as well as a PBY seaplane from Elizabeth City. The plane found the helpless ship in the dark, flew around her dropping flares, and by radio kept her apprised of her position.

The *Miget* was being driven relentlessly toward Portsmouth Island. The cutters could not reach her before she grounded, but Coast Guardsmen gathered on the beach where the freighter was headed. Captain Tangen had to make a decision. A mile or two from land the *Miget* touched bottom. Now was the time to abandon ship—before her position became completely untenable. "A Coast Guard rocket fired by a beach party was answered by a blinker light from the stranded freighter about 2 A.M. That gave the crew its bearings and the ship was abandoned."

The first lifeboat was lowered into the frothing sea—and was instantly smashed to splinters against the ship's steel hull. Despite this forboding calamity the crew launched the one remaining lifeboat. It reached the water in one piece. All twenty-six men crowded inside, released the falls, and rowed desperately toward shore. Waves broke over the gunwales and soaked the men with frigid water; wind-swept spray hit their faces like icy tentacles.

Soon only the giant combers in the surf zone separated them from the safety of the beach. A huge wave hit the lifeboat broadside and flipped it over like a spatula flipping a hotcake on the griddle. The men were thrown clear of the boat, then tossed about like socks in a dryer. With unbelievable good fortune, every last one of them managed to hold his breath long enough to wade ashore. "Then were taken to a Coast Guard station, fed and outfitted with new clothes."

The storm continued to drive the *Miget* beachward throughout the day. The hull took a terrible pounding. Lloyd's Weekly Casualty Reports noted cryptically, "Have sent surveyor to examine. Merritt-Chapman & Scott's salvage steamer *Curb* now off Savannah, bound north. Have requested Merritt-Chapman and Scott to examine and report."

By the next day, however, the *Miget* was sitting high and dry. The sea subsided, the weather cleared. The ship appeared to be intact. But shortly afterward she was battered by another storm. The final report stated that the "steamer *Miget* has stranded in exposed position, listed 15 deg., starboard rail under water, hatch covers missing, grain cargo spewing out of seams and washing over deck. Vessel has broken in two, pieces four feet apart amidships. Merritt-Chapman & Scott not interested. Salvage of vessel, together with repairs, would far exceed hull insured value."

In 1979 it was reported that salvors succeeded in recovering the three bronze propeller blades, as well as nearly eight tons of copper and brass fittings. They used explosives to accomplish the task.

Today no part of the *Miget* is visible above the surface of the sea.

Courtesy of William Quinn.

Ballena, sister ship of the *Mount Dirfys*. (Courtesy of The Mariners Museum, Newport News, Virginia.)

MOUNT DIRFYS

Built: 1918
Previous names: *Bernini, War Penguin*
Gross tonnage: 5,242
Type of vessel: Freighter
Builder: W. Dobson & Company, Newcastle, England
Owner: Atlanticos Steam Ship Company
Port of registry: Piraeus, Greece
Cause of sinking: Ran aground
Location: 45247.0

Sunk: December 26, 1936
Depth: 30 feet
Dimensions: 400′ × 52′ × 28′
Power: Coal-fired steam

59211.9

What began for the *Mount Dirfys* as a long but otherwise routine voyage ended embarrassingly shy of her goal. Sixty-two days out of Travancore, India via Lourenco Marques, the steamship was angling in toward Wilmington when she ran aground on Frying Pan Shoals. According to her consignment papers she should have been nowhere near the shoals. In fact, her cargo of iron ore was slated to be delivered to Wilmington, Delaware, not Wilmington, North Carolina. It was such absurd navigational dyslexia that put the Greek freighter on a course to disaster.

There was little to be done other than radio for help. This was done at 11:01 that morning. Much to the chagrin of the thirty-six people aboard the *Mount Dirfys*, it was then discovered that the ship's receiver was not working. So, they had to fend for themselves and hope that their plea was getting through to the proper authorities.

Fortunately, the U.S. Coast Guard cutter *Modoc* intercepted the message. She was docked in Wilmington (North Carolina), but most of her officers and crew were ashore. Orders went out to recall the men while the ship was prepared for sea. Three hours later the *Modoc* left, and four hours after that she arrived at the site of the stranded steamer. By that time the motor boat from the Oak Island Coast Guard Station had assured the people on the *Mount Dirfys* that help was on the way.

The *Modoc* carefully took soundings around the stranded vessel, then moved in close and secured an eighteen-inch towing hawser. This work was not completed until 10 o'clock that night, by which time the pounding surf had strained the freighter's hull; she was taking on water faster than her pumps could get rid of it. Worse, "the rudder and one or more of the blades of the propeller were gone." Now there was some fear that should the ship come off at the next high tide she might sink before she could be towed into port. For this reason "the master was requested and did put in writing a request that the *Modoc* pull and that the master assumed all responsibility for all that might happen."

At 6 o'clock the next morning the *Modoc* pulled with every bit of power her engines could generate. Nothing happened. Even with the *Modoc's* anchor used as a kedge the *Mount Dirfys* was still stuck fast. Then the cable broke from the strain and the *Modoc* lost her anchor. The Coast Guard commanding officer firmly believed that with help from a salvage tug the *Mount Dirfys* would have come off, but that she probably could not "have been gotten to a place of safety before she sank. She would have more than likely drawn too much water to have been able to enter the Cape Fear River and any other port would have been too far to have towed her with the rudder gone."

By nightfall the master of the *Mount Dirfys*, unnamed in official reports, feared for the safety of his crew. Although the weather report was favorable, "the breakers on the shoals started to make up out of all proportions to the wind blowing or predicted, so much so in fact, that

Lost nets continue to take their toll against the marine life. This shark got so entangled that it could not free itself, and eventually it died a lingering death.

taking the crew off required clever handling of the power surfboat and good judgment of the officer in charge." The *Modoc* was crowded that night, and her cook worked overtime.

The salvage tug *Relief* arrived the morning of the twenty-eighth, as did the Coast Guard cutter *Cahoon*. Now a curious situation occurred. "The master of the *Mount Dirfys* would not sign an agreement for the salvage operations as written by the salvage officer on the *Relief* until he had received authority from Lloyds agent the next day." This seemed immaterial, "as it is doubtful whether there was ever any chance of saving the vessel. Early in the morning the master, ten officers and men were put back aboard the stranded steamer."

The next day salvage operations were abandoned. The crew of the *Mount Dirfys*, as well as their personal effects, were taken off. Quarantine regulations required that they be landed at the Quarantine Station at Southport. The *Modoc* then refueled and returned to sea in order to resume her primary duty assignment: searching for smugglers.

Today the stern of the wreck is relatively intact, at least below the quadrant; there is no sign of superstructure. Strong currents have scoured a washout under the fantail, and the depth there can reach 40 to 45 feet. This hole can be filled with as much as four feet of shells, largely conch and scotch bonnet. The shaft alley is intact and large enough to swim through.

The engine has been blown apart. Three boilers provide high relief amidships, two in such a position that a diver can swim under them. The bow is broken up. As much as ten feet of sand movement can alternately bury and expose large portions of wreckage.

Divers should note that the surge can sometimes be very powerful.

Lost nets are particularly dangerous to sea turtles, which dive down to wrecks food, but must return to the surface every hour or so for a breath of air. Even a temporary entanglement can prove fatal.

NAECO

Built: 1918
Previous names: *Charles M. Everest*
Gross tonnage: 5,373
Type of vessel: Tanker
Builder: Bethlehem Ship Building Corp., Wilmington, Delaware
Owner: Charles Kurz & Company (Pennsylvania Shipping Co., Mgrs.)
Port of registry: Wilmington, Delaware
Cause of sinking: Torpedoed by *U-124* (Kapitanleutnant Mohr)

Sunk: March 23, 1942
Depth: 140 feet
Dimensions: 411' × 53' × 31'
Power: Oil-fired steam

| Location: | 27053.7 | bow | 39422.8 |
| | 27065.4 | stern | 39387.8 |

According to Utilityman Walter Swank, the *Naeco* was ill prepared for the U-boat war running riot off the U.S. eastern seaboard in the early months of 1942. Although sinkings were hot and heavy in an area known at the time as "torpedo alley" (the approaches to the Diamond Shoals) "there was no life safety equipment on the ship." This category was intended to include such items as life rafts, life preservers, and medical and food supplies cached in the Lifeboats. Swank's grievance might conceivably be perceived as an overstatement—perhaps the result of the anger and pain he suffered over the loss of so many of his fellow merchant seamen.

He also claimed that "the black-out was not enforced as it should have been since there were no black-out lights supplied," and "the lifeboats were not swung out; they were in their cradle." During the war, and especially when passing through a zone known to be patrolled by the enemy, the precautions he described became standard operating procedure. In order to be less visible to German eyes, ships ran at night without navigation lights, with their ports dogged shut and locked, and with only special blackout lights screwed into sockets near any hatch that could be opened to the outside. Because ships often sank within minutes after being torpedoed, the

Courtesy of The Mariners Musuem, Newport News, Virginia.

common practice was to carry the lifeboats swung out on their davits so they could be launched at a moment's notice.

The situation with respect to the lifeboats seems irrelevant in light of the circumstances, for when the deadly torpedo detonated beneath the *Naeco's* hull amidships the immediate danger lay not in getting away from the ship, but in getting away too soon. The navigating bridge was utterly destroyed by the explosion, and all the men on duty, including Captain Emil Engelbrecht, were killed. With the official chain of command terminated at the top, Swank alleged that "every man had to think for himself and act fast."

Some reacted—or overreacted—too fast. Those who launched the first lifeboat did so before the ship's forward motion had slowed sufficiently for a safe getaway. The boat swamped as soon as it touched the swiftly moving water. By the time the chief engineer shut down the engines and turned on the steam smothering system, the flames were out of control at the forward end of the ship, and were being fanned aft.

With the two midship lifeboats either demolished or burnt, and one of the after lifeboats swamped, those still alive were in desperate straits. Confusion reigned on the oil-slickened decks. Afterward, no one knew for sure the exact chronology of events, or even what those events were. The possibility of death lurked everywhere. The tanker might blow up at any moment and kill everyone on board, or it might sink, and plunge the men into the fiery cauldron the sea had become: an immense conflagration fed by 97,000 barrels of domestic heating oil that was pouring out of the damaged tanks. Drowning might seem an easier way to go.

Life rafts tossed overboard were swept into the fire by the wind. According to Swank, "one boat was launched and got away with two members in it which were later found burned to death." Only one lifeboat got away safely—and this not until 4:45 a.m. (an hour and a half after the torpedo struck.) The intense heat seared the lungs, and the engulfing smoke stung the eyes and sent the men into coughing spasms. The ship was a charnel house of the dead, an archipelago of the living: each man was cut off from his companions by blindness and the scorching flames. Most men were forced to jump overboard in order to have any chance of survival. Some were picked up by the lone lifeboat. Others had to fend for themselves in the water. The boatswain wound up swimming back to the ship.

Some time during this bewildering chain of events the *Naeco* broke in two, and the pieces drifted apart.

Help finally arrived at 7:30 in the morning as a flotilla of escort craft converged on the scene, drawn to the burning ship like moths to a flame. The U.S. Coast Guard cutter *Dione* picked up the ten men in lifeboat No. 3, then rescued two men afloat. The USS *Osprey* (AM–56), a minesweeper, found one man on a raft. The Naval tug *Umpqua* (No. 25) brazenly jammed her bow against the stern of the still-floating tanker so the boatswain could escape the flames.

The Naval tug *Umpqua* cautiously approaches the stern of the *Naeco*. (Courtesy of the National Archives.)

When the final count was in there were fourteen survivors. Twenty-four valiant men of the merchant marine had perished at the hands of the German war machine.

The stern of the *Naeco* sank at about 8:30. According to one official document, the bow "was seen by the survivors to sink prior to the sinking of the stern." The two pieces came to rest on the bottom about two and a half miles apart. The people in Seawarren, New Jersey, who were expecting to heat their houses with kerosene from Houston, Texas, found themselves on short rations.

During her 1943 shipwreck survey, the USCG cutter *Gentian* identified one wreck "by underwater photography as the stern of the tanker, *Naeco*." She returned in 1944 to complete the survey. At that time she determined that the wreck lay in 130 feet of water. The report then contradicts itself on the same page, finding first a "fathometer rise to 91'," then stating that "the least depth recorded over the wreck was 59 feet at mean low water." Perhaps it is a typographical error.

Elsewhere the report stated that "although the wreck has not been wire dragged, it is not believed to be a menace to navigation. ... A Sonar plot indicated the wreck to be about 180 feet long."

Today the bow section has sunk into the sand to a depth of about 140 feet, and is considerably broken down. Washouts scoured by the current go as deep as 150 feet, allowing entry to the interior spaces. As one might expect of that portion of a tanker that is largely just a tank, it makes for a rather mundane dive.

The Coast Guard cutter *Tallapoosa* located the stern of the *Naeco* in 1943, and the *Gentian* surveyed it more fully in 1944. At the time it rose to within eighty-seven feet of the surface, was not considered a menace to navigation, and was not wire-dragged. "A Sonar plot indicates that it is only about 135 feet long." One might wonder what happened to the remaining 126 feet of wreckage; perhaps the midship wheelhouse and adjacent tank section lie scattered and flattened somewhere between the two existing pieces, or in the triangle formed between the bow and the stern and the torpedoed position some eleven miles upcurrent.

The stern is an interesting and a pretty dive. The depth is fairly consistent at 140 feet. Many of the hull plates have collapsed outward, exposing the massive engine. Abaft the engine the wreck is largely flat, and much of it is buried, including the propeller. Forward of the engine the deck inclines up to about 120 feet. For the brass collector there are numerous valves, tees, and elbows—now all cleaned of the kerosene that once gushed through them. Beginning at the forward break a long, low debris field extends for quite a way. Visibility is usually excellent; it can lure an inquisitive diver far off the wreck in search of other large pieces. It is a dive well worth making.

By the way, *Naeco* is "ocean" spelled backward.

What of Johann Mohr and the *U-124*? See elsewhere in this book for the sinkings of the *E.M. Clark, Esso Nashville, Papoose,* and *W.E. Hutton*; see *Shipwrecks of North Carolina: from the Diamond Shoals North* for the sinking of the *Kassandra Louloudis.* The *U-124* was lost on the night of April 2–3, 1943, in an action west of Gibralter. There were no survivors.

Lost traps catch fish in a deadly and self-replenishing cycle. The fish that swim into a trap to feed on the remnants of decomposing flesh then become victims that attract more fish.

NEVADA

Built: 1864   Sunk: June 6, 1868
Previous names: None   Depth: 72 feet
Gross tonnage: 914   Dimensions: 160' × 32' × 17'
Type of vessel: Wooden-hulled screw steamer
Power: Coal-fired one-cylinder vertical direct-acting steam engine, built by
      Albertson & Douglass
Builder: Maxson, Fish & Company, Mystic, Connecticut
Owner: Francis Alexander and Sons, New York, NY
Port of registry: New York
Cause of sinking: Stranded
Location: 26940.1   40191.4

According to the shipping articles entered by an 1850 Act of Congress, each sailor hired for a voyage signed an agreement with the master of the vessel that declared his conditions of employment, guaranteed the wages to be paid, and described the behavior expected of him. "No grog allowed, and none to be put on board by the crew, or by any of the parties hereunto, and no profane language allowed, nor any sheath-knives permitted to be brought or used on board."

The captain had Congressional authority to suppress "immorality and vice of all kinds" against forfeiture of wages "together with everything belonging to him or them on board the said vessel." For every day a man was absent without leave he forteited three days wages; if he was absent more than forty-eight hours he also had to pay the wages of a seaman hired to replace him.

On the good side, flogging was not allowed.

The crew of the *Nevada* appears to have been as standarized as the articles they signed, for under the column for height, seventeen were put down as being five feet nine inches tall, while twelve measured up at five feet seven. Only the captain's height went unrecorded. I wonder if the Chief Mate used a tape or dead reckoning as a rule.

When the *Nevada* was launched, on September 5, 1864, she went into the service of Wakeman, Gookin & Dickerson, of New York. The company wasted no time in chartering her to the U.S. Quarter Master Department, which, due to the amount of supplies needed to maintain the War of the Rebellion, was paying competitive rates for the transportation of troops and materiel: $411 per day. After the cessation of hostilities, the *Nevada* was put on the Savannah route, running between that city and New York. In 1866 she was sold to the New York & Mexican Mail Steam Ship Line. Finally, on April 24, 1868, she was purchased by Francis Alexander & Sons; Captain W. Megill was assigned as master.

The circumstances involving the loss of the *Nevada* after only six weeks of service under new ownership are described in tantalizingly meager detail. The *New York Times*, June 12: "She left New York on the 3d inst. with a full cargo of merchandise and a number of passengers, bound to Havana and Vera Cruz. On the 4th inst., at midnight, the ship grounded on Hatteras Shoals, in a thick fog. There being a heavy swell on the vessel labored hard: but at daylight a landing was effected on the beach, and assistance sent for. The passengers were landed, an anchor run out to heave her off, the cargo hove overboard to lighten her, and every effort made to save her; but finding her leaking badly and the sea running high, they were compelled to abandon her. One seaman lost his life by the upsetting of a boat. At 5:30 P.M., on 5th inst., the ship worked over the shoals, and at 4 A.M. on the 6th she sank in twelve fathoms of water, due south from Hatteras lighthouse. The Captain left for Newbern, and the first officer of the ship was put on board the wrecking steamer *Winants*, bound to the ship off Body Island. The ship's masts are above water. Nothing whatever was saved from the vessel."

According to the Steamboat Inspection records, "as near as can be ascertained, the disaster was caused by foggy weather, a strong current, the compass being in error, and the negligence of the master in not taking soundings. The Shipmasters' Association of New York city, after due investigation, promptly revoked the certificate of the master for want of due precaution on his part. Vessel and cargo were a total loss, and valued at $200,000. No lives were lost."

Did a seaman drown, or didn't he? If so, there are no provisions in the shipping articles that offer compensation to his heirs.

The wreck of the *Nevada* lies exactly where contemporary accounts placed it: due south of Hatteras Light in twelve fathoms (seventy-two feet) of water. Before Steve Lang found a pewter spoon with the name *Nevada* engraved on the handle, the site was known as the Urn Wreck because of the earthenware urns found there. The name Unis has also been applied to this wreck, and may still be found on tourist charts and in amateur publications.

Very little remains of the hull. It appears to have fallen outward and now lies mostly beneath the sand. The engine dominates the site, rising some fifteen feet above the bottom, while the two boilers forward of it rise up about eight feet. Nothing else other than the iron propeller sticks up higher than two feet. There is no discernible bow; the debris field forward of the boilers simply peters out into the sand.

The *Nevada* is what is known as a digging wreck. By fanning the sand one may dredge up parts of the original cargo not thrown overboard at the time the ship first grounded upon the shoals. Brass lantern parts abound, as do brick-sized pieces of soft sandstone known as holystones, once used to scour the wooden decks. There is no telling what merchandise remains to be recovered.

NORMANNIA

Built: 1897
Previous names: None
Gross tonnage: 2,654
Type of vessel: Freighter
Builder: Howaldtswerke, Kiel
Owner: D/S A/S Norden (P. Brown, Jr. & Company, Managers)
Port of registry: Copenhagen, Denmark
Cause of sinking: Foundered
Location: 27142.8

Sunk: January 17, 1924
Depth: 115 feet
Dimensions: 312' × 45' × 20'
Power: Coal-fired steam

39180.5

There comes a time in a ship's career when no amount of human effort can save her from the elements of nature. Despite ongoing maintenance, despite annual inspections, despite the perfect functioning of her machinery and mechanical devices, sometimes none of these is enough to forestall the demise of an otherwise well-tuned vessel. For a ship has a life: not life as we know it, not organic growth and reproduction, not consciousness or personality or soul, but life as continuance. And, as in any form of life, the difference between existance and nonexistance, between animation and everlasting stillness, is a delicate balance that can be tipped all too abruptly. For a human being this can be the spontaneous creation of a cancer cell, for a ship it can be as seemingly insignificant an occurrence as the loosening of a single rivet. Once control is lost it is often impossible to regain.

Courtesy of the Peabody Museum of Salem.

On January 16, 1924, the Danish freighter *Normannia* encountered a fierce gale that proved to be the impetus for tipping her scale of life. She began taking water into the engine room, apparently from leaks in her hull. The crew tried valiantly at first to stem the rapidly gaining flood, but soon were compelled to cry out for help; the sea poured in faster than the pumps could eject it.

Out went the distress call: SOS, Save Our Ship, SOS.

The radio waves got through and, complying to the mariner's rule of the sea, two vessels immediately changed course for Frying Pan Shoals: The *Henry R. Mallory* and the *Charles E. Harwood*. At the Charleston Navy Yard the Coast Guard cutter *Modoc* got up steam and headed out to sea under forced draft.

First to arrive at the scene was the *Henry R. Mallory*. She had been only ten miles away when her wireless received the call; now, an hour later (8:30 p.m.), she circled in the dark, searching for signs of the vessel in distress. Not until a sharp-eyed lookout spotted a flash of light off the starboard bow was there any indication that the *Normannia* was nearby. Captain H.W. Barstow instructed his radio operator to request that the *Normannia* fire rockets. Once this was done Captain Barstow was able to pinpoint the *Normannia's* position. He maneuvered his ship to within a quarter mile of her stern, all the while playing his searchlight on the beleaguered ship's fantail.

By this time four feet of oily water was sloshing around in the *Normannia's* engine room, and the fire under the boilers was extinguished. The ship wallowed sickeningly. As the *Henry R. Mallory* hove to in mountainous seas, Captain Christian Blom, master of the *Normannia*, put four men in the ship's yawl and sent them for help. Iwulhman Hansen and three hearty seamen pulled on the oars for all they were worth. They reached the *Henry R. Mallory* safely.

Captain Blom had instructed Hansen to ask for a tow. Captain Barstow listened patiently to Hansen's plea, but the southeast gale made such a scheme impossible. The *Henry R. Mallory* was a passenger liner, not a salvage tug. Instead, Captain Barstow put his third officer, W.P. Dukin, in charge of a volunteer rescue crew. During the next four hours these courageous men battled the breakers in the liner's lifeboat, and managed to bring back twenty people: nineteen crew men and, under protest, Captain Blom's wife. Anna Blom did not want to leave her husband, but he insisted, and said that "if she did not go he would drop her over the side into the boat." Anna also saved her two pet dogs.

Now it was after midnight. Captain Blom and his six (or seven) officers remained on the *Normannia* in hopes that they could help rig salvage lines when the *Modoc* arrived. They spent the night wondering what dawn would bring.

After the *Charles E. Harwood* arrived, the *Henry R. Mallory* continued on her way to New York. She had a schedule to keep. The *Charles E. Harwood* stood by faithfully.

The sun did not bring good news. The *Nomannia* was fast settling by the stern. Without power her pumps would not work. There was nothing Captain Blom could do to save his ship, so, regretfully, he and his officers abandoned her. He watched sadly from the deck of the *Charles E. Harwood* as the *Normannia* slipped slowly stern first beneath the waves. When the *Charles E. Harwood* left, at 10:50 a.m., only twenty feet of the bow stood out of the water. The stern was resting solidly on the bottom.

The *Modoc* arrived in time to catch a last glimpse of the *Normannia*. Then, as water surged into her holds and compartments, forcing trapped air forward and out through the hatchways, she gasped her last and sank completely of sight.

When a person dies, only his body remains; when a ship dies, only a rusting hull is left. Forged steel has no soul—but do not try to tell that to a seaman.

The *Normannia* was carrying mahogany on that last voyage, from Chester, Pennsylvania to Charleston, South Carolina. Little remains today; the teredoes have eaten most of it. But some of this exceptional hardwood has been interred by the sand, and thus preserved from marine boring organisms. It can be found under recognizable hatch cover frames.

Despite the low relief (about five feet) the wreck is large, contiguous, and fun to explore: like a vast debris field among which ship parts can be identified. In places the deck crossmembers are exposed. Patient divers fanning the sand have found bullets, drawer knobs, and Scandanavian coins. One diver even found a fourteen karat gold ring inscribed "Christian;" it undoubtedly belonged to Captain Blom.

Part of the stern is fairly intact. The engine rises like a great tombstone, and the two boilers sit side by side. The beam of the wreck is narrow enough that one can often see from one side to the other. Visibility can be "from top to bottom."

Is the *Normannia* really dead? Not according spearfishers who visit the wreck regularly. They have found new and effulgent life swarming around the encrusted remains. The *Normannia* has become a microcosm whose entire ecosystem revolves around the lowest link in the food chain—those creatures who have only two prerequisites for survival: something to cling to, and a good flow of nutrient solution.

Perhaps, then, sunken ships are not deceased, but vessels reborn into a new form of existance that serves a grander purpose than that for which they were originally constructed. Perhaps. But that is a question for philosophers.

PANAM

Built: 1925
Previous names: *Otokia*
Gross tonnage: 7,277
Type of vessel: Tanker
Builder: Livingstone & Cooper, Ltd., Hessle
Owner: War Shipping Administration (Marine Transport Lines, charterer)
Port of registry: Panama
Cause of sinking: Torpedoed by *U-129* (Kapitanleutnant Witt)
Location: 34-09.1 N

Sunk: May 4, 1943
Depth: 480 feet
Dimensions: 438′ × 57′ × 33′
Power: Twin diesel engines

76-40.5 W

German U-boats were kicked out of the eastern seaboard shipping lanes in mid 1942, after only six months of encroachment. By then, antisubmarine warfare patrols were so many and so well organized that it was practically suicide for the enemy to even think about attacking heavily protected convoys. A glance at the statistics demonstrates this point. During the three years from mid 1942 until the end of the war the Germans sank eleven ships—at a cost of six U-boats.

Only the boldest of U-boat commanders considered attacking east coast shipping during this time; the wisest lurked low, popped his target, and made a hasty retreat. It was the only tactic with survival value: the sniper stratagem of shoot and run. This is how Kapitanleutnant Hans Witt made his kill and lived to tell about it.

Perhaps if he had known about the Submarine Tracking Office he would not have made the attempt. The German codes had long since been broken, and Allied intelligence monitored transmissions on every wave length the Germans used. By deciphering the messages coming out of Admiral Karl Doenitz's U-boat headquarters the STO kept tabs on orders sent to each U-boat, including area of operations, times of departure and arrival, and length of stay. Furthermore, by intercepting a U-boat's transmissions the STO could triangulate its position; with a series of triangulations it could predict its direction of travel.

By correlating these data the Submarine Tracking Officer proclaimed on May 1, 1943 that only one U-boat was then operating within the boundaries of the Eastern Sea Frontier: "one recently unlocated, probably patrolling Savannah to Hatteras." For two days aerial and surface craft patrolled the area, but found nothing. On May 3 high winds and heavy seas hindered the search.

About this time Convoy NK-538 left Norfolk and headed south. It passed safely through the high probability zone. Among the merchantmen in the convoy was the *Panam*, travelling in ballast to Lake Charles, Louisiana. Shortly after midnight on May 4 she developed engine trouble. The tanker lost speed and was soon left behind. By daylight, repairs had been effected, permitting the *Panam* to resume her southward journey. Now she alone in the broad reaches of the sea.

She rounded Cape Hatteras at eight or nine knots, and turned slightly westward to 203° true. Because of difficulty with her steering gear it proved impossible for the ship to zigzag. The captain made up for the ship's mechanical deficiencies by increasing the number of lookouts to seven: three on the bridge, two at the aft gun, and two on the fantail. Her degaussing equipment was operating smoothly, thus offsetting the magnetic field generated by such a large mass of moving steel, and making her a blind target for German magnetic torpedoes.

All these precautions were not enough, however. At 8:25 a.m. a torpedo struck the *Panam* on the port side of the engine room. The explosion killed two duty personnel, wrecked the engine, and caused immediate flooding. The radio was knocked out by the blast so no distress signal could be sent. The *U-129* remained submerged. Gunners on the *Panam* scanned the horizon for signs of the enemy, but saw nothing.

The *Panam* went dead in the water. She was a sitting duck. Eight to ten minutes later a second torpedo struck the tanker on the port side amidships. The pump room was wrecked and the deck plates were severely buckled, but no one was killed. It was time to abandon ship.

While lifeboats were being launched some of the men panicked and jumped overboard. Fortunately, the tanker was without a cargo so she did not burst into flames. Three lifeboats got away before the ship sank; they went around and picked up the men in the water. In all there were forty-nine survivors; the only casualties were the two men killed in the initial blast.

Luck was with the crew of the *Panam*. They had hardly escaped from the ship when an Army B-25 bomber flew by and tipped its wings as a signal of recognition. The pilot reported the situation over the radio. Five hours later the *SC 664* rescued the men and took them to the Section Base at Morehead City.

Anyone thinking about looking for the wreck should take note that in 1944 the U.S. Coast Guard cutter *Gentian* found what was believed to be the *Panam*, at a depth of 480 feet. "No other sinkings have been reported within many miles of this position, nor were any other wrecks located in the 60 square miles searched in the area."

The *U-129* was decommissioned in Lorient on August 19, 1944. Rather than turn the U-boat over to Allied authorities when Germany agreed to unconditional surrender, its crew scuttled the boat there in the first week of May 1945.

Compare this pre-war photo with the one below. (Courtesy of the U.S. Coast Guard.)

PAPOOSE

Built: 1921

Previous names: *Silvanus*

Gross tonnage: 5,939

Type of vessel: Tanker

Sunk: March 18, 1942

Depth: 125 feet

Dimensions: 412′ × 53′ × 31′

Power: Oil-fired steam

Builder: S. Western Ship Building Company, San Pedro, California

Owner: American Republics Corporation

Port of registry: Wilmington, Delaware

Cause of sinking: Torpedoed by *U-124* (Kapitanleutnant Mohr)

Location: 27074.0   39431.1

The *Papoose* is a ship that was once destroyed by fire, but, like the phoenix, rose again from its ashes. It happened on April 8, 1926 about forty

In this view taken in January 1942, the flag and the ship's name have been painted out, and the previously white superstructure has been darkened to match the hull and make the ship less visible through German periscopes. (Courtesy of the U.S. Coast Guard.)

miles south of New Orleans, Louisiana. She was named *Silvanus* then, and was owned by the Dutch Shell Company. While navigating a bend in the Mississippi River she drove her bow into the Standard Oil tanker *Thomas H. Wheeler*. Buckling steel plates generates sparks that ignited a cargo of highly flammable benzene. A series of destructive explosions spread fire along her decks, raging out of control. Twenty-six men died that night. The ship was declared a total constructive loss.

In the law suits that followed, the hull was put up for auction by a federal marshall. Highest bidder was the Petroleum Navigation Company. The derelict was towed to Beaumont, Texas, where the Pennsylvania Shipyards maintained a plant on the Neches River. Three hundred workmen were assigned the task of reconstructing the *Silvanus*. Although the engine and boilers were undamaged they were thoroughly overhauled. Where people get face lifts, ships get deck lifts. In this case it was a half million dollar deck lift. According to a contemporary account, "it was necessary to rebuild practically the entire superstructure and to put in new decking and new deck beams. New quarters for the officers and crew were built and elaborately fitted out.

After five months of surgical torching and welding the *Silvanus* was ready to take to the sea once again. On March 31, 1927 she was rechristened *Papoose*. A trial trip to Galveston found her in good working order. She returned to Beaumont, took on 67,000 barrels of gasoline, and departed for New York. She continued in the tanker trade for another fifteen years. Then came war and, instead of accidental damage, intentional destruction.

It was fortunate for the crew of the *Papoose* that she was headed south on the night of Marh 18, 1942—not because her direction of travel had any bearing on events, but because it meant that she was riding in ballast: that is, her cargo tanks were empty. She was steaming from Providence, Rhode Island to Corpus Christi, Texas, there to pick up another load of crude.

Instead of following a deep-water route that would have carried the vessel far offshore, the Navy Routing Office recommended hugging the coastline in order to be better protected from U-boats lurking off the eastern seaboard. The enemy was taking a severe toll of merchant shipping, and March was the worst month yet for Allied casualties. Captain Raymond Zalnick, master of the *Papoose*, conned his ship through the Long Island Sound, along the East River, out the New York Bay, then south, keeping as close as practical to the shore. It was nighttime when he rounded the Diamond Shoals at eleven knots.

"There was a fresh northwest breeze and though the sea was moderately rough, visibility was good for a night watch. The *Papoose* was not zigzagging but she was completely blacked out." She ran independently—and right into a German torpedo.

As is common during times of stress, observations are telescoped so that afterward people confuse the exact sequence of events and even the nature of those events. For example, several witnesses aboard the *Papoose* testified to seeing a ship in flames on the horizon. This can only have been the tanker *W.E. Hutton*, the only other ship torpedoed that night in the vicinity. (They were probably less than five miles apart.) Yet, it is reported that the *W.E. Hutton* was not torpedoed until thirty minutes *after* the *Papoose*. (Elsewhere, it was even reported that the *W.E. Hutton* was torpedoed on the evening of the nineteenth. Records get confused during a time of war.)

The deck log of the *U-124* records two attacks on the eighteenth, but there was no way for Johann Mohr to know one tanker from another. Mohr's log is overflowing with attack reports since in the course of a week he sank seven ships and damaged two others. The *E.M. Clark, Esso Nashville, Naeco,* and *W.E. Hutton* are covered elsewhere in this book. The *Kassandra Louloudis* can be found in *Shipwrecks of North Carolina: from the Diamond Shoals North.* The *Ceiba* was sunk far offshore.

Amid this mass of contradictory evidence is a kernal of truth. Since it is unlikely that men saw flames where none existed, and were put on the alert because of it, I think such testimony is valid. If such is the case, at 10:30 p.m. on March 18, 1942, the *Papoose* "was struck aft on the port side by a torpedo which penetrated the fuel tank, damaged interior bulkheads and caused flooding by oil and water of the fire and engine rooms, the fluid rising in about four minutes to the height of the tops of the cylinder heads. One fireman and one oiler were lost and presumed drowned by this flooding." Edward Peters and George Kreuger were never seen again.

The position was approximately fifteen miles southwest of Cape Lookout light. Captain Zalnick ordered the wheel turned hard right, toward shore. Unfortunately, with the engine so quickly disabled, the ship was without power. She slowly lost headway. The radio operator sent out a distress call, and was relieved to have it acknowledged.

With the *Papoose* now a sitting duck, Captain Zalnick ordered abandon ship. The crew wasted no time in carrying out the order. With practiced efficiency lifeboat No. 3 was launched within five minutes of the initial explosion. The men pulled hard at the oars. No sooner had they cleared the ship than a "second torpedo narrowly missed hitting their boat." This one struck on the starboard side nearly opposite the spot where the first torpedo had struck. The tremendous explosion ripped open a hole in the hull that gaped eight feet above the water line.

"The wooden awning over the amidships deck house and the radio shack were partially demolished. ... Falling debris ... caused the after fall of boat No. 1 (starboard side, amidships) to foul when the boat was still 15 feet above the water, whereupon the Captain gave the order to lower forward end to waterline and cut after fall." Some of the men were injured by the falling debris. They all got away in the lifeboat.

Now a curious event occurred. An amber light appeared some thirty feet above the water, a couple hundred yards off the stern of the *Papoose*. Everyone saw it; everyone had an opinion about it. Was it the U-boat's searchlight meant to blind the survivors or to observe damage to the vessel? Was it a decoy buoy released by the U-boat in order to lure another ship to her destruction? Or was it an angel from Heaven come to take the U-boat's victims to a better world? "It hovered mysteriously in the neighborhood for an hour, or an hour and a half, following the attack, never revealing what lay behind it in the darkness before it finally disappeared."

The thirty-four men in the two lifeboats rowed away from the *Papoose* toward shore. At 7:30 the next morning the U.S. destroyer *Stringham* (APD-6) hove into view and took them all on board. With amazing presence of mind, Captain Zalnick managed to escape the *Papoose* with all his code books and confidential papers. He turned them over to the Commanding Officer of the *Stringham* at the time of rescue.

When last seen the *Papoose* was settling by the stern, but still afloat with her after deck awash. The ship obviously capsized because today the wreck lies upside down. The hull rises off the bottom more than thirty feet almost totally intact, like some monstrous encrusted cigar, with enough large cracks to permit easy entry into the vast interior. The engine room is especially interesting as gauges can still be found on the bulkheads. Penetration techniques should be fully utilized.

The port side is buried in the sand while the starboard edge and some of the railing is visible. The largest break is on the port side amidships. Just forward of the break is a debris field that is the remains of the bridge. The seventeen-foot-diameter bronze propeller was salvaged, but the rudder is still there.

The *U-124* was lost with all hands on during the night of April 2–3, while operating west of Gibralter. Credited with the kill were the British warships *Stonecrop* and *Black Swan*.

Captain Zalnick (with glasses) sits in the back of a Navy truck with some of the other survivors from the *Papoose*. (Courtesy of the National Archives.)

PETERHOFF

Built: 1861
Previous names: None
Gross tonnage: 819
Type of vessel: Iron-hulled screw steamer
Builder: Oswald, Sunderland, England
Owner: U.S. Navy
Cause of sinking: Collision with USS *Monticello*
Location: 45323.0

Sunk: March 6, 1864
Depth: 30 feet
Dimensions: 220' × 29' × 17'
Power: Coal-fired steam

59075.9

The short career of the *Peterhoff* was a checkered one about which there is still much confusion and doubt. She was reportedly built as a yacht for the Czar of Russia, and named after the city of Petrodvorets in the Gulf of Finland. Petrodvorets was previously known as Peterhof; it is located twenty miles southwest of Leningrad.

It was also reported that "later she was leased to the company of Pile, Spence, and Co., of London, under contract to the British government, for use as a cargo vessel, at a time when the British were trading with the Confederate states." No reason is given as to why the Czar of Russia should want to inconvenience himself with the absense of his yacht in order to help British privateers run the federal blockade.

All inferences aside, the *Peterhoff* was in fact plying the trade routes as a freighter in 1863. She left Falmouth, England on January 27 under the command of Captain Jarman, her final port of destination listed as Matamoras, Mexico, She had on board six passengers with passports obtained from the Mexican consul in London. She carried six hundred tons of varied cargo in her holds: "Blucher boots (army shoes), cavalry boots, 192 bales of gray blankets, ninety-five cases of horse shoes, thirty-six large cases containing artillery harnesses in sets for four horses with two riding saddles attached to each set, two hydraulic presses (in pieces) adapted to cotton, drugs (including quinine, calomel, morphine, and chloroform), coiled rope, boxes of tin, boxes of sheet zinc, hoop and bar iron, anvils, and bellows."

Three and a half weeks later, after a partially stormy passage, the *Peterhoff* caught sight of St. Thomas, then a Danish possession. Before she could enter the harbor she was fired upon by the USS *Alabama*: first a blank charge, then a shot across the bow. The *Peterhoff* hove to. A boarding officer from the *Alabama* examined the *Peterhoff's* papers, then allowed her to proceed, "declining to endorse his visit and examination on the plea that he had no authority to do so." Nor was any apology made for accosting a British vessel in Danish waters, an act that was not in keeping with the international laws of the sea.

According to passenger S.J. Redgate, "The *Peterhoff* remained in St. Thomas Harbor for the purpose of completing her supply of coal till about noon of the 25th February. During her stay, Admiral Wilkes, of *Trent* notoriety, arrived in harbor with the U.S. steamers *Wachusett* and *Oneida* and declared publicly here that the *Alamaba* should have made a prize of the *Peterhoff*."

Rear Admiral Charles Wilkes had in hand a list of British ships suspected of being blockade runners. Usually, such ships recoaled in Bermuda before attempting to run the federal blockade; but lately they had been known to steam into St. Thomas in an effort to avoid capture by U.S. warships. Admiral Wilkes was not going to allow the *Peterhoff* to get away with so obvious a subterfuge. He ordered the USS *Vanderbilt* to lie in wait just outside of territorial waters.

Because the *Peterhoff* was experiencing engine trouble which her crew was endeavoring to repair, she cleared port under sail on the twenty-fifth and was quickly overtaken and ordered to heave to. Wrote Acting Lieutenant C.H. Baldwin, captain of the *Vanderbilt*: "I boarded her some 5 miles off the harbor and found his papers quite irregular. He had only a certified manifest for seven boxes of tea, whereas he had a cargo of kegs, cases, and boxes for which he had no certified manifest. He had seven passengers, yet he told the boarding officer he had no passenger list. ... I learn from one of her crew that she has fieldpieces and arms on board."

This suited Admiral Wilkes's fancy just fine; he claimed that the *Peterhoff* was a lawful prize under international articles of war because she had broken the neutrality clause. He sent orders that Captain Jarman bring his papers to him. With stereotypic British resolution Captain Jarman refused. He allowed that as "he held a commission in the royal navy reserve, and had charge of her Majesty's mail for Matamoras, that he would not leave his ship, especially after the threat which had been held out, but that they were welcome to come on board, examine his papers, and search the ship."

Wilkes went a step further. He sent a prize crew consisting of an officer, four mates, two engineers, and twenty-one armed guards, and placed Captain Jarman, his crew, and passengers under arrest. The demand was again made, and was again refused. Captain Jarman steadfastly stood his ground. The situation did not change during the night. The *Peterhoff's* men were confined to quarters under threat of being shot.

The next day the prize crew sailed the *Peterhoff* toward Key West for adjudication. The passage took ten days, during which time the Britishers were permitted on deck only a few at a time, and then only on the after deck. The passengers were freed some time after arrival at Key West. Because there was no U.S. district judge in Key West at that time, the *Peterhoff's* crew (twenty-four men) were sent to Boston. The captured mail was sent to Washington.

Such U.S. transgression created great commotion in Great Britain, where the hijacking of royal mail and official correspondence was perceived as an unconscionable act of aggression, and where the capture of a British ship and her crew was considered an act of piracy; and in St. Thomas, where the continued harrassment of merchant ships in and around its harbors threatened "free commercial intercourse." The *Peterhoff* was only one among many ships seized by an overzealous U.S. Navy in pursuit of fighting the Civil War. Wilkes accused the regime at St. Thomas of condoning a contraband trade "under the eyes and with the approval and sanction of the authorities." Lieutenant Governor Rothe of St. Thomas denied such allegations.

The political climate was hot and took quite a while to cool down. Wilkes and Rothe exchanged lengthy correspondence that eventually soothed the sores on both sides. After a great deal of diplomatic debate between Parliament and the President of the United States, the royal mail was returned unopened to the British consul in New York. The British seamen were given passage to England. But the *Peterhoff* was kept as a prize of war.

U.S. District Judge Betts found that "First—That the said ship *Peterhoff* ... was knowingly laded in whole or in part with articles contraband of war, and had them in the act of transportation at sea. Second—That her voyage ... was not truly destined to ... Matamoras, a neutral port ... but, on the contrary, was destined for some other port or place, and in aid and for the use of the enemy. ... Third—That the ships papers were simulated and false as to her real destination."

Interestingly, Betts described articles of a contraband character as any "cargo ... particularly adapted to army use." According to J. Thomas Scharf in his *History of the Confederate States Navy*, "As there are but very few articles of commerce which, in a direct or indirect manner, are not 'adapted to army use,' that criterion of contraband, if recognized by all nations, would prohibit all commerce on the part of neutrals in time of war between any two nations."

The *Peterhoff* langoured at Throgs Neck, in Long Island Sound, for nearly a year while all this wrangling went on. In February 1864 the U.S. Navy purchased the *Peterhoff* from the prize court for $80,000. She was commissioned, and armed with "a 12 pound howitzer on the fantail, a 30 pound parrott Rifle on the bow and at least five 32 pound smoothbores on the gun deck amidships."

On the twenty-fourth she left New York under the command of Acting Volunteer Lieutenant Thomas Pickering. Pickering's orders from Secretary of the Navy Gideon Welles were to "proceed with the U.S.S. *Peterhoff* to Hampton Roads and report to Acting Rear-Admiral S.P. Lee for duty in the North Atlantic Blockading Squadron."

Pickering's command lasted little more than a week. How the *Peterhoff* was lost off New Inlet, Fort Fisher was described all too briefly in the *Monticello's* log. "March 6.—At 5 a.m. made a vessel on the port beam, distant about three-quarters of a mile, supposed it to be a blockade runner. Starboarded the helm and challenged her. On her answering my challenge, put the helm aport to keep on my course, thinking she was at anchor. Were going slow at the time. Stopped the engine, still keeping the helm hard aport. Inside of a minute struck the vessel fair in amidships. Got all the officers and men out before she sank. I was suspended from duty at 5:30 a.m. by order of the captain. The moment she struck gave orders to clear away all the boats and sound the pumps. (Signed by J. Hadfield.) Continuation of Mr. Hadfield's log: Discovered the vessel to be the U.S.S. *Peterhoff*. Let go our kedge close to the *Peterhoff*. At 5:35 the *Peterhoff* sunk in 5½ fathoms water. At 5:40 got underway and stood for the flagship. At 8 a.m. Captain Cushing and the captain of the *Peterhoff* went on board the flagship."

William Keeler, paymaster aboard the *Florida*, saw it from a different perspective. "It was early in the morning, just light & the vessels were on their night stations under Fort Fisher (about a mile & a half from it). We were about a mile from the vessels at the time of the accident & immediately steamed up to them & sent our boats to their assistance. The officers & men barely had time to get into the boats when the *Peterhoff* went down in five fathoms of water. Fortunately no lives were lost. We were within easy range of the guns of the fort & batteries but they did not open on us, why, we can't imagine."

Bad as it was losing the *Peterhoff*, it would be worse to let the wreck and its armament fall into Confederate hands. What was left of the *Peterhoff* had to be destroyed. The USS *Mount Vernon* and the USS *Niphon* were assigned the task the following day.

Acting volunteer Lieutenant James Trathen, *Mount Vernon*: "At 7:40 p.m. dispatched two boats and 20 men from this ship, well armed, and two boats and 20 men from U.S.S. *Niphon*, all under command of Acting Master Edward W. White, of this vessel, who proceeded to the wreck. The enemy appeared to be very active, telegraphing from Fort Caswell to Fort Fisher with night signals; at 10:55 p.m. the fore and main masts fell from the wreck of the *Peterhoff* with a great crash. At 12:15 this morning the boats returned, and Acting Master White reported that on reaching the wreck he found 5 feet of water over her spar deck, and that, in addition to cutting away all her masts, he had unbent or cut away all her sails, also all of her standing and running rigging, leaving nothing above her spar deck, and spiked and thrown overboard the 30-pounder Parrott rifle gun on the forecastle and the howitzer from the quarter deck. The main deck guns could not be got at. He reports that nothing now remains of the wreck above water except the smokestack, which could not be removed in consequence of there being too much sea for the boats to remain any longer near the vessel.''

Confirmation came from Acting Ensign H.S. Borden, Executive Officer of the *Niphon*, who added; ''Articles saved and brought on board, viz, one foresail, taken off the yard whole; greater part of main spencer, main topgallant sail and fore spencer; about twenty blocks, mostly small, and part of main rigging. ... The vessel is sunk in about $4\frac{1}{5}$ fathoms of water, the poop and forecastle being about 1 foot under water at low tide. The main deck guns are about 5 feet under water at low tide.''

The *Peterhoff* was gone but not forgotten. Pile, Spence, and Co. filed an appeal after the war. Despite the fact that Matamoras was a drop port for supplies later taken overland to Brownsville, Texas and subsequently traded to Confederate agents, the possibility of such a connection was not due cause for confiscation. The Court also took exception to Admiral Wilkes's eager assumption that the testimony of one sailor should hold more weight than certified ship's papers. Therefore, on April 15, 1867, the United States Supreme Court reversed the ruling of the lower court and ordered that the Pile, Spence, and Co. be reimbursed for vessel and cargo.

The *Peterhoff* next entered the realm of human consciousness in 1962, when it was seen from the air by Charles Foard and Hall Watters. Watters and his brother dived the wreck the following year, in June. Shortly thereafter Watters took Lieutenant Commander J.L. Bull to the site and showed it to him. The Navy then took an interest in the wreck and, along with the North Carolina Department of Archives and History, conducted reconnaissance and recovery operations in July and August.

Samuel Townsend offered the following description in his paper ''Progress in Underwater Archaeology in North Carolina,'' presented in 1965 to the Second Conference of Underwater Archaeology held at the Royal Ontario Museum in Toronto, Canada: ''Divers from the crew of the USS *Petrel*, a submarine rescue vessel based in Charleston, South Carolina recovered two 32-pounder cannons weighing 7,200 pounds and 6,400 pounds, respectively. A third weapon, a 32-pounder weighing 6,000 pounds, was raised by a second crew of Navy divers from the Naval Ordnance Disposal School at Indian Head, Maryland.

''Since the cannons were too heavy to lift with available winches on small boats, it was decided to use huge rubber flotation bags to raise the big guns. The deflated bags were taken down and lashed to a cannon. Compressed air was then pumped into the bags causing them to rise to the surface lifting the coral-encrusted Civil War cannon. When the bags surfaced, they were towed as close to shore as possible by a small boat. Divers then swam to shore with a tow line which was hooked to a bulldozer. The flotation bags and cannon were towed through the surf and onto the beach by the tractor.'' (The charter boat was the *Coquina*, Captain Alex Trask.)

By today's archaeological standards, such a brute-force method of artifact recovery would undoubtedly meet with strict censure, especially in light of the apparent lack of regard for archaeological provenance.

During a field school survey in July and August of 1974, the 30-pounder Parrott Rifle "and parts of the carriage of the brass howitzer were recovered." State archaeologists were concerned about the wreck because it lay in shallow water that was easily accessible: it was only one mile offshore. In seeking protection status for the *Peterhoff* on the National Register of Historic Places, the nomination form claimed that the wreck was a site for "sport diving & artifact plundering." In 1975, the *Peterhoff* became one of twenty-one Cape Fear Civil War shipwrecks on the inventory of the NRHP; it is designated Site 0002NEI.

According to the official description, "the vessel is heavily encrusted with marine growth but is generally in remarkably good condition with only moderate collapsing of hull plates and much of the upper structures still intact." And, "although the bow and stern sections have broken from the main body of the wreck they remain in proper alignment. Besides significant portions of the hull and interior structural members, the boilers and steam machinery are prominent features. Two cannon as well as a variety of miscellaneous ship's equipment are still present on the site."

Divers may visit the site but may not rescue artifacts.

A cannon from the *Peterhoff* guards the entrance to the Fort Fisher archaeology buildings.

Doylestown, a sister ship of the *Portland*. (Courtesy of the San Francisco Maritime National Historical Park.)

PORTLAND

Built: 1919
Previous names: *Jacox*
Gross tonnage: 2,648
Type of vessel: Freighter
Builder: Albina Engineering & Machine Works, Portland, Oregon
Owner: Cia. Columbus de Vapores
Port of registry: Panama
Cause of sinking: Ran aground
Location: 16213.6

Sunk: February 11, 1943
Depth: 55 feet
Dimensions: 289′ × 44′ × 19′
Power: Oil-fired steam

55197.1

During 1942, when the U-boat threat off the eastern seaboard was the most dire, the *Portland* operated in the comparatively safe waters of the west coast. She shuttled freight between such ports as Astoria, San Francisco, San Pedro, Colon, and Buenaventura. In January 1943 she passed through the Panama Canal into the Atlantic Ocean. By that time the U-boats had been chased off the east coast, so it may have appeared to the *Portland's* captain and crew that coastal freighting was a milk run. This proved not to be the case.

On her very first Atlantic voyage, from Philadelphia to Havana, the *Portland* strayed from the normal shipping route and ran aground on the shoals off Cape Lookout. Merchant ship casualties such as strandings received little media attention. There was a war on, and there was more important news to be garnered elsewhere. Nor were investigations conducted to determine cause and assign blame; the Coast Guard was too busy escorting convoys and maintaining anti-submarine patrols. The War Shipping Administration assumed all insurance claims under the war risk clause. Consequently, records of an event as insignificant as a simple grounding were either not kept or were never generated.

However, the difficulties encountered by the *Portland* can be interpreted by the nature of her radio distress calls. When first intercepted by the Third Naval District and passed on for action, the receiving operator could make no sense of the message because the ship transmitting on 500 kilocycles "sent jumble of unreadable characters ending with VA." The Amagansett station concurred: "SS *Portland* sent jumbled traffic of unreadable characters." The time given was 11:13.

Stations all along the coast tried to "work" the *Portland* (that is, exchange radio signals with her) but without success. Radio stations at Nantucket, Virginia Beach, Cape Hatteras, and Cape Lookout took bearings on the signal in order to ascertain its location. By doing so they were able to approximate the *Portland's* position, and alert rescue craft in the vicinity.

Finally, at 12:03, the freighter's radio operator calmed down enough to transmit an intelligible message: "Steamer *Portland* requires immediate assistance aground position 34.34 N 76.34."

What occurred during the next four hours went unrecorded. But at 16:14 both Nantucket and Cape Lookout concurred in their interpretation of the newly transmitted garbage; "Nan-Cape Lookout says he believes SS *Portland* said abandoning ship."

Apparently the men did so without casualty, for the Lloyds records make no mention of loss of life. Thus ended the career of the *Portland*.

The wreck is considered by many to be a world class dive despite often poor visibility. Twenty feet is the average; a southeast or northeast wind can bring in clear water with fifty to sixty feet of visibility; the prevailing southwest wind can mean arm's-length vis.

The stern lies over on its starboard side, is intact, and stands as high as thirty feet. The house is still attached to the deck, beautifully encrusted with coral and sponge and attended to by gaily colored tropical fish. The mast extends horizontally from the wreck and spears into the sand some fifty feet away. Only about five feet above the centerline shows above the bottom, indicating how much of the hull is buried.

The stern can be entered easily; on some bulkheads the portholes are still in place, and artifacts are always turning up inside. One compartment is full of .50 caliber and .20 caliber gun shells. The white gleam of porcelain toilets is a common sight.

Forward of this is a large area of breakdown where the hull has collapsed outward. The general relief is five to ten feet. The shaft alley appears like a bridge spanning the space between the intact stern and the engine; depending upon the level of the sand, which varies from year to year, it can be anywhere from five to eight feet above the bottom. The engine is so overgrown that it is indistinct. The boilers are largely exposed.

On the port side about fifty feet forward of the boilers a gun tub sits upright, complete with a machine gun and belts of bullets. Another gun tub lies on its side nearby. The port waist can be followed to the very majestic bow, which looms some twenty feet off the bottom. This makes for an interesting penetration dive when the conditions are good.

Because the wreck rises so close to the surface in a commonly travelled area, it is marked with a navigational buoy.

PROTEUS

Built: 1900

Sunk: August 19, 1918

Previous names: None

Depth: 120 feet

Gross tonnage: 4,836

Dimensions: 390' × 48' × 29'

Type of vessel: Passenger-freighter

Power: Coal-fired steam

Builder: Newport News Ship Building & Dry Dock Co., Newport News, VA

Owner: Southern Pacific Company (Subsidiary of the Morgan Line)

Port of registry: New York, NY

Cause of sinking: Collision with SS *Cushing*

Location: 26949.6

39960.6

The *Comus* and the *Proteus* were sister ships built for the Cromwell Line for passenger and freight service between New York and New Orleans. The *Comus* began service in May 1900, the *Proteus* a month later.

At that time these ships were considered the most modern in the industry for both passengers and freight. According to *The Marine Journal* each was "schooner rigged and her two pole masts will carry all necessary sail to steady her in heavy weather, besides which she has bilge keels for reducing the rolling of the vessel. The life boats and life rafts are well built, stanch and have the latest improved conveniences for quick handling."

Triple expansion engines propelled the *Proteus* at a respectable seventeen knots. The stack and both masts were raked in order to evoke an image of speed. Most of the freight was carried forward in four cargo decks contained within the hull; one cargo deck was situated aft, above the shaft alley.

Only the steerage passengers bunked inside the hull, one hundred of whom lived above the after cargo deck. Above the cramped steerage area was a deck house with ten bunk rooms for thirty second class passengers,

Courtesy of The Mariners Museum, Newport News, Virginia.

and ten double-occupancy first class staterooms. Forward of that was a two-level superstructure for the main dining room, the rest of the seventy-three first class passengers, and the pilot house.

The Marine Journal: "The passenger arrangements on this ship could not be improved upon. The staterooms are elegantly upholstered and furnished, and the dining room the same, besides being very spacious for the number of passengers carried. There are many new features and conveniences on this ship that are not found on those of less modern construction. Toilet and bath rooms are provided for all on board; independent mess rooms for the officers, sailors, and firemen, as well as steerage passengers, and what will add largely to the convenience and comfort of first-class passengers is a large lobby and smoking room and spacious unobstructed decks. The first-class staterooms are provided with electric heaters, while steam heaters are used in all other parts of the vessel where necessary, with electric lighting throughout. The deck houses are built of metal fitted with either round or square air ports which are very spacious and give natural ventilation in saloons and staterooms where are also provided electric fans. The pantry is located just aft of the main dining saloon in the most convenient locality, while the galley forward has a shaft over the range so that all odors are carried up and away from the saloon."

Along with the *Louisiana*, "the Cromwell Line has now three speedy large passenger and cargo carrying ships, one of which can be dispatched from this port or its southern terminus weekly. This will enable travelers by sea to secure accomodations during the season second to none, and shippers ample and prompt dispatch of their goods, besides insuring a much quicker delivery than by rail."

Some confusion exists as to the length of the *Proteus*. While the Lloyd's Register gives her length as 390 feet, advertising brochures claim that she was 406 feet long. The difference is undoubtedly that Lloyd's used the length at the waterline instead of the overall length: from the point of the bow to curve of the fantail.

As an interesting historical sidelight, the first captain of the half million dollar *Proteus* was Edwin V. Gager, who had served as an officer aboard the Civil War ironclad *Monitor* (although not during the time of her historic battle with the CSS *Virginia*.)

In 1902 the Cromwell Line was absorbed by the Southern Pacific Company. The change of ownership in no way affected the *Proteus*. She kept up her five-day voyages without interruption, and continued to provide reliable passenger and freight service without incident for the next twelve years.

The first major accident to befall the *Proteus* was the loss of her propeller in the Gulf of Mexico, on October 28, 1914. She had to be towed ignominiously to New Orleans by the *El Oriente*. On January 26, 1916 the *Proteus* suffered minor damage from a brush with the *Brabant*, off Quarantine, New York. On November 13, 1917 the *Proteus* ran aground near the mouth of the Mississippi River. She was stuck there for two days before the tugs *Corona* and *W.A. Bisso* pulled her off.

Then came the Great War. Germany sent U-boats across the broad Atlantic to disrupt American shipping and to lower the morale of the American public. The first goal was achieved, but not the second. If anything, the stalwart American people were incensed by foreign aggression against their shores; they were in no way demoralized. Ships took certain precautions against the killer U-boats, such as altering their routes closer to shore, running blacked out at night, and increasing the number of lookouts.

Even so, many ships did not escape the deadly onslaught of the German war machine. One of these was the *Eidsvold*, sunk by the *U-151* on June 5, 1918. (See *Shipwrecks of Virginia* for details.) Fortunately for the crew of the *Eidsvold*, the *Proteus* happened by and rescued them.

Then came the night of August 18–19, 1918. Four days out of New Orleans the *Proteus* worked her way north under the command of Captain Harry T. Boyd. Aboard were ninety-five souls: twelve passengers and eighty-three crew. The ship moved through a sea described as calm, in weather that was clear with light clouds and moonlight. She was observing wartime recommendations by running without navigational lights. Unfortunately, so was the Standard Oil tanker *Cushing*. In an effort to avoid German torpedoes these two ships had the great misfortune to cross paths in the dark off Ocracoke Island. It was just after midnight.

Most of the passengers were asleep, and only those crew members on night watch were up and about. The drone of the engine drowned out any sound of forthcoming doom. The *Proteus* appeared to be alone on the sea.

Captain Boyd's jaw must have dropped when out of nowhere he saw the *Cushing* heading straight towards him. The *Cushing* was painted in a camouflaged color scheme that did its job too well. Captain Boyd blew the whistle and ordered the helm put hard aport, but too late. The tanker's bow punched a gaping hole in the starboard hull of the *Proteus*, about amidships. Water poured into the wound as the two ships were separated, each by her own momentum. With his ship so sorely wounded Captain Boyd wasted no time in giving the order to abandon ship.

There was no confusion as the crew lowered the lifeboats. They worked hastily but competently. Half-dressed men and women in their night clothes rushed from their cabins to their assigned lifeboat stations. Only one man panicked: a water tender by the name of Rodriguez; he jumped overboard and was drowned.

Captain Boyd stayed on deck until everyone else had left. He was no stranger to this kind of event. The year before he was in command of another Morgan Line steamer, the *Antilles* (a passenger liner converted to a troop transport) when she was torpedoed after landing troops in France. He literally went down with the ship, carried downward by the suction, and was saved only when the cold Atlantic reached the hot boilers, and the resultant explosion blew him to the surface. Once again, in the true tradition of the sea, Captain Boyd was the last person to leave his ship.

Fortunately for the *Proteus* passengers and crew, although the *Cushing* was severely damaged she was not in sinking condition. She hove to and picked up all ninety-four survivors. Her decks were overflowing with humanity since she did not have accomodation for so many people. The *Cushing's* men donated clothes for the six women passengers to wear over their nighties. The cook was a busy person.

The *Proteus* sank fifty minutes after the collision. She carried $600,000 in hull insurance, and $3,020.20 coverage on her general cargo. The *Cushing* was valued at $277,770; on this voyage she was riding in ballast from New York to Beaumont, Texas. Her estimated damage was $70,000. The U.S. Shipping Marine Insurance Board assumed all war risk coverage. But, Southern Pacific protested that the *Proteus* was worth far more than her insured amount, and filed a suit accordingly. In August 1923, the value of the *Proteus* was increased by the U.S. Circuit Court of Appeals to $1,225,000.

The *Proteus* lay undisturbed on the bottom until the next war against Germany. In 1942 it was Hitler's U-boats instead of the Kaiser's that threatened east coast merchant shipping. During the course of six months—from mid-January to mid-July—the Germans sank one hundred twenty ships in an area from Maine to Georgia designated the Eastern Sea Frontier, and killed 2,409 men, women, and children. Hardest hit was the Cape Hatteras region, where ships were forced to bunch around the outthrust Diamond Shoals. So many tankers and freighters were attacked there that the area became known as "torpedo alley."

Against this second barrage of enemy marauders the U.S. Navy waged increasingly aggressive antisubmarine warfare. Standing orders were that every suspicious whirl in the water and every submerged sonar target be attacked without question; the action was debriefed afterward in order to determine what—if anything—was attacked, and what the outcome might have been.

By June the number of sunken hulls that lay in the vicinity of Cape Hatteras kept planes, patrol boats, and escort vessels guessing about their identity. The masts of ships that lay in shallow water sometimes protruded above the surface; all too often they were mistaken for periscopes and bombed by overzealous pilots. Deeper wrecks often showed up as strong sonar targets, and were consequently depth-charged by Naval vessels. All this was in keeping with standard operating procedure, and was necessary in order that no U-boat would escape due to hesitancy to open fire.

What sometimes aggravated the situation of sunken ships being mistaken for U-boats resting on the bottom was the water clarity in the Gulf Stream. With the sun at the right angle it was easy for a pilot to spot a long dark shape at a considerable depth. Thus on June 25, 1942 one plane dropped two depth charges on a target later determined by the office of Naval Intelligence (ONI) to be the wreck of the *Proteus*.

Nor was that the only occurrence. At a later date the U.S. destroyer *Stansbury*, the *CGC 453*, and the *CGC 486* cornered what they thought was a U-boat sitting out the daylight hours. The three vessels delivered a combined attack, dropping in all eight depth charges. ONI determined that their sonar gear had mistaken the *Proteus* for a U-boat.

On June 10, 1942 the survey vessel *Anton Dohrn* lowered cameras down to a wreck that observers determined was the *Proteus*. An examination of the photograph reveals a hull that is spotless of marine growth and which obviously had not been underwater more than a few months. The positional data given indicates that the wreck was actually that of the *British Splendour* (q.v.). It seems likely, therefore, that the wreck depth-charged on both occasions mentioned above was actually the British tanker, not the *Proteus*.

Additionally, a wreck surveyed by the *Gentian* in 1944 was believed at the time to be the *Malchace*. It lay at a 45° angle in 120 feet of water, at the position now known to be that of the *Proteus*. "No attacks or instrument contacts are on record as having been made on the wreck by ASW vessels." (ASW stands for Anti-Submarine Warfare.) Apparently, the *Proteus* was spared the ignominy of depth-charging.

When rediscovered in 1983 the *Proteus* was called the Window Wreck; this was because of the 150-pound bronze windows that lay scattered on the bottom. (The superstructure had long since rusted away.) These windows are exquisite because of the leaded glass panes that occupy the upper panel.

The *Proteus* lies in an area where visibility is seldom less than seventy-five feet, and is sometimes more. It is not an exceptionally colorul wreck—brown schemes dominate—but it does have its share of coral, sponge, tropical fish, large skates, sea turtles, sand tiger sharks, and the occasional shovel-nosed lobster.

The wreck is contiguous from bow to stern. It leans to port on a heading of about 210°. The upper hull plates rise some fifteen feet above the bottom on the starboard side, while the port side dips beneath the sand. Small chunks of debris exist as far as fifty feet off the port side where the top of the superstructure slid off when the wreck was more intact and was still supported by the upper decks.

The bow rises some ten feet high. The forward compartments are intact enough to permit penetration without leaving the light zone. The large anchor windlass is readily apparent, and is surrounded by attendant machinery and nondescript wreckage. Aft of that the deck support beams are evident, held several feet off the lower deck by iron stanchions.

Just forward of the three immense boilers is the remains of the pantry. Divers looking for china and silverware should dig in this area, or fan the sand on the port side where many of the pantry items slid due to the ship's initial list. The dislodged donkey boiler came to rest on the port side of the wreck near the after edge of the main boilers; it sometimes provides a hiding place for octopi.

The steam engine does not dominate the midship section as it does on many wrecks. It appears to have fallen over. Pipes, fittings, valves, electrical cables, and ancillary machinery are exposed to view from above. Aft of the engine the wreck appears bathtublike: curved on the bottom and open on top. Cross beams that were the deck supports are easily recognizable. White sand fills the inside of the hull.

The most visually impressive part of the *Proteus* is the extreme stern, which rises to a height of thirty feet and is topped by the steering quadrant. Framed by the arch produced by the upsweeping hull and the vertical rudder turned to port, is the four-bladed bronze propeller that is eighteen feet across.

Sister ship *Comus* was scrapped in 1935.

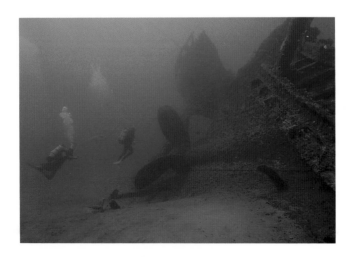

From *Steamboat Disasters and Railroad Accidents in the United States.*

PULASKI

Built: 1837
Previous names: None
Gross tonnage: 687
Type of vessel: Side paddlewheeler
Builder: John A. Robb, Baltimore, Maryland
Owner: Savannah & Charleston Steam Packet Company
Port of registry: Savannah, Georgia
Cause of sinking: Boiler explosion
Location: Thirty miles off New River Inlet

Sunk: June 13–14, 1838
Depth: Unknown
Dimensions: 203′ × 25′ × 13′
Power: Vertical beam engine

The Savannah and Charleston Steam Packet Company ran regular passenger service between Baltimore/Norfolk and Charleston/Savannah. Prior to 1837 it owned two steamships, the *South Carolina* (1835) and the *Georgia* (1836). With the construction of the *Pulaski* in 1837 it was able to offer twice weekly sailings, with the three ships working in rotation.

The *Pulaski* could accomodate 116 passengers in three public cabins, plus four families in separate staterooms. Her appointments were luxurious for the times, especially in comparison to the cramped space allotted to those travelling by stagecoach. In addition to a common lobby she had closets for linen, china, and glassware. She was a kind of miniature, floating hotel.

The *Pulaski* began service in October 1837. For the next eight months she maintained her schedule with little cause for notice. Captain Dubois ran a taut ship. On the morning of June 13, 1838 she left Savannah with "about" ninety passengers and a crew of thirty-seven. That afternoon she docked in Charleston, staying only long enough to pick up an additional sixty-five passengers. If anyone debarked there it was not recorded. Thus there were approximately 202 people aboard the *Pulaski* as she headed north on a fateful voyage that saw the end of the vessel, as well as the termination of so many human lives.

The throb of the engine was felt throughout the ship as the *Pulaski* bucked a heavy sea produced by a fresh wind from the east. The night fell clear, with stars twinkling in the sky like diamonds nestled in black velvet. A full head of steam was required to turn the paddle blades at the desired speed. The "black gang" worked hard to keep the boiler fires stoked with coal. Above deck, the passengers were settling down to sleep in their cabins. All were unsuspecting of the disaster to come.

There was nothing to indicate that the starboard boiler was nearing its limitations of stress—only an explosion when the joints let go "with tremendous violence, blowing off the promenade deck above, and shattering the starboard side about midships—at the same time the bulk head between the boilers and forward cabin was stove in, the stairway to it blocked up, and the bar room swept away. The head of the boiler was blown off, and the top rent fore and aft."

How many people died instantly from the blast, or were scalded to death by escaping steam, is not known. What was calm and contentment one moment was pain and confusion the next. Major James Heath saw a number of passengers killed in their berths by the hot steam; fast action saved his life: he raced out of the cabin ahead of the gushing steam and ducked behind the steps. At least one gentleman was hurled overboard from the promenade deck, never to be seen again. Captain Pearson, the second captain, and Mr. Chicken, the second engineer, were catapulted out of their berths into the sea. Captain Pearson grabbed onto a loose plank and eventually managed to swim back to the ship.

Mr. Hibbert, the first mate, had the watch at the time of the boiler eruption. He was knocked unconscious when he was hurled off the bridge; he awoke on the main deck confused but uninjured. As he stumbled aft he found that the "midships was blown entirely to pieces."

The hull heeled to port because of the weight of the boiler on that side—a fortuitous event that prevented the sea from pouring into the starboard boiler room except when the *Pulaski* rolled with the waves: an event that saved the ship from capsizing immediately.

Pandemonium reigned among the passengers. There was no sign of Captain Dubois, so Hibbert took charge of the situation. He ordered the lifeboats lowered, ostensibly so he could row around the ship to inspect the damage, but in full knowledge that the *Pulaski* was lost. He feared that in their panicked state the passengers would do more harm than good if they rushed to the boats uncontrolled.

Within five minutes three of the four ship's yawls were launched. The planking of one was so dried out from exposure to the sun that it flooded almost immediately, and sank. Another was kept afloat by vigorous and continued bailing; it had on board two crew men and ten passengers, of whom four were women, one a child, and one a babe-in-arms. Hibbert took charge of the third yawl; he permitted two passengers to climb aboard and take up stations at the oars. The yawl backed away from the ship but stayed in the vicinity and rescued the two crew men who had launched the first yawl.

Meanwhile, the *Pulaski* settled lower in the water with each passing minute. Major Heath was swept overboard by a large sea. One of the masts snapped off at that point and toppled into the water next to him, crushing "one of the passengers, M. Auze, a French gentleman, of Augusta." Fortunately for Major Heath, a rope caught around his leg so he was able to pull himself back to the ship. He claimed that about forty-five minutes after the boiler explosion the *Pulaski* "broke in two, and the deck, forward of the mast, was carried away from the rest of the vessel, seemingly very swiftly."

A somewhat different viewpoint was recounted by surviving passenger Mr. Fosdick, as related to him by Mr. Eldridge. "As the hull of the steamboat toward the engine began to sink, the promenade deck gradually separated, and when the whole had sunk to an angle of nearly 40 degrees, leaving the stem high above water, the promenade deck broke off a few feet forward of the wheel, and the hull turned completely over and came keel up, throwing those persons upon it (many of whom were females) into the water. A number of them regained the promenade deck, which afterwards served them as a raft." It was estimated that over a hundred people drowned when this portion of the ship capsized.

It was also reported that the fourth yawl was in the process of taking women off the promenade deck during the time of collapse, that it was inundated by the wave generated when the *Pulaski* went down, and that several of those women were drowned in the process.

If the time frame is accurate, the main hull and machinery of the *Pulaski* took the final plunge at 11:45 on the night of the thirteenth. Most modern sources give June 14 as the day of sinking—a moot point of possible importance to historians, but insignificant to those who lost their lives.

An overview of the situation as it existed at midnight finds more than half the people dead. Out of the contradictory morass of testimony I have concluded that the survivors were distributed approximately thus: on the two yawls under Hibbert's command were 22 people; on the forecastle deck (that portion forward of the paddlewheel) were 22 people; on the promenade deck (that portion aft of the paddlewheel) were 24 people (counting those aboard the yawl tied to the promenade deck); and an uncounted number adrift on their own or afloat upon various fragments of the ship ranging in size from individual planks to the 45-foot-long section of the ladies cabin.

Nor were all these people and pieces of wreck together. Rather they were drifting apart in the current and wind according to the particular drag coefficient presented by each. Darkness prevented any one group from observing the others. Each group, and in some cases each individual, was a microcosm floating upon the surface of the sea with no knowledge or awareness of anything beyond the range of their senses. It was a desperate and lonely time for all.

From this point we have to track each story as a separate entity, in most cases independent from the others.

At 3 a.m. on June 14 the two yawls under Hibbert's command left the scene of the wreck. For thirteen hours they rowed on a northwesterly course, "being favored by a heavy sea and strong breeze from S.E." They sighted a remote and desolate strectch of beach protected by a pounding surf. Hibbert wanted to proceed along the coast in search of an inlet, but "the persons in both boats became tired, and insisted that Mr. Hibbert should land. . . . He was at length forced to yield to the general desire, and to attempt a landing upon the beach, a little west of Stump Inlet."

He elected to go in first. The boat overturned in the surf, and five people drowned. The other six dragged themselves up on the beach nearly exhausted, but happy to be alive. The other boat, under the command of Mr. Couper, waited until nearly sunset before making the attempt to land. Because Mrs. Nightingale had an infant barely seven months old, the baby was lashed to her body so the two should not become separated in case they were tossed out of the boat. Hibbert and his people spread themselves out along the beach so they could help pull in the boat and its passengers.

Then, "the bow of the boat was turned to the shore, and Mr. Couper skulling, and the two men at the oars, she was pulled into the breakers—she rose without difficulty upon the first breaker; but the second, coming out with great violence, struck the oar from the hand of one of the rowers. The boat was then thrown into the trough of the sea, and the succeeding breaker struck her broadside, and turned her bottom upward. Upon regaining the surface, Mr. Couper laid hold of the boat, and soon discovered that the rest of the party with the exception of Mrs. Nightingale, were making for the shore; of her, for a few seconds, he saw nothing; but presently feeling something like the dress of a female touching his foot, he again dived down, and was fortunate enough to grasp her by the hair.

"The surf continued to break over them with great violence; but, after a struggle in which their strength spent its last efforts, they reached the shore, utterly worn out with fatigue, watching, hunger, thirst, and the most intense and overwhelming excitement. Besides this, the ladies and children were suffering severely from the cold. The party proceeded a short distance from the shore, where the ladies lay down upon the side of a sand hill, and their protectors covered them and their children with sand, to prevent them from perishing. Mean time some of the party went in quest of aid, and about ten o'clock the whole of them found a kind and hospitable reception, shelter, food and clothing, under the room of Mr. Siglee Redd, of Onslow county.'' Seventeen had survived.

Now to the people on the forecastle. ''The heavy mast lay across the deck on which they rested, and kept it about twelve inches under water, and the planks were evidently fast parting! Capt. Pearson, with the rest, set himself at work to lash the wreck together, by the aid of the ropes on the mast—letting the ropes sink on one side of the raft, which, passing under, came up on the other side, and by repeating this operation, they formed a kind of net work over it. They also succeeded in lashing two large boxes to their raft, which formed seats.''

As the day passed ''their thirst now became intense. The heat of the sun was very oppressive, its rays pouring down on their bare heads, and blistering their faces and backs, some not having even a shirt on, and none more than shirt and pantaloons.'' Darkness brought with it some surcease of suffering, but also despair of their plight. They were alone upon the broad reaches of the sea, with no hope of rescue in sight.

The next day ''they fell in with another portion of the wreck, on which were Chicken and three others, whom they took on their raft.''

From a different perspective we learn that ''a Mr. Lovejoy was at first alone on a box or hencoop. When day light appeared, he paddled to a piece of the wreck with three persons on it. One of the three soon died from exhaustion. They then reached another piece of the wreck, containing fourteen persons. Ten of them died! The surviving seven then reached a large piece of the forecastle deck, upon which were twenty-three persons.'' (Notice that the numbers do not coincide.)

''Towards the close of evening they had approached within half a mile of shore, as they thought, and many were very anxious to make an effort to land. This was objected to by Major Heath, as the breakers ran very high, and would have dashed the raft to pieces on the shore.''

Mr. Greenwood wanted to swim to shore with a rope tied around him. An argument ensued, and eventually he was dissuaded from risking his life. Then an offshore breeze sprang up and shoved the raft farther out to sea. Night brought an end to the second day adrift, with the chance of rescue no more likely than it had been forty-eight hours earlier.

The morning of their third day at sea it began to rain, ''with a stiff breeze from the N.E. which soon increased to a severe gale. Every effort was made to catch some of the falling rain in the piece of canvas which they had taken from the mast, but the sea ran so high that the little they did catch was nearly as salt as the water of the ocean. Still the rain cooled them, and, in their situation, was refreshing and grateful.'' This last mitigating statement does not do justice to their predicament. Remember that these people were completely exposed to the elements: the wind lashed their faces, they were constantly inundated by waves, and no doubt some of them were seasick.

During the fourth day adrift they spotted a total of four ships on the horizon. "They raised on a pole a piece of the flag that was attached to the mast, and waved it, but in vain. The vessels were too far off. . . . They had now been without food and water for four days and nights; their tongues were dry in their mouths—their flesh burnt and blistered by the sun, and their brains fevered, and many of them began to exhibit the peculiar madness attendant on starvation. They could not sleep either, as the raft was almost always under water, and it required continual watchfulness to keep themselves from being washed overboard by the sea."

By the next morning some of the people could not even raise their heads. "A vessel hove in sight, and her track seemed to lie much nearer than those they had seen before. They again waved their flag, and raised their feeble voices. Still the vessel kept on her track, which now appeared to carry her away from them. 'She is gone,' said one of the crew, a poor fellow who had been dreadfully scalded, and he laid himself down on one of the boxes, as he said 'to die.' Captain Pearson, who had been closely watching the vessel, cried out, "She sees us! She is coming toward us!" And so it was."

Their saviour was the schooner *Henry Camerdon*, bound from Philadelphia to Wilmington, North Carolina with Captain Davis in command. "He immediately gave each of them a half pint of water sweetened with molasses, and repeated it at short intervals. His prudence, doubtless, preserved their lives." Another twenty-six were saved from the wreck of the *Pulaski*.

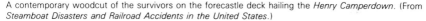

A contemporary woodcut of the survivors on the forecastle deck hailing the *Henry Camperdown*. (From *Steamboat Disasters and Railroad Accidents in the United States.*)

Another contemporary woodcut of the survivors on the forecastle deck hailing the *Henry Camperdown*. (From *Narrative of the Loss of the Steam-Packet Pulaski*.)

What of those on the promenade deck? On the second day adrift the second mate (unnamed) "proposed to take the boat which they had secured ... and with five of the most able of those on the raft to endeavor to reach the shore, and send out some vessel to cruise for them." One of the five was Mr. G.B. Lamar, who left behind on the raft his daughter Rebecca and son Charles.

Those on the yawl must have felt that they had made the wrong decision, for they did not reach land until day six—all alive, but much the worse for wear. By that time most of the people on the promenade deck had died from exposure; their bodies had gone adrift. The four who managed to stay alive were picked up the previous day by the *Henry Camerdon* shortly after she rescued the people from the forecastle. Another ten are added to the tally.

Now add the tale of Mr. Fosdick. He was on the forward part of the promenade deck when the *Pulaski* went down. "A wave washed me from my hold, and I sunk. When I rose, I found myself near a piece of plank, to which I clung; but this not being large enough to support me, I left it, and after getting from one fragment of the wreck to another (and the water all around me was filled with fragments) I succeeded in finding a piece large enough to support me sitting, and upon this I remained some ten minutes, and took off my boots and loosened my dress—for my clothes were so full of water that I could scarcely move.

" . . . I heard some persons calling out not far from me, and concluded they were in one of the boats; but on enquiring, found it was a part of the ladies' cabin (the side) and that there were two persons upon it (Andrew Stewart and Owen Gallagher, deck hands) and that there was room enough for another, and that they would take me upon it, if I could get to it, but that they had no means of coming to me.

"I knew the only chance of safety was to reach it, and I made a desperate effort and succeeded, by swimming, and by getting from plank to plank, which were scattered all around me, in reaching it, and was pulled upon it almost exhausted. This piece of the ladies' cabin was then about 10 feet wide by 45 feet long; but in the course of the night we lost 10 or 15 feet of it;—leaving us a piece of 30 feet in length. Upon this we sat all night, with the water about a foot deep.

"The wind blowing quite fresh, in a direction towards the land, and our raft being long and narrow, made very good progress; and in the course of two hours after the bursting of the boiler, we were out of sight of the wreck. About this time we discovered approaching near us, a portion of the deck of the steamboat, with an upright post near the centre of it, and upon it were Mr. George Huntington and two other persons. They said they were all from Savannah.

"We lashed the two rafts together with a rope which they threw to us, but finding that the sea dashed our rafts together with considerable violence, we concluded it would be better to separate again, and we did so. Mr. H. wished me to take a passage with them, but I concluded to remain where I was. I saw them no more."

Taking stock of what was aboard their raft, Fosdick, Stewart, and Gallagher found "two mattresses, a sheet, a blanket, and some female wearing apparel. The mattresses we emptied of their contents, and with the covering of one of them we made a sail." Even so, they sailed all day and night before sighting land.

"Now we redoubled our exertions—we paddled, we held up in our hands pieces of cloth, we did everything to propel our craft, for we feared the wind might change and blow off shore, and then all hope would be lost; for our raft, we felt sure, could not hold together another day." It was 4:00 p.m. before they reached the surf zone. "The first breaker came over us with great violence—and so did the second—the third broke the raft to pieces—but we clung to the fragments—and soon found we could touch the bottom with our feet; and in a few minutes we were safe upon terra firma, considerably bruised and sun-burnt; but with our lives."

Consider this saga. With the *Pulaski* sinking from under him, Mr. Ridge lashed together two settees with a coil of rope, added a piece of sail and a small cask, and launched the makeshift raft at the moment of sinking. After a while he spotted a young woman a couple of body-lengths away, so he swam after her and brought her back to the settees, "which proved sufficient to sustain them both, but with their heads and shoulders only above water." Her name was Miss Onslow.

Later they came upon a section of floor. Ridge managed to get the settees on top of it; the extra flotation gave them some relief. After a while one of the yawls came by but was too crowded to take them aboard. They drifted on alone. The next day they found themselves nearing land, but like the forecastle their raft was blown away. They spent another night at sea, and another day. On the third day they were rescued by an unnamed sailing vessel. "When found, they were sadly burned by the sun—starving and exhausted, though still in possession of their faculties, and able to move and talk."

After having endured so much together, Mr. Ridge and Miss Onslow decided to spend the rest of their lives together, so they were joined by the bonds of holy matrimony.

At least two others are known to have reached land upon a makeshift raft: Mr. Merritt and an unnamed man, who floated in on the same fragment. This brings the verified total of survivors to sixty.

Although the *Pulaski* broke up and much of the wreck floated away, the engine and boilers and parts of the hull must still lie somewhere on the bottom off New River Inlet, awaiting discovery.

Mr. Ridge and Miss Onslow on their makeshift raft constructed from two settees lashed together. (From *Steamboat Disasters and Railroad Accidents in the United States.*)

Heavily laden. (Courtesy of the National Archives.)

RARITAN

Built: 1919
Previous names: *Detroit Wayne*
Gross tonnage: 2,649
Type of vessel: Freighter
Builder: American Ship Building Company, Detroit, Michigan
Owner: Raritan Steam Ship Corp. (Smith & Johnson, Managers)
Port of registry: New Orleans, Louisiana
Cause of sinking: Ran aground
Location: 45248.2

Sunk: February 25, 1942
Depth: 75 feet
Dimensions: 251' × 43' × 26'
Power: Oil-fired steam

59275.2

    Despite the war being fought off the eastern seaboard in the early months of 1942, it was not a U-boat that got the *Raritan*, but mother nature.

    The *Raritan* was a tramp freighter; that is, a ship that plied no regular route, but that discharged her cargo at its port of destination, then picked up another one that her managers had contracted for, and took it wherever specified. A brief check of her itinerary for 1941 found the *Raritan* in new York, Trinidad, Mobile, Delaware, Cuba, Philadelphia, Cristobal, St. John's (Newfoundland), Boston, Wabona, Baltimore, Laguaira, Paramaribo, Philadelphia, New York, St. John's, Boston, St. John's, New York, and Argentia.

    In 1942 she steamed from Cornerbrook, Newfoundland to New York, discharged and loaded, and headed south for Cristobal, Canal Zone, Then she picked up a cargo of coffee in Buenaventura, Colombia, bound for New York. On this voyage, however, she ran into a storm that blew the ship off course and caused her to ground on Frying Pan Shoals.

    In accordance with wartime regulations the *Raritan's* radio was sealed: that is, the fuses were removed and the electrical panel locked. In an emergency the panel door could be opened and the fuses replaced, but the radio operator had to have a good explanation for why he was breaking radio silence. He was supposed to listen to traffic, not talk and give away the ship's position.

This was an emergency. The distress call alerted the Frying Pan Shoals Coast Guard Station of the *Raritan's* predicament. Immediately, motor lifeboat *#4405* put out to sea. With U-boats sinking ships on an almost daily basis, losses due to natural causes received scant attention and hardly any follow-up investigation. Of the twenty-nine men aboard the *Raritan* it was reported thus: "All saved."

The U.S. Coast Guard cutter *Calypso* arrived on the scene but had little more detail to offer: "One lifeboat partly showing. Marked wreck with red flag." The *Calypso* also mentioned that the wreck lay in twelve fathoms, suggesting that it slipped off the shoal into deeper water.

How or when the *Raritan* broke into two parts is not recorded, but that is the condition of the wreck today. Both sections lie on about a 45° angle to port, and stick up some twenty to twenty-five feet from the bottom. The distance between the two is about a hundred yards.

The intact bow offers easy access to two deck levels. By going into the forepeak storage area one may find an assortment of tackle and an occasional bronze cage lamp. Both anchors are tight in their hawse pipes; an extra anchor is lashed to the center of the upper deck.

The stern section is also intact. It is larger than the bow, and its interior is more complicated. Corridors lead past compartments all the way to the crew's quarters, where the remnants of bunks are visible. The head is complete with toilets and wash basins. Brass fire extinguishers have been found all the way aft. Gaping rust holes in the hull are large enough to swim through and offer means of egress. Strapped to the little house on the topside of the wreck is an anchor.

Just forward of the stern breakdown is a debris field that stretches toward the distant bow section. Here are the after cargo booms and the exposed engine and boilers. The forward cargo booms lie closer to the bow piece.

All in all, the *Raritan* is a rare dive that is fun, exciting, and not particularly life threatening. It is well worth a visit.

In ballast. (Courtesy of the National Archives.)

The *Schurz* as the *Geier*. (Courtesy of the Naval Photographic Center.)

SCHURZ

Built: 1894
Previous names: SMS *Geier*
Displacement tonnage: 1,603
Type of vessel: Gunboat
Builder: Kaiserliche Werft, Wilhelmshaven, Germany
Owner: U.S. Navy   Official designation: Third-class gunboat

Sunk: June 21, 1918
Depth: 110 feet
Dimensions: 255′ × 32′ × 14′
Power: Coal-fired steam

Armament: Eight 10.5-centimeter/35 caliber Krupp guns (4.1-inch), five 1-pounders, four Maxim machine guns, two torpedo tubes; later the main battery was replaced by four 5-inch guns.
Cause of sinking: Collision with SS *Florida*
Location: 27067.7   39463.8

  The *Schurz* could be described as a ship that turned against the country of her birth, very much like the man after whom she was named.
  She was launched in Germany as the SMS *Geier*, and designated as an unprotected cruiser. With a bulbous ram bow that was distinctive of the times, she displayed the kind of profile that contemporary naval architects and modern ship fanciers find attractive. The raked stem mimics the squat pugnacity of a bulldog hunched back for a fight.

In seeming contradiction to the ironclad warships that came into vogue during the Civil War (ships with wood hulls that were clad in iron) the *Geier* had an iron hull that was clad in wood, then plated with copper. The wood served merely as a point of attachment for the copper sheathing, which was considered essential for vessels intended for tropical service, where marine organisms such as barnacles thrived by attaching themselves to steel hull plates, thus slowing a ship's speed. Copper served as a deterrent to such home-making activity because its oxide was toxic to the animals.

With a maximum speed of sixteen knots the *Geier* was not the racehorse of the German fleet. Yet, for a small ship she packed an awful amount of wallop. She served adequately in demonstrating a military presence among German colonies, and was useful in policing the Kaiser's possessions. Her career was undistinguished not by lack of fortitude but by lack of opportunity.

When the Great War broke out in August 1914, the *Geier* found herself alone in the South Pacific, between Africa and Asia, and separated from the rest of Admiral von Spee's Far Eastern Squadron by too far a distance to join forces. Therefore, she did the same as other German auxiliaries that found themselves in a similar predicament: she became an independent commerce raider.

Raiders were like ocean-going snipers. The only way they could survive against the overpowering enemy fleet was to keep out of sight. They prosecuted the Kaiser's war effort by overhauling lone merchant ships at sea, or by cornering the unarmed vessels in desolate ports.

Two of the more successful raiders of World War One were the *Emden* and the *Wolf*, about whom much has been written. Both eluded the combined naval forces of the British, French, and Japanese long enough to wreak great havoc among the merchant marine. The *Emden* was destroyed by the HMS *Sydney*; the *Wolf* made it back to Germany.

For the *Geier*, however, destiny saved a more ignominious fate.

On September 4 she steamed into Kusaie, in the Eastern Carolines, and pounced upon the British freighter *Southport*. Instead of sinking the ship, or capturing her as a prize, the Germans decided to disable her engines and leave her for dead. According to Carlos Hanks, "the Germans had removed the main and high-pressure eccentric gears, the intermediate stop valve, and many tools. Despite this damage, and after 11 days' work, the Britons had created a semblance of a compound engine by fitting the astern eccentric of the low-pressure to the high-pressure cylinder, and cutting out the middle cylinder. Under this arrangement, the ship could not go astern. After obtaining 350 coconuts and 400 pounds of edible roots to bolster her dwindling stores, the *Southport* sailed on September 18, and arrived at Brisbane on the thirtieth, with belated but authentic news of the *Geier*."

With her cover blown, the *Geier* became a hunted vessel. For the next month and a half she managed to evade detection, all the while searching unsuccessfully for indefensible victims. Meanwhile, the stoking gang scraped her coal bunkers for every bit of bituminous, and the engineers struggled to keep up repairs on the engine. Finally she was forced to put into Honolulu, at that time neutral territory.

Almost at once the Japanese battleship *Hizen* and the armored cruiser *Asama* appeared on the scene. They could not legally enter the harbor to engage the *Geier* in battle; but they could patrol beyond the three mile territorial limit and wait for the *Geier* to emerge. Usually, under the neutrality laws, a warship is permitted to remain in a neutral harbor no longer than twenty-four hours. To violate that convention invited internment. However, Karl Grasshof, captain of the *Geier*, utilized a loophole in the international agreement that allowed a warship to dock long enough to undergo repairs necessary to make a vessel seaworthy.

There was no doubt in anyone's mind that the *Geier* would be pummeled to pieces as soon as she exchanged fire with the Japanese ships: both were better armed and armored than the German cruiser. The only chance the *Geier* had for survival was to stay put and hope that the Japanese would become impatient and have to leave in order to pursue more important military objectives.

The stand-off continued for three weeks. Then the U.S. took the initiative by seizing the *Geier* and her crew. Technically, this made the ship a prize of the United States government, and the crew prisoners of war. In actuality, since the U.S. was not at war with Germany, the ship and crew were merely detained and, under international treaty, not permitted in any way to advance the war effort of their country. The *Geier's* arms and ammunition were turned over to U.S. military authorities.

It was a long detention. For nearly two and a half years the *Geier* sat placidly docked at her assigned pier while the global war raged on. To the German crew it must have seemed like an extended holiday, or a carefree Hawaiian vacation. But as the sentiment of the American people grew more pronounced against Germany and the Kaiser's intent on world domination, it became apparent that President Wilson's campaign promise to keep the United States out of the war was about to be broken. Isolationism was not working. The U.S. had to take a stand, or let the democracies of the world fall under German tyranny.

With U.S. entry into the war imminent, and diplomatic relations becoming strained, the German government issued secret orders for the *Geier's* crew to wreck their ship so it could not be used against the fatherland upon the declaration of war. On February 4, 1917 the crew started coal fires under the boilers from which the water had been drained, damaging them and some of the attendant machinery. But, as in the case of the *Southport*, they did not do a very good Job. The German officers and enlisted personnel were locked up in the army stockade, and the ship was moved to Pearl Harbor for safekeeping. Naval inspectors discovered concealed machine guns—a violation of neutrality—and found that parts of the main battery had been removed and tossed overboard.

Nine other German ships interned at Honolulu were similarly damaged by fire. The high time of good living was over.

Furthermore, the discovery of Grasshof's diary revealed that he and the *Geier* had not been idle during internment. He had taken "a hand in international politics by relaying to Japan wireless messages from German agents in the United States . . . while her bands played lively tunes to drown out the telltale sound of crackling electricity."

The jailed Germans were arraigned for sabotaging their ships. Within a week they were released from detention (but not internment) at the request of the U.S. District Attorney. After all, the ships belonged to Germany, and

These pictures were taken when the *Geier* was interned in Honolulu. Notice the ornate carvings on the bow and stern. (Courtesy of the Hawaii State Archives.)

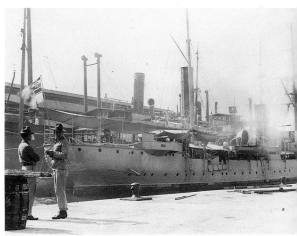
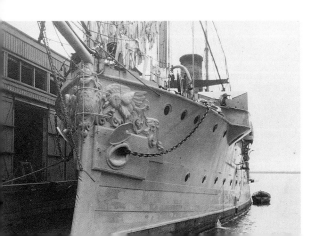

the U.S. could exercise no control over the actions of their crews since the ships had been interned voluntarily.

On April 6 the U.S. entered the war against Germany, and the situation changed. On May 22 an executive order was issued to officially sieze the *Geier* in the name of the United States of America. All other interned German vessels were seized as well.

During that summer the ship's boilers and other broken machinery were repaired. Divers retrieved some of the breech mechanisms, others were machined. All the ammunition that had been stowed on Magazine Island was returned to the ship. This consisted of 867 shells for the main battery, five modified Whitehead torpedoes, 14,000 rounds for the rifles and machine guns, and 12,000 rounds of 8.8-mm pistol ammunition. Small arms consisted of eighty 1906 Mauser rifles and thirty-nine 9-mm Luger pistols, complete with cartridge belts and pouches, bayonets, bandoliers, holsters, and spare clips. A large number of pith helmets were found "unfit for use;" they were a couple of wars out of date.

Excerpt from the deck log, September 15, 1917: "At 10:00 the Commandant read his orders to commission the U.S.S. *Schurz*. ... At 10:20 Commander Arthur Crenshaw read his orders ... assigning him to duty in command of the U.S.S. *Schurz* and took command."

The ex-*Geier* was named after Carl Schurz, "a liberal forced to flee Germany after the 1848 revolution." He emigrated to the United States and became an influential "writer, editor, and speaker on behalf of: emancipation, a workable and equitable post-Civil War reconstruction program, civil service and Indian policy reform, preservation of the public domain, the development of national parks, the Liberal Republican movement, and the Anti-Imperialist movement." He was a general in the Union army, later became a Senator (Missouri), then Secretary of the Interior. He died in 1906 after more than half a century's service to his adopted country.

This view was taken after the *Schurz* reached San Diego. Notice that she has two masts instead of her original three; during a refit in 1908–1909 her rig was reduced from barkentine to brigantine. (Courtesy of the Naval Photographic Center.)

Dock trials were completed by September 24. A week later the ship's full complement was on board: ten officers and 151 enlisted men. As on all ships the number of personnel fluctuated constantly; after a month the ranks swelled to twelve officers and 185 enlisted men.

When the *Schurz* left Pearl Harbor on October 31 she was part of a convoy that consisted of the Third Division Submarine Force (*K-3*, *K-4*, *K-7*, and *K-8*), the submarine tender USS *Alert*, the *Columbine*, and the *Gulfport*. They reached San Diego on November 12. The *Schurz* continued on submarine escort duty for the next two months, then passed through the Panana Canal and touched such ports as Key West and New Orleans.

On February 20, Captain Crenshaw was relieved by Commander William Wells as commanding officer of the *Schurz*.

According to recommendations by the Bureau of Ordnance, "the military value of this ship would be increased greatly by installing a new battery. The present battery will not stand the test of any sort of battle and the structure as previously shown will accomodate guns of more modern type. The ammunition will not last long and is an unknown factor as irregularities may develop even after test. Pointing with open sights is inaccurate." Therefore, when the *Schurz* entered dry dock at Charleston, South Carolina on March 19, 1918, in adition to hull maintenance she also had her battery removed. Four 5-inch guns were installed as well as fresh ammunition. The German Mausers and Lugers were replaced by seventy-two .30 caliber Springfield rifles (1903) and fifteen Colt .45 pistols (1911).

The Maxim guns remained.

The *Schurz* left Charleston on April 27. For the next four months "she was attached to the American Patrol Detachment, U.S. Atlantic Fleet, performing routine exercises and patrol duties." She visited Cuba, the Canal Zone, Key West, and New York.

One June 19, 1918 the *Schurz* left New York for Key West. She had on board 215 officers and men. The morning of June 21 found her passing ten miles southwest of Cape Lookout Lightship, "steaming with mast head and running lights lighted under four boilers and all sail except main trysail, speed 11 knots, course 234°."

Out of the darkness loomed the steamship *Florida*, "running dark, speed about twelve knots," on a nearly reciprocal course. When first seen by the *Schurz* she was nine hundred yards away. To a pedestrian, half a mile might seem like plenty of space to get out of someone's way. But ships turn slowly at sea; they are carried forward by their weight and momentum, and respond to the helm with agonizing delay.

The *Florida* turned on her running lights and blew four short blasts on her whistle. The *Schurz* put on hard left rudder, stopped both engines, then backed the starboard engine at two-thirds. Commander Wells stepped out from the chart room to get a better view of the situation just as the bow of the *Florida* knifed into the *Schurz* abreast the starboard bridge. The bridgewing crumpled. Seaman Second Class Manual Gouveia, Jr., the starboard bridge lookout, was killed instantly and his body hurled "over the bridge rail onto the fireroom hatch." A section of the bridge rail ripped loose and slammed into Commander Wells's chest. The bow of the *Florida* continued to penetrate the hull of the *Schurz* to a depth of about twelve feet, "cutting thru bunker No. 3 to the forward fireroom; the *Florida* immediately backed clear." The time was 4:45 a.m.

Commander Wells reported that "the hole was far too large to make any attempt to cover it with the collision mat or to stop it with splinter mattresses." The forward fireroom flooded so quickly that the coal passers were chased up the ladders by the incoming sea. Adjacent bulkheads were strained and leaking. The well deck was awash.

An SOS was transmitted immediately, again at 4:55, and agian at 5:03. Then the power failed.

Despite the crushing injury to his chest, Commander Wells remained very much in command of his ship. He ordered the engines ahead at one-third speed. But the steering gears were jammed, and the helm refused to respond. The ship would move, but its direction could not be controlled. Then "the *Florida* drifted across the bow of the *Schurz* and the engines were stopped to avoid a second collision."

Water washing through the hull breach was quickly filling the well and berth decks. The *Schurz* was taking on a decided list to starboard. With his ship in imminent peril of sinking underneath him, and with more than two hundred men to be evacuated, Commander Wells gave the order to abandon ship. This was "accomplished with only minor casualties to men and boats due to the heavy seas." Not everyone got away dry. Those who escaped on life rafts had to cling to them in the water. Others resorted to swimming.

Commander Wells was the last man to leave his ship, although because of his injuries he had to be helped off the deck by the assistant navigator and the quartermaster.

Meanwhile, the *Florida* was also sending distress calls because it was feared that her ruptured stem would cause the ship to founder. Twenty miles away the steamship *Saramacca* intercepted the calls for help. She wasted no time in changing course for the transmitted coordinates. The *Saramacca* must have been operating on a different time zone, for her master, Captain L.P. Ritchie, stated that he received the wireless message at 3:45, exactly one hour before the collision occurred. Notwithstanding the disparity in times, the *Saramacca* poured on steam and arrived an hour later.

By then 180 of the men from the *Schurz* had made it safely to the *Florida*. Those in the water were being rounded up as quickly as possible "for there were a number of sharks in the vicinity." Commander Wells stated that he took charge of the motor sailing launch and "picked up the Executive Officer and 28 men from a life raft and landed them on the *Saramacca* at 5:45." Commander Wells was then placed on the sick list; command devolved to the Executive Officer, Lieutenant Howell.

"The *Florida* whose whole bow had been torn out had in the meantime been pumping her cargo of oil overboard and this helped to break the seas. At 5:50, the *Florida* signalled the *Saramacca* that her condition was dangerous and that it was vital that the crew of the *Schurz* be removed from her immediately. All boats were then put to work to transfer the *Schurz's* crew from the *Florida* to the *Saramacca*."

While this was going on two officers returned to the *Schurz* and found her watertight bulkheads still holding. In their opinion it was possible the gunboat "might get to the beach under her own power before sinking. A volunteer crew was then formed, the intention being to return to the *Schurz* with four Officers and sixteen men and a lifeboat and to attempt to reach the lee of Cape Lookout (32 miles distance) and beach the vessel there. It was decided to return to the *Schurz* as soon as all hands were rescued from the *Florida*.

"At 7:50, the *Schurz* took a sudden list to port. Her bow gradually sunk and her stern rose to a perpendicular position. She sank slowly with large bursts of white vapor appearing about every 30 seconds. At 7:58, the stern disappeared; . . . It is the opinion of the Commanding Officer that the *Schurz* broke in two as she sank, probably just abaft the bridge. She sank in 19 fathoms of water."

Commander Wells's statements shed light on the relative values of observation. In order for a ship to go vertical she must sink in a depth that is deeper than her own length—in this case 255 feet. This contradicts his own statement that she went down in nineteen fathoms, a depth borne out by today's knowledge about the wreck. Neither does the hull appear to have broken in two.

Be that as it may, no one could dispute that the *Schurz* was gone. Furthermore, "she drifted about twelve miles before she sank, due to the fact that her fore trysail was left up and to the strong currents in the vicinity." Four of the *Schurz's* boats were taken aboard the *Saramacca*. Conditions on the *Florida* stabilized so that she was able to proceed to port under her own steam.

Twelve men were injured during the event. Eight suffered from contusions and lacerations, one had a crushed finger and another a crushed foot. Both Commander Wells and Lieutenant Shaw suffered crushing injuries to the chest.

Commander Wells ended his report thus: "The Commanding Officer considers that the remarkable lack of loss of life in connection with the whole accident was due to the courage and coolness of the Officers and crew, to their prompt obedience of orders and to their adherence to the abandon ship bill. The ship was abandoned in a rough sea and at the time of abandoning it was very dark although dawn came shortly afterwards. The Commanding Officer considers that the Officers and crew acted in accordance with the best traditions of the service."

This heavily retouched photo purports to show the *Schurz* in the background. Actually, the vessel with the gaping hole in the bow is the *Florida*. (Photo by Robert McLean, courtesy of the Naval Photographic Center.)

Secretary of the Navy Josephus Daniels agreed. On August 18 he issued letters of commendation to five officers and seven enlisted men for their courage and devotion to duty subsequent to the collision: Lieutenants Schwerin and Rogers for inspecting damaged compartments; Lieutenant Johnson for keeping. the engineering department running efficiently; Lieutenant Howell for organizing abandon ship procedures; Lieutenant Shaw for his rescue work; enlisted men Kiser, Rabon, and Judson for staying at their posts; James Donnellan, "for getting his men out of the fireroom and remaining in fireroom until water was up to his waist;" Bryant and Sarran for rescue work; and Virgil Dinell, the quartermaster who helped Commander Wells into the lifeboat.

Then came a curious turn of events. Upon hearing about the commendations, Chief of Naval Operations W.S. Benson expressed his conviction that "certain officers, particularly the commanding officer and the executive officer, should be brought to trial by court-martial." There was a difference of opinion between Benson and the findings of the court of inquiry that investigated the sinking of the *Schurz.*

Commander Wells was absolved of all blame for the collision because the *Florida* had been running without lights and was therefore responsible for wrongful navigation—this despite the recommendation that merchant vessels run blacked out due to the U-boat threat. (Under these circumstances the *Florida* was merely following orders.) Benson took no exception to this. His objection was that "the vessel was permitted to drift without an attempt to get her into shoal water from approxmiately 5:00 a.m. until approximately 7:50 a.m. (or a period of two hours and fifty minutes) at which time she sank."

Benson: "I consider that the decision of the Commanding Officer to abandon ship with all hands at the time he did displayed bad judgment . . . was not in keeping with the best tradition of the Service, and should not be encouraged by offical white-washing. Had the Commanding Officer remained on board with enough men to keep such steam as was possible on his boilers, and set such sail as might have been possible to work the vessel in shore, and kept such other men as might have been necessary for shoring up bulkheads, etc., it is possible that the vessel might have been in such position and condition at 7:50 a.m. that she could either be saved or salvaged."

I found no records indicating that the Judge Advocate General reversed the opinion of the court of inquiry, or that a court-martial was in fact conducted.

A memorandum from the Bureau of Ordnance requested that "the four 5-inch 51-caliber guns and mounts on the U.S.S. *Schurz* be salvaged if possible, as they are most urgently required at this time for arming transports, merchant ships, etc." All four guns are visible on the wreck today. Both bow guns are emplaced in a single turret that lies on its side. The two stern guns are single barrel pieces lying close together.

The wreck is contiguous with the port side partially buried and the starboard side rising some five feet off the bottom. The hull and decks are considerably broken up. The four boilers provide the highest relief, with the two engines lying on their sides being somewhat lower.

The small arms ammunition locker is found on the starboard side some seventy-five feet forward of the boilers; both rifle and pistol bullets can be found. Mounds of 5-inch projectiles are partially concealed under some steel decking nearby. Another magazine in the stern served the after deck guns. Watch out for the blasting caps found in the space just in front of the boilers.

Next to the forward gun lies an anchor with a thick stock and flukes shaped like a "U." Adjacent to the boilers on the port side are the lifeboat davits. The remains of the bridge are there, but they come and go with the sand. Farther off the wreck is the crow's nest and a portion of the mast. The galley is in the stern; it has been the source of china recovered by divers. For the collector, brass items are found practically everywhere.

The *Schurz* is an exceptionally colorful wreck due to the large coral formations and the profusion of tropical fish that inhabit the many nooks and crannies. Although the visibility is generally seventy-five feet or better, I have seen it where the sheer numbers of fish hovering over the wreck reduced visibility to less than fifteen feet. One can be completely surrounded by thousands of fish that appear oblivious to human encroachment.

The *Schurz* is sometimes referred to as the World War One Wreck.

Below: Small arms ammunition. Upper right: The top gear head of the helm stand. Lower right: A bronze condenser weighing many tons.

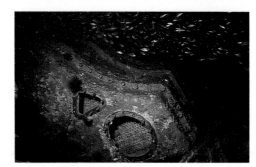

SENATEUR DUHAMEL

Built: 1927   Sunk: May 6, 1942
Previous names: None   Depth: 60 feet
Gross tonnage: 913   Dimensions: 192′ × 31′ × 16′
Type of vessel: Converted armed trawler   Power: Coal-fired steam
Builder: Hall, Russell & Company, Aberdeen, England
Armament: One 4-inch gun, one machine gun, depth charges
Owner: British Navy
Cause of sinking: Collision with USS *Semmes*
Location: 27092.8   39633.3

    Her Majesty's Trawler (HMT) *Senateur Duhamel* was assigned to the
U.S. Navy for escort duty (in which capacity she accompanied merchant
ships along the east coast) and for antisubmarine patrol. For a full discussion of the "trawler trade," rather than repeating the information here, the
reader is asked to refer to the first four paragraphs of the *Bedfordshire*.

    Suffice it to say that the *Senateur Duhamel* was traveling alone on the
night of May 5–6, 1942 when she came upon the USS *Semmes* (DD-189),
one of the obsolete flush deck, four stack destroyers that had *not* been
transferred to the British Navy. The British would have gained two ships
if the *Semmes* had been sent to England.

Courtesy of the Steamship Historical Society of America.

The action report later filed by the *Semmes* described her operation as "a routine escort and patrol assignment under orders of Commander Inshore Patrol, Norfolk." This patrol was anything *but* routine. She left Norfolk inauspiciously on May 1, escorting a convoy of eight southbound tankers. The convoy anchored off the Lookout Bight that night, then continued south the next day. Ships assigned to specific Naval districts did not accompany convoys all the way to their destination, but, like a relay race, passed the baton of authority to other vessels in the neighboring Naval districts when the convoy reached the district boundary. Therefore, after seeing her charges safely transferred to other escorts, the *Semmes* steamed for Morehead City for fuel and depth charges, and waited for her next assignment.

While she was engaged in a lone antisubmarine warfare patrol the *Semmes* destroyed the still-floating hulk of the *Ashkhabad*, which had been torpedoed by the *U-402* on April 29, but which was being considered for salvage. (For the complete particulars of that debacle, see *Ashkhabad*.) In addition to apparent misinterpretation of orders, the *Semmes* was experiencing mechanical malfunctions. Thus in the early morning of May 6, when her radar went out of commission during a time described as "unusually deceptive, with light haze, low moon," the destroyer became partially blind. When the radar came back on line, its signal bounced off a ship only two miles away.

"The gun crew was ordered to man the gun and stand by. Course was held in order to make a close-up investigation and preparation made to challenge upon visual contact. ... The object was first sighted about one point on the starboard bow at about one mile and appeared to be approaching, and, from the two radar bearings, drawing slowly to the right, but immediately, before the silhouette could be positively recognized the unknown ship began signalling with a very bright light, completely obscuring the vision of the O.O.D. and lookouts. The signal was "WHAT SHIP?" This same tactic has, it is believed, been used by hostile submarines in coastal waters in an effort to confuse our ships at night. Before a reply could be sent or counter illumination used, it was seen that the ship was very close on the starboard bow and appeared to be crossing. The rudder was put full left, crash back rung up, and general alarm sounded at 0343."

One minute later the "*Semmes*' bow struck the other ship ... amidships, *Senateur Duhamel's* counter then riding up on *Semmes*' forecastle with both ships stopped. ... *Senateur Duhamel* was hailed and inquiry made as to his condition and whether he desired to send any personnel over before *Semmes* backed clear. Upon receipt of a negative reply, *Semmes* backed clear, to prevent further damage due to the mild swell running."

Damage to the *Semmes* was severe. The weather deck and shell plating had been sheared off and was hanging over the port side, held there only by one section of shell plating, the degaussing cable, and the anchor chain; the ship had been flenced like a whale. The port anchor was hanging on by a fluke. The chain locker was dished in, there was a hole in the weather deck over the CPO's quarters, and the splinter shield supports for the gun were caved in. On the good side, all watertight "doors and hatches were properly closed, and . . . the forward sound room and passageway over it were intact and dry. Shoring of forward bulkheads in these compartments was started immediately. Forward bulkhead of anchor windlass room was opened slightly on port side by the strain of the wreckage hanging to port.

"A wire rope was taken from the bitts to the windlass with a bight around the fish davit (solidly attached to the wreckage) and strain was taken using capstan bars in order to relieve strain on port shell plating. Another wire rope bight was put around wreckage where strain was heaviest, in vicinity of degaussing cable, and strain taken with chainfall and shell plating on port bow."

Miraculously, no one had been killed. And there were no injuries "except severe bruises on feet of Chief Boatswain's mate."

By this time the *Semmes* had backed nearly half a mile from the *Senateur Duhamel*. The two ships were lost to each other in the dark and haze, but a flashing signal light from the *Senateur Duhamel* was visible to the bridge watch on the *Semmes*. The British asked that the *Semmes* stand by. The U.S. destroyer *Roper* (DD-147) "was immediately called by TBS, requested to close *Semmes* and did so."

When muster was taken aboard the *Semmes* everyone was accounted for, including one man extra: J. Woods, a British tar assigned to the *Senateur Duhamel*, who had climbed aboard the *Semmes* while the two ships had been attached.

When it was ascertained that the *Semmes* was in no danger of sinking, the Executive Officer took a boat to go in search of the *Senateur Duhamel*. With him was Seaman Woods. "At 0540 the Executive Officer returned and reported that he had seen *Duhamel* settle slowly on even keel and sink, that her masts showed above water (charted depth is 55 feet) and had picked up personnel from raft and put them aboard *Roper*." The entire crew was accounted for, with no injuries.

"It was found that *Semmes* would not steer backing down, so, at 0555, bulkheads having been shored, went ahead at 5 knots and proceeded into Lookout Bight." There she moored next to the stern section of the *Esso Nashville* (q.v.), which had been torpedoed by the *U-124* on March 21 and subsequently partially salvaged. The *Semmes* was later repaired and returned to service.

The saga of the *Senateur Duhamel* did not end there. On June 8, 1943 the British freighter *Norman Star* stranded on the wreckage of the trawler. She was pulled free by the tug *P.F. Martin*, and, accompanied by the salvage tug *Warbler*, was towed to Norfolk for repairs. The *Senateur Duhamel* was demolished in 1944 by the salvage ship *Vigilant* (WPC-154), which used two tons of dynamite to "remove high spots."

Today the wreckage of the *Senateur Duhamel* is relatively flat. It lies in an area of marsh sand that stirs up quickly and can silt out the visibility. The bow is buried completely so that only about two thirds of the wreck is exposed. The sides are collapsed outward, giving an extreme width of about forty feet.

Exposed at the stern is the hub of the propeller with the blades sheared off. Forward of that the gun operating mechanism sits in a small debris field, along with cannisters for the 3-inch projectiles. The shaft alley is recognizable, as well as the remnants of a propeller that may be a spare. Scattered machinery and mechanical parts litter the area.

No signs of the engine are evident. Two big boilers dominate the area forward of where the engine should be. Twenty feet beyond the boilers the wreck disappears into the sand. That is where ammunition lockers the size of trunks are located. Divers should be careful of the hand grenades and small arms within.

The crushed bow of the *Semmes*. (Courtesy of the National Archives.)

The *Suloide* as the *Amassia*. (Courtesy of the Steamship Historical Society of America.)

SULOIDE

Built: 1920
Previous names: *Maceio*, *Amassia*
Gross tonnage: 3,235
Type of vessel: Freighter
Builder: Akt. Ges. "Neptun," Rostock
Owner: Lloyd Brasileiro
Port of registry: Rio de Janeiro, Brazil
Cause of sinking: Hit the sunken wreck *W.E. Hutton*
Location: 27146.1

Sunk: March 26, 1943
Depth: 65 feet
Dimensions: 338′ × 48′ × 21′
Power: Coal-fired steam

39550.1

When Johann Mohr launched his attack from the *U-124* at the tanker in his sights, he had no way of knowing that his torpedoes would sink not one ship, but two, and that those ships would sink a year apart. No, it was not a case of time bombs or magic; it was much more subtle than that. The *W.E. Hutton* (q.v.) went down in a fiery hiss that snuffed out the lives of thirteen men; the date was March 19, 1942.

Twelve months later the lumbering ore carrier *Suloide* happened by the same spot. By that time the U-boat menace was a thing of the past. There was no threat of danger. Then came the awful grating sound of steel on steel as the *Suloide* scraped to a grinding halt. She had run onto the wreckage of the *W.E. Hutton* and was stuck there like a bug on a pin.

Worse than that, the forepeak flooded and the ship was taking water into No. 1 hold. Out went the call for help, in response came the tug *P.F. Martin*. Towing hawsers were passed to the men on the *Suloide*. The tug's powerful engine whined, her propeller whipped the water to a froth, the line grew as taut as piano wire and very nearly as thin. With a lurch the *Suloide* came free ... and a few moments later she sank out of sight, dragged to the bottom by holds full of water and manganese ore. Fortunately, there was no loss of life. Mohr had gotten his second ship. The date was March 26, 1943.

As can be imagined, there was a great hoopla over the loss of the *Suloide*. If the *W.E. Hutton* had been properly razed the accident never would have happened. The position of the *Suloide* was marked with a black buoy to which was attached a green light that flashed at two-second intervals.

Within months the Coast Guard cutter *Vigilant* was dispatched to survey the area. She took a salvage crew that began work leveling the cause of the accident, the *W.E. Hutton*. During the course of the next six months, thirty tons of dynamite was used to demolish the tanker and ensure that she sank no more ships. The job was completed on January 11, 1944.

On March 17, 1944 the *Vigilant* began blasting operations on the *Suloide*. Although this was nearly a year after the casualty, the flashing green light warned away any vessels straying too close. For two months the salvage crew blasted away at the *Suloide*. By May 27 they had expended twenty tons of dynamite. "A wire drag party of the U.S. Coast and Geodetic Survey visited the wreck on 31 May 1944 and determined that its least depth at mean low water is 39 feet."

The damage done to the *Suloide* is evident today. For the most part the wreck is a large area of disorganized plating punctuated here and there by recognizable ship parts: two small boilers side by side, an indiscriminate lump that is the engine, a shaft alley large enough to swim through, one blade of the propeller, and the upthrust rudder.

Even though visibility averages in the twenty to thirty foot range the *Suloide* is a nice dive. The high bow lying on its starboard side is festooned with coral that add flowing color to this three dimensional oasis. (The bow points south.) The perimeter of the wreck is distinctive: an aid to orientation. And enough artifacts are found on a continuing basis to keep the collector interested: portholes, brass mechanical parts, and, if you dig in the galley, silverware. All compliments of Johann Mohr.

TAMAULIPAS

Built: 1919   Sunk: April 10, 1942
Previous names: *Hugoton*   Depth: 155 feet
Gross tonnage: 6,943   Dimensions: 434′ × 56′ × 31′
Type of vessel: Tanker   Power: Oil-fired steam
Builder: Bethlehem Ship Building Corp., Sparrow's Point, Maryland
Owner: Mexico Shipping & Trading Company
Port of registry: Wilmington, Delaware
Cause of sinking: Torpedoed by *U-552* (Oberleutnant zur See Topp)
Location: 26981.3   bow   39788.8
          26980.7   stern   39773.9

Named after a Mexican state that borders the Gulf of Mexico, the
Tamaulipas was in the business of transporting petroleum products from
Tampico, a port city within that state, to the refineries of the United States.
Under the command of Captain Allan Falkenburg, the unarmed tanker left
Tampico on April 2, 1942 with 10,200 tons of oil for a solo voyage to New
York. Captain Falkenburg had received no routing instructions, so it was

The *Tamaulipas* as the *Hugoton*. (Courtesy of the Steamship Historical Society of America.)

up to him to take whatever precautions he thought necessary to evade the U-boat threat.

The passage had been routine until the evening of April 9, when the heavily laden tanker was approaching Cape Lookout. At 10 p.m. a lookout reported that a torpedo had just cut the wake of the ship. Although no one took him seriously, Captain Falkenburg put the *Tamaulipas* on a zigzag course as a precautionary measure. Every ten minutes the helmsman steered from 20° left of the base course to 20° right. When another crew member reported the sound of a motor astern, the captain ordered an immediate 50° turn to starboard. If a U-boat was trailing him, he wanted to make the *Tamaulipas* a difficult target for German crosshairs. Then he ducked into the radio shack to check with the operator; there was no traffic over the airwaves, but he stayed to chat a while—a chat that undoubtedly saved his life, because stalking the tanker was Topp in the *U-552*, his tubes still hot from torpedoing the *Atlas*.

The midnight watch had been on duty only twenty minutes when there came a terrific blast on the starboard side abaft the midships house, in No. 5 tank. "A flashing instant later, the ship broke in two and her cargo went up in searing, brilliant flame, fanned by a light southeast wind. ... The ship's engines stopped immediately and within five minutes all of the crew, except two, abandoned the tanker in two lifeboats. Two of the men apparently jumped overboard, although the second cook, Quinto Boschetto, said he saw one raft go over with a man on it whom he never saw again." Gone forever were Third Mate Lloyd Crampton, "who had been on the bridge at the time of the attack, and Harry Ritner, a boatswain."

As the men rowed away, the *Tamaulipas* was a "broken, blazing hulk. When they last saw her, the ship was down amidships with her bow and stern still showing above the water." After an hour and a half in the boats, the thirty-five survivors were picked up by the British armed trawler HMS *Norwich City* and were taken to the Section Base at Morehead City, where they later met the men from the *Atlas* (q.v.).

The wreck of the *Tamaulipas* rests on the bottom in two parts separated by more than half a mile. Both sections are upright and largely intact, with an average relief of twenty-five feet; the wheelhouse rises even higher. The curve of the fantail is easily recognizable, and below it the bronze propeller is visible. The hull plates have fallen away from the engine room, exposing the massive engine. Portholes are found in a large debris field to starboard. Because of its depth the *Tamaulipas* is not dived as much as it should be.

In addition to the *Tamaulipas*, Erich Topp sank the *Atlas* and the *British Splendour*, both covered in this volume; the *Lansing* and the *Byron D. Benson*, both covered in *Shipwrecks of North Carolina: from the Diamond Shoals North*; and the *David H. Atwater* (see *Shipwrecks of Virginia*.) Both Topp and his boat lived to see war's end.

TARPON

Built: 1936   Sunk: August 26, 1957
Previous names: *P-4*   Depth: 140 feet
Displacement tonnage (according to various sources):
      Surface: 1,310—1,316—1,500.   Submerged: 1,960—1,968—1,990
Type of vessel: Submarine   Dimensions: 298′ × 25′ × 15′
Armament: Six 21-inch torpedo tubes (four forward, two aft) and sixteen
      torpedoes, one 4-inch/50-caliber gun, two 5-inch anti-aircraft guns,
      two 3-inch anti-aircraft guns.
Power: Four 16-cylinder diesel engines, four Elliot electric motors
Builder: Electric Boat Company, Groton, Connecticut
Owner: U.S. Navy   Official designation: SS-175
Cause of sinking: Foundered under tow
Location: 26946.0
                                              39959.2

The *Tarpon* is a wreck that is close to my heart, not just because it was the first wreck I ever dived in the Gulf Stream waters south of the Diamond Shoals, but because I was the first diver ever to descend to her sunken remains. Making a discovery dive is an incomparable thrill, made all the more emphatic when one drops down the anchor without foreknowledge of what lies at the end of it: wreck or rock pile. It happened like this.

I was on the shrimp boad *Mary Catherine* for a weekend dive to the newly discovered *Proteus* (q.v.). That wreck was a hot item because it was loaded with ornate brass windows sporting colored, leaded glass. By August 1983 only two charters had been made to the site, so there were still plenty of artifacts waiting to be rescued from the ravages of the sea. I packed extra liftbags for the occasion.

Courtesy of the Submarine Force Library and Museum.

I arrived at the dock exhausted after the ten hour drive from Philadelphia. The sweltering heat was exacerbated by clinging traffic. At midnight in Morehead City the temperature was 90°. I was perspiring profusely even before I loaded my gear on the boat. Captain Al Wadsworth arrived at two a.m., cranked over the engine, threw off the dock lines, and headed out to sea. The ocean was as flat as a mill pond.

The bunks inside were quickly taken, so I spread out my sleeping bag on the after deck and lay down on top of it. Wearing only jogging shorts I was still uncomfortably hot; the cool breeze one normally expects from the sea was nonexistant. As the sky brightened I wrapped a towel over my eyes and kept trying to sleep. I was only partially successful. By the time we approached the dive site it was eight o'clock. I stirred slowly on the deck, and sat up halfheartedly.

Then Al announced that he had loran numbers for a wreck a mile away from the *Proteus*: a wreck that had never been dived. Did someone want to check it out? Although I was always eager to dive unknowns, in this case I demurred because of the expectations I had for the *Proteus*. I did not want to lose valuable bottom time on a sunken trawler or a geological outcrop, for that would take away the time I could spend on the *Proteus*. Nevertheless, my spirit of adventure and quest for discovery got the better of me, and I agreed to go down alone for a quick look. It turned out to be a bounce dive into history.

As I donned my gear Bill Nagle said he would take a chance and go with me. So, the two of us jumped over the side into azure blue, crystal clear water. There was no current, so we slid easily down the anchor line, Bill leading the way as I fussed with my camera equipment. Imagine my surprise when I landed on the hull of a ship next to what I soon saw was the conning tower of a submarine. Bill's exuberance was unbounded; he went into a dance like the lead cheerleader at a homecoming rally.

As we explored the wreck we made some startling discoveries. The first was that the hatches were locked from the outside with heavy-duty turnbuckles—a situation totally unacceptible on an operational submarine. Secondly, we found two portholes that had fallen out of the conning tower fairweather. German U-boats never had portholes, and only U.S. subs built prior to the war had them. So we knew what we had found, but not which one by name.

When we told Al Wadsworth what we had seen, he said, "This must be the long lost *Tarpon*. People have been looking for it for ten years, but it's supposed to have gone down ten miles from here."

The *Tarpon* began life as a modified *Porpoise*-class submarine: a subgenre called the *Shark*-class, of which there were only two. The *Porpoise*-class subs were among the first of the high-speed fleet subs designed for extended patrols. Their diesel engines could drive them along the surface at 19 knots; their electric motors, feeding off 240-cell batteries, propelled them underwater at 8 knots. They could travel 11,000 miles at a cruising speed of 10 knots without refueling, and carried enough provisions to last seventy-five days. Submerged endurance was ten hours at 5 knots, thirty-six hours at minimum speed.

The *Tarpon* was designated *P-4*. She and the *Shark* (*P-3*) were the only two of the class to be given names not beginning with the letter "P." What distinguished them from the *Porpoise*-class was the innovative all-welded hull, the first in American submarine construction; this paved the way for the later construction of wartime submarines. The 5/8-inch steel hull plate gave them a crush-depth rating of 250 feet.

It is interesting to note that in U.S. Navy parlance submarines are called boats. By strict definition, a "boat" is a vessel small enough to be hoisted out of the water and placed upon a "ship." Certainly, in the early days of submarine construction they fit this classification. But as submarines grew larger their category remained the same. Not until the launching of the *Nautilus*, the first nuclear powered submarine, were submarines officially called "ships."

The *Tarpon's* keel was laid on December 22, 1933; her hull was launched on September 4, 1935; she was commissioned on March 12, 1936. She left immediately for the Pacific Ocean, where she operated during her entire career, working out of such ports as San Diego, Pearl Harbor, and the Philippines. She was in Manila when the Japanese attacked Pearl Harbor. Sub Fleet Command wasted no time in sending her out on patrol against Japanese shipping. Pearl Harbor was still smoldering when the *Tarpon* departed for Luzon, on December 9, 1941. Her record on that patrol was less than enviable. During more than a month at sea she fired not a single torpedo. Because the Philippines was a prime military target for the Japanese, the *Tarpon* put in at Darwin, Australia at the conclusion of the patrol. Command shifted from Lieutenant Commander Weeden to Lieutenant Commander Wallace.

Her second patrol was a bit more exciting. South Molucca, Manipa Strait, and the Sawar Sea were crawling with Japanese convoys, and into this target-rich territory the *Tarpon* prowled. She fired her first shot in anger on February 1, 1942: a spread of four torpedoes at an enemy freighter. She claimed one hit, then fired two more that were seen to strike and break the ship's back; yet post-war analysis failed to reveal any Japanese ships lost at that time and place. Although an incredible boost to the crew's morale, the *Tarpon* went uncredited with the kill.

On this patrol the *Tarpon* also received her baptism of depth-charging. On "the night of 11 February 1942, when upon investigating a ship silhouette, the vessel turned her searchlight on the sub which illuminated the interior of the bridge just before the hatch was closed. A dive of 235 feet and a hard turn to the left at full speed were not enough to avoid the unexpectedly loud and stunning explosions of four depth charges which erupted in rapid succession. Bow planes, rudder angle indicator and the port annunciator were knocked out and some loose paint cracked off. The

Japanese kept moving and, after listening to the screws of another patrol vessel pass overhead, the crew could breathe easier."

To round off the "firsts" on this patrol the *Tarpon* next managed to suffer the ignominy of running aground. "In attempting to pass through a narrow strait by moonlight in the early morning of 24 February, the submarine's calculations were thrown off by a clump of mangrove trees which was mistaken for Point Tauk. A grating noise and a gradual stop indicated that the submarine had run aground. Backing, twisting and blowing water from the ballast tanks failed to free *Tarpon*. As the tide was ebbing, attempts to back off were discontinued and all efforts were made to lighten the ship forward. TNT demolition blocks were placed to destroy the submarine in case capture appeared imminent.

"A native in a boat was induced to take an officer ashore to make contact with Pastor H. von Den Rulst, a Dutch missionary who was the only white man in Ahdunara. Through him as interpreter, it was learned from the natives that high tide would be from 1600 to 1800. It was also learned that Japanese planes had been seen over the strait each day for the past four days and that enemy ships had been in the next bay three days earlier. It was a great relief to everyone when the tide came in. With three engines backing, heaving in on the anchor windlass and flooding and blowing the aftermost ballast tank, *Tarpon* slid off the bottom smoothly."

Wallace had some explaining to do. Apparently, he did it well, for he was permitted to take the *Tarpon* out on two more patrols. Unfortunately, neither of those patrols produced any enemy contacts. This is not necessarily a reflection on the captain's aggressiveness; it could be that her patrol area off the Hawaiian Islands lacked enemy targets.

The *Tarpon* spent the summer of 1942 undergoing overhaul at the Mare Island Navy Yard, in San Francisco, California. Her original Winton engines were a constant source of trouble, breaking down often and at the most inopportune times, so they were replaced. The conning tower was slightly modified, and the deck fittings were altered, giving the boat a somewhat different profile. The most significant change was the addition of two torpedo tubes mounted outside the pressure hull under the forward deck. She now carried eighteen torpedoes into battle.

Command for the next year (and five patrols) went to Commander Thomas Wogan. He struck out on his first (the *Tarpon's* fifth) patrol, operating north of Bougainville. Torpedoes were fired, depth-charges rained down in response, but no gains or losses were made on either side.

The *Tarpon's* sixth patrol had an auspicious beginning. "Heavy weather was encountered enroute to the patrol area and minor topside damage was sustained. The seas had moderated sufficiently by 23 January to make topside repairs and secure all loose gear. The end of the month brought bad weather again and a typhoon with mountainous waves. Rain, hail and snow, made self-preservation a full time activity."

Then came Wogan's (and the *Tarpon's*) moment of glory. On February

Notice the external bow tubes added during refit, giving the *Tarpon* eighteen torpedoes.

1 he fired a spread of four torpedoes that scored a single hit against a Japanese ship. Moving in for the kill he fired two more. Both hit. The ship's back was broken, and she split in two and sank beneath the waves. It was the *Fushima Maru*, a passenger-cargo vessel that grossed 10,935 tons.

The *Tarpon* escaped retribution in this case, but paid for it in spades the next day. "Apparently *Tarpon's* periscope was sighted by a patrol plane on 2 February for 22 explosions were heard and felt. Two explosions were close and flooded the main induction, necessitating withdrawal from the area to effect repairs. By 5 February, the sub was back to work the Truk traffic for a few days." That brought even bigger glory.

On February 8 a radar contact on an unidentified ship sent the *Tarpon* off in hot pursuit. After closing on the target and setting his angles, Wogan fired four torpedoes. Every one hit. The *Tarpon* crash dived "because of the counter attack by an escort who dropped 19 depth charges." The *Tarpon* escaped unscathed, but not so the *Tatsuta Maru*. The troop transport was loaded to the gills with soldiers bound for Truk. How many casualties there were no one knows. Escorts picked up hundreds of survivors treading water in full military kit; many were dragged under the surface by the weight of their gear, and drowned. Also gone was the transport which, at 16,975 tons, was the largest enemy vessel ever sunk at that time by an American sub. It was a record that stood for more than a year.

Thus, Wogan returned from patrol with two verified sinkings that totaled 27,910 tons. That, too, was a record amount of tonnage sunk during any one patrol. That record held for about four months. If this made Wogan a hero, his ninth patrol made him a demigod.

According to the official Naval history, "On the night of 16 October, she was patrolling the approaches to Yokohama when she sighted a ship which she tentatively identified as a large auxiliary. The submarine tracked the target until 0156 the next morning when she attacked it with four torpedoes which stopped it dead in the water. However, it soon got underway again and headed straight for *Tarpon*. The submarine submerged, went under the ship, and attacked the target from the other side with three more torpedoes which produced one hit in the stern. The enemy still did not sink, so *Tarpon* fired again with a torpedo which struck the target in the same place as the first. The vessel exploded and disappeared. Postwar examination of enemy records revealed that the victim was the German raider *Michel* (Shiff 28) which had been preying on Allied shipping in both the Atlantic and the Pacific. *Michel* was the first German raider sunk by a United States submarine in the Pacific.''

Since the *Michel* had more than 120,000 tons of Allied shipping to her credit, her sinking prevented the loss of an uncounted number of Allied ships in the future. Because of these actions, and others not recounted here, Wogan wound up in thirteenth place among U.S. submarine commanders in terms of tonnage sunk. It was an admirable record that he bestowed upon the *Tarpon*. He left the *Tarpon* at the end of this, her ninth patrol.

The *Tarpon* saw very little action in 1944. Her tenth patrol was a photographic mission to the Marshall Islands, where she took pictures of atolls. Her eleventh and twelfth patrols saw her performing lifeguard duty near Truk—looking for downed flyers. She made no rescues. Christmas Eve found her departing Pearl Harbor for the east coast. She passed through the Panama Canal. The new year found her in the Atlantic Ocean, which she had not felt against her hull since 1936.

The *Tarpon's* east coast operations were minor. The war ended, and left the peacetime Navy with more submarines than it needed. The *Tarpon* was decommissioned in Boston on November 15, 1945. She was reactivated in 1947, and towed to New Orleans where she served as a dockside Naval Reserve training boat until 1956. She was finally struck from the Navy list on September 5. The highly decorated submarine had earned eleven Battle Stars for her various wartime operations in the Asiatic-Pacific theater.

Tarpon's tubes remained closed during her tenth war patrol. Instead she took photographs, of which the one at right is an example. (Both courtesy of the Submarine Force Library and Museum.)

TARP-10 CONF. (PRISIC)
AREA 22. MARSHALL ISLANDS - KWAJALEIN ATOLL. GENERAL.
App.Lat. 09°00'N. Long. 167°30'E. Sortie TARP-10.
Print #9, Roll #141. Shows shipping on the high seas
taken by the U.S.S. Tarpon on the 10th War Patrol on
2-3 Jan. 1944. For data sheet covering this print,
see ONI #285423.   ONI (P-5) #285-606.

In June 1957 the *Tarpon* was sold for scrap to the Boston Iron & Metals Company, in Baltimore, Maryland. The tug *Julia C. Moran* towed the dilapidated submarine to her last port of call. But before she could reach the scrap yard the *Tarpon* had other ideas about her future. As tug and tow passed Ocracoke Island the unmanned sub began taking on water. As dawn of August 26 shed light on the rusted steel hull, the crew of the *Julia C. Moran* noticed that the sub was slowly settling by the stern. As they watched helplessly, the bow rose higher and higher, like some great black whale holding up its head for a last gasp of air before making a deep dive.

The *Tarpon* submerged for the last time.

A buoy was placed over her sunken remains, but no attempt was ever made to raise her since the cost of salvage was more than her value as scrap. There she remained, unobserved for over a quarter of a century until that fortuitous dive during a summer heat wave, when a reluctant bounce dive became a chance discovery.

When I first dived the *Tarpon* the wreck was largely intact. The bow was pointed and well-defined, the forward gun mount stood proudly in place, and the conning tower with its two lofty periscopes and radar mast and antenna reached upward majestically, presenting an awesome profile. The 20° list to port was made obvious by the tilted conning tower. The propellers were missing, probably removed long before the boat had been sold for scrap. The most evident area of deterioration was the outer skin:

The periscopes that once pointed toward the sky now lie against the sand or are buried.

the metal shroud that covers the pressure hull and exterior pumps, valves, and machinery, all of which was exposed.

In the few short years since that time the wreck has undergone great destruction, not all of it due to accelerated rusting from the dynamic environment in which it sits. The two most dramatic changes are the twisted bow, which is now bent back some 110° to starboard, and the missing gun mount and fallen conning tower. What appears to be the pedastal of the gun mount lies upside down in the sand below the base where it was once attached. The conning tower lies on its side on the sand on the port side of the wreck, with the periscopes partially knifed into the bottom.

One can conjure in one's imagination a great storm reaching down through the water and causing such damage by underwater wave action. With the wreck listing to port one would expect that tall structures held in an unnatural position would eventually break away from their welds. Yet, unless there are strange gravity fluxes in the area, such a scenario cannot account for the bow being bent backward. I strongly suspect that this major structural damage is due to trawler action. A net hung up on the bow probably yanked the rusting, weakened metal to the side. A net that caught the gun mount and conning tower could have fractured the fatigued welds and ripped the large structures off their bases.

Indeed, a hundred feet off the port side of the wreck I found the brass fairweather: the protective shield that surrounds the conning tower and external bridgeworks; it had been in place when I first dived the wreck in August 1983. It could not have "fallen" so far from the hull. Therefore, it must have been dragged off the wreck.

Today the wreck is more exposed than it was at the time of its discovery. The outer doors of the forward torpedo tubes are exposed because the hydrodynamic bow has been torn away. Oddly, there is no sign of the added-on tubes; perhaps they were removed after the war.

Where the conning tower once stood there is now a vast mound of cables and piping, and the open hatch leading into the control room. Also open is the crew's hatch just aft of the conning tower, and the after torpedo loading hatch. These permit entrance into the submarine's dark interior. Long combings make sliding through the hatches something like crawling down a tubular sewer pipe. The interior is full of silt and thick mud that stir up easily. Divers beware.

Due to the new position of the conning tower it is possible to get inside it by ducking under the point where it is leaning against the hull, and coming up through the bottom opening. Here are valves and gauges, radio equipment, and the periscope tubes and hydraulic lifting gears.

Perhaps the most exciting attraction of the *Tarpon*, even for those with no interest in submarines or penetration diving, is the vast accumulation of sand tiger sharks that are commonly encountered on the wreck. On one occasion, when I was diving alone, I hovered above the hull completely surrounded by five- to ten-footers. As I slowly spun around I was able to count forty within a radius of seventy-five feet: the average visibility. So many sharks frequent the wreck that their distinctively shaped teeth can be found lying atop the hull or in the sand. I once picked up half a dozen in a matter of minutes.

Rather than scaring off divers, many trips are planned to the site *because* the sharks are there. Diving among large numbers of ferocious looking sharks, each exhibiting multiple rows of jagged teeth, can be an exciting experience.

It has been suggested that the *Tarpon* has become a breeding ground for sand tiger sharks. This belief is based upon the assumption that sharks congregate there and not anywhere else. While there is a greater chance of seeing sharks on the *Tarpon*, and in greater quantity, than on neighboring wrecks, this is far from quantatative evidence on which to base scientific principle or biological behavior patterns. I have seen large numbers of sand tiger sharks on the nearby *Proteus* and the *Manuela*, and have made sightings on virtually every other wreck in the area. I suspect that the sharks are in no way attracted to the *Tarpon* per se, but that the wreck simply happens to occupy a spot that is part of a vast ecological region inhabited by sand tiger sharks.

It is more correct to note that divers concentrate their observations to that particular geographic locus because the *Tarpon* is there. That they happen to see sand tiger sharks on the wreck and nowhere else is because they do not dive elsewhere. I have seen sharks more than a hundred fifty feet away from the wreck during sweep explorations, so I have every reason to think that the same concentration exists three hundred feet away, five hundred feet away, a thousand feet away, a mile or more away. It is simply that people dive wrecks, not the endless tracts of sand between them.

Whatever the reason, the sharks are usually there during the summer months when divers frequent the area. And only rarely will one be disappointed by their absence.

The inner door of the after torpedo tube.

January 14, 1912: her back is broken, and the wreck is being lightered. (Courtesy of William Quinn.)

THISTLEROY

Built: 1902

Previous names: None

Gross tonnage: 4,027

Type of vessel: Freighter

Builder: Irvines' Ship Building & Dry Dock Co., West Hartlepool, England

Owner: Albyn Line, Ltd (Allan, Black & Co., Managers)

Port of registry: Sunderland, England

Cause of sinking: Ran aground

Location: 27078.8

Sunk: December 28, 1911

Depth: 20 feet

Dimensions: 345′ × 47′ × 19′

Power: Coal-fired steam

39656.8

Anyone who has ever been to sea at night knows how difficult it is to judge distance and decipher lights and landmarks. Even though the professional mariner studies aids to navigation on a continuing basis, and has a lifetime of experience to help guide him through the darkened sea lanes, the blackened sky and invisible skyline conspire to play tricks on the eyes. This is exactly what happened to Captain W.C. Ferguson, master of the British steamer *Thistleroy*.

When the *Thistleroy* left Galveston, Texas she was heavily laden with phosphate and cotton that was bound for Liverpool, England. She crossed the broad reaches of the Gulf of Mexico and made a short stop at Tampa, Florida. From there she rounded Key West, drove east along the Straits of Florida, and turned north for Norfolk, where she expected to coal up before making the long Atlantic crossing. Like most ships, the *Thistleroy* hugged the coast on the northward leg of the voyage. In the pre-electronic age, when dead-reckoning was the accepted procedure for determining one's position at sea, plotting a course from a series of known landmarks offered a far more accurate way of logging a ship's course and direction. Captain Ferguson was careful to make the jog as he approached North Carolina, where the coast line changed its north-south trend to east-west. He rounded Cape Fear, then headed north again. He was equally careful when approaching Cape Lookout, the next east-west jog.

That was where he fell prey to the illusion of optics. After sunset on December 28, 1911 Captain Ferguson paid particular attention to the lights on shore. He may have been comforted by the sight of the Cape Lookout lighthouse he so eagerly sought, and which was the next landmark he expected to see. Instead, however, the light he saw was that of the lightship on Cape Lookout Shoals. Captain Ferguson had no way of realizing his mistake until the *Thistleroy* ground to a halt on a shallow mound of sand some three miles offshore and four or five miles southeast of the cape.

According to the official report, "When the steamer struck, shortly after nightfall, the sea was moderate, there was little wind, and the weather was clear. The lifesaving crew discovered her situation as soon as she got into trouble and promptly put out to her in their power lifeboat. They found her resting easily on the shoal, with everything on board apparently in good condition and her crew taking their misfortune philosophically. As the weather outlook was good and no one on board desired to leave, the life-savers soon put back for the shore, carrying with them, for delivery at Beaufort, N.C., messages from the master to his owners."

The revenue cutter *Itasca* arrived the next morning, and stood by to offer assistance in case the situation should worsen. The day passed uneventfully. The *Thistleroy* sat hard aground; there was no relief from the rising tide. At two a.m. on December 30 the wrecking tug *Rescue* arrived. Towing hawsers were emplaced. "The two vessels were unable, however, to move the stranded vessel."

By the thirty-first, after two and a half days aground, the weather threatened to change for the worse. The life-saving crew returned to the scene of the wreck, which was still attended by the *Itasca* and the *Rescue*, and offered their assistance. Eleven people of the thirty-one aboard the *Thistleroy* elected to be taken ashore—ten crewmen and the captain's wife. Then came some excitement.

"A short distance from the wreck, on the way to the *Itasca* and while the lifeboat was still in the rougher water on the shoal, the engine stopped. As the occasion was one in which time could not be taken to work over the machinery, the crew immediately resorted to the oars to get out of the dangerous area. After rowing a distance of perhaps 50 yards they took a line from the waiting cutter's boat, with which assistance they proceeded to the *Itasca*."

"At this point arose the second obstacle to be encountered by the life-saving crew in the course of their day's work. When they attempted to transfer their passengers to the cutter they found that the exchange could not be made except at great risk owing to the state of the sea. There was nothing to do under the circumstance but hoist sail and run the four or five miles necessary to be traversed to reach sheltered water. This they did, the cutter accompanying them in.''

The engine trouble turned out to be the fusing pin; it had come out of the igniter. The *Itasca's* engineer soon fixed the problem. The life-saving boat returned to the wreck site just in time to stave off disaster. Fourteen men of the *Thistleroy's* crew had lowered a lifeboat and were making good their escape from the rapidly deteriorating sea state. ''Unused to working in broken water, the sailors had got into the trough of the sea and were in imminent peril of swamping when the power lifeboat overhauled them. They were transferred to the service craft and their own boat taken in tow. When the party were halfway to the shore their engine stopped a second time. They immediately resorted to the sails, as on the preceeding trip, and came safely to harbor, where the load of passengers joined their shipmates aboard the *Itasca*.'' (It was previously stated that the life-saving crew took to the oars, not the sails. This time, the engine trouble was a choked oil pipe.)

Then a boat from the *Rescue* took the remaining six people off the stranded steamer. Soon the entire complement of the *Thistleroy* was safely berthed on the *Itasca*. On January 1, 1912 the freshly repaired engine permitted the life-saving boat to lighter the *Thistleroy*. In the words of Killey Guthrie, Keeper of the Cape Lookout Life-Saving Station: ''The personal effects of all was transferred from ship to Cutter. (The ship was full of water) using our boat to tow back and forth the boats loaded with men and bagage.''

The *Itasca* weighed anchor and headed for Wilmington. The rescue operation took a total of four days—one of the longest on record.

By this time heavy winds arrived and drove the *Thistleroy* farther onto the shoal. During the ensuing storm the steamer's back was broken, and she was declared a total loss. The value of the hull was estimated at a quarter of a million dollars. Salvage of the cargo, valued at $60,000, was begun as soon as conditions permitted. It was later reported in the media that the wrecking schooner *H. Toomey* was partially successful in recovering some of the cotton:

''There were about 8,500 bales of cotton on board the vessel when she stranded and about 3,000 of these have been recovered. The cotton was, of course, watersoaked and blackened, but can be used. The work of salvage has now been discontinued and the schooner *Toomey* laid up at Morehead City while the crew have returned to Norfolk. Owing to the position of the wreck, which was dynamited, the cotton which has been recovered was secured with great difficulty, the divers being in danger at all times from falling decks and other superstructures.''

192

Ironically, the salvage of the *Thistleroy* was interrupted on January 17, 1912 by circumstances nearly identical to her own loss. The 3,586-ton British freighter *Trebia*, whose home port was Liverpool, England, was carrying phosphate rock and cotton from Savannah, Georgia to St. John, New Brunswick when she ran aground close enough to the *Thistleroy* that a strong-armed man could have tossed a phosphate rock from either vessel onto the deck of the other. However, the *Trebia* suffered a better fate than the *Thistleroy*, and was pulled off her precarious perch the day following her stranding, none the worse for wear and with injuries only to the pride of her master.

Today little of the *Thistleroy's* remains are exposed. Usually, only a twenty-foot piece of unidentifiable wreckage marks the steamer's last resting place. The wreck comes and goes as storms scour away sand or build it up on the flattened steel hull plates. Perhaps someday, in the far distant future, the contour of the shoals will change, and the *Thistleroy* will make a glamorous reappearance for future divers to explore.

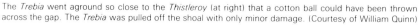

The *Trebia* went aground so close to the *Thistleroy* (at right) that a cotton ball could have been thrown across the gap. The *Trebia* was pulled off the shoal with only minor damage. (Courtesy of William Quinn)

U-352

Built: 1941   Sunk: May 9, 1942
Type of vessel: Type VII-C U-boat (submarine)   Depth: 110 feet
Displacement tonnage: 769 (submerged), 1,070 (surfaced)
Dimensions: 218′ × 20′ × 15′
Power: Two diesel engines and two electric motors
Speed: 17 knots surfaced (on diesels), 7.6 knots submerged (on motors)
Armament: Five torpedo tubes (four bow, one stern), one 88-mm gun
Builder: Stulcken Sohn, Hamburg, Germany
Owner: German Navy
Cause of sinking: Depth-charged by USCG *Icarus*
Location: 27063.5   39491.5

    Compared to all the U-boats that Germany sent to war, the life span of the *U-352* was probably about average. More than eighty percent of the operational U-boats (most of them constructed after the onset of hostilities) did not live long enough to enjoy peace; likewise for the crews. The very underwater machines of destruction that wrought such havoc and caused the deaths and suffering of so many innocent people became justly deserved iron coffins for those who conned them.

Typical of the breed was the *U-352*. It was commissioned in October 1941 by the U-boat Acceptance Commission, in Kiel, Germany. After a five-week shakedown cruise in the Baltic Sea, and a short sortie for tactical exercises, the end of November found it docked in Flensburg for "minor repairs and adjustment." It remained there throughout December, thus permitting the crew frequent leaves at home before their first war patrol. In mid-January the *U-352* returned to Kiel to take on torpedoes and provisions. It left soon after for its operational area off Iceland.

According to official Navy documents, "The complement of the *U-352* consisted of 3 officers, 1 midshipman, 18 petty officers, and 24 men." Kapitanleutnant Hellmut Rathke was thirty-two years old, but thirteen of the forty-six men were under twenty-one years of age.

During the five weeks at sea Rathke scored no successes. He once spotted a merchant ship and prepared to attack, but was stymied by British corvettes; they harried him with depth charges that exploded uncomfortably close. At other times land-based aircraft attacked with such vehemence that he was forced to submerge. On one occasion he fired a spread of four torpedoes at a destroyer, but they all missed their mark. The true value of the Iron Cross—supposedly bestowed for excellence in the line of battle—can be measured by the fact that three of them were awarded to crew members after a cruise that was an utter failure; it may have been a morale booster, but it certainly did not reflect skill or accomplishment.

March found the *U-352* in St. Nazaire, the U-boat base on the French coast. For several weeks the boat underwent repairs and reprovisioning. It left the first week in April for the three-week Atlantic crossing to the U.S. eastern seaboard. At that time U-boat depredations were at their highest. Any U-boat commander worth his salt could not fail to achieve success in the "great American turkey shoot." Tankers and freighters were being sunk with such regularity that the ocean bottom was literally paved with iron hulls.

Furthermore, Rathke was ordered to patrol the area off the Diamond Shoals, dubbed "torpedo alley" by U.S. Navy pundits to describe the great number of ships lost there to enemy action. However, by the time the *U-352* reached the American coast in May, U-boat activity was on the wane. The *U-85* had been sunk two weeks earlier. (see *Shipwrecks of North Carolina: from the Diamond Shoals North.*) The coast was patrolled by ever-growing numbers of warships, Coast Guard cutters, gunboats, converted yachts, bombers, and blimps. What the Germans called the "second happy time" was nearing its end.

Instead of watching for isolated merchant vessels plying the shipping lanes, and picking them off with "eels," the *U-352* spent most of its time crash-diving to avoid aerial detection, or running submerged so as not to be spotted by patrol boats and planes; it was the life of a gopher. Those times that Rathke was able to prosecute attacks against unsuspecting merchant ships resulted in negative results. He was a man thirsting for water in a house full of spigots. Perhaps that was what led him to make an insane daylight attack against the fully armed U.S. Coast Guard cutter *Icarus*. A vessel only 165 feet long must have seemed easy pickings.

Lieutenant (jg) E.D. Howard was at the conn of the *Icarus* on the afternoon of May 9, 1942. The Coast Guard cutter was on route from New York to Key West, travelling independently at fourteen knots. The sea was smooth, the visibility about nine miles with a slight haze; at 4:25 p.m. there was still three hours of sunlight left. As the Executive Officer, Lieutenant Howard paid particular attention to making sure the helmsman followed the prescribed zigzag pattern.

The sound equipment suddenly indicated an underwater contact described as "rather mushy." It was a mere one hundred yards away "a wee bit off port bow." The XO immediately rang General Quarters and called the ship's captain to the bridge. Lieutenant Maurice Jester took charge of the *Icarus*. Four minutes after the initial contact a torpedo detonated some two hundred yards off the port quarter.

Rathke, already lacking in skill, had run out of luck as well. The torpedo he fired at the *Icarus* exploded prematurely, not only allowing the cutter to escape but divulging the U-boat's position.

Lieutenant Jester: "Contact drew to port quarter. The submarine attempted to hide in our previous wake. We heard the propeller noises of the submarine." He ordered the course of the *Icarus* reversed. The cutter bore down on the clearly discernible swirl of bubbles caused by the torpedo's explosion. In an official interview, Lieutenant Jester described events with military precision and succinctness.

"At this time, we dropped five depth charges, in a diamond pattern. It was later learned that this attack destroyed the submarine's periscope, and killed the Conning Officer. We then reversed course. At 1645 EWT, we dropped three depth charges, in a "V" pattern. At this point, we observed large air bubbles on the surface. The submarine then attempted to surface, as the machinery had been disabled. We reversed course again, and dropped one depth charge, at 1708 EWT. At 1709 EWT, the submarine surfaced down by stern. We then opened fire with our 3" gun, and scored seven hits, on the hull and conning tower of the submarine. At 1711 EWT, the crew of the submarine was seen to be abandoning ship. At 1714 EWT, the submarine sank, and we then ceased fire."

During the forty-five-minute engagement Rathke did all he could to slink away. The U-boat twisted and turned like a worm on a hot tarred road. As depth charges landed with unerring accuracy "gauges and glasses were smashed in the control room. The deck was littered with broken gear. Lockers burst open. Crockery and other loose objects were flung about the boat. The crew was shaken up. All lights except the emergency system failed." The engines also halted momentarily.

The *Icarus*. (Courtesy of the National Archives.)

With one man already dead and the rest sure to follow, Rathke had no choice but to surrender. The men donned Draeger lungs and lifejackets as Rathke ordered the tanks blown. As soon as the U-boat reached the surface he gave the order to abandon ship. Thirty-three men burst from the hatch under a hail of shells from the smoking guns of the *Icarus*. The Germans had no opportunity to return fire: it was all they could do to jump into the water and hide behind the U-boat's perforated hull. Thirteen men did not make it out.

The *U-352* went down for the last time. On the surface, German sailors floated on the sea like flotsam, and supplicated for rescue.

On each of her sweeps the *Icarus* had gone as far as a thousand yards before turning in for another attack. Now, as she returned to where the *U-352* had come to rest, she saw the group of men drifting away in the current. On the ocean there are no sign posts, so each time the cutter drove in to attack there was no way of knowing if the sonar target she was approaching was the same one she had just passed over, or another, altogether different one. Plotting a course by dead reckoning did not yield the pinpoint accuracy of modern loran. Since merchant marine survivors often attested to U-boats working in consort, the Navy mind was set on the possibility that another U-boat might be lurking in the vicinity. To stop and pick up survivors meant exposing the *Icarus* to potential counter attack. Lieutenant Jester could not make such a decision on his own; it had to come from fleet command.

Communications Officer, Ensign C.C. Poole, sent a plain language message on the Navy frequency at 2716 kilocycles: "Have sunk submarine. 30 to 40 men in water. Shall *Icarus* pick up any of the men." When no answer was received from either Norfolk or Princess Anne, the same message went out to Charleston, on 355 kilocycles. The message was received and receipted, but no message was forthcoming. Seventeen minutes later Ensign Poole asked, "Have you any message for us?" The answer was "No."

By this time the *Icarus* had completed another figure-eight loop. Again the sound gear made contact with a target. Was it the U-boat already sunk, or a brother wolf? Lieutenant Jester drove over an area of erupting bubbles and dropped a single depth charge. By this time the survivors of the *U-352* were far enough away to escape injury from the concussion. Rathke made the best of his time in the water by shouting "warnings to his men not to give any information to their rescuers." He also applied a tourniquet to the stump of Machinest's Mate Gerd Reussel's severed leg.

Nine minutes after his last message, Ensign Poole transmitted another. "Shall *Icarus* pick up any survivors?" Seven minutes after that: "32 German submarine men in water. Shall we pick them up?" The poor German sailors were as likely to drown in red tape as in the Atlantic swells. At last, the Commandant of the Sixth Naval District favored the *Icarus* with a reply: "Pick up survivors. Bring to Charleston."

Now if Lieutenant Jester lost his ship to further German aggression he was at least acting under direct orders that would save his career in the event of a court-martial. "At 1750 EWT, we stopped and picked up 33 survivors, including 4 wounded. One of the wounded, who had lost a leg, died at 2215. One member of the crew lost an arm, and one had a fractured wrist, with possibly a bullet inside. One member had a slight wound on his hand. Each member of the submarine crew was searched as he came aboard the *Icarus*. All were equipped with life jackets and lungs, of the most excellent quality. Thirty members of the crew were placed under guard. Two members were placed in sick bay.'

Ensign Poole's next message was triumphant: "Contacted submarine, destroyed same. Lat 32-12-1/2, long 73-75. Have 33 of her crew members on board. Proceeding Charleston with survivors."

Rathke had finally done something noteworthy: he became the first German submariner to be captured off the American coast.

The Sixth Naval District appeared to be unable to keep up with events. An hour and a half after the *Icarus* left the site of the engagement she received a message from the Commandant: "Buoy spot with secure anchor. Recover sample oil and surface and all floating debris." Then: "Request that all information concerning *Icarus* incident be treated strictly confidential."

Rathke, for one, intended to fulfill this last request. Because Ensign Jester did not separate the German officers from their men, during the trip to Charleston there was ample opportunity for Rathke to get "the prisoners together to give them instructions about the story they would tell. He told them not to mingle with German girls, if they should be placed where they would have occasion for such association. He told them not to forget their comrades who had died, and also not to forget anything he had told them the preceeding night."

The *Icarus* tied up at the wharf in Charleston, South Carolina, at 11:30

198

the following morning. The German prisoners were marched off her deck
with the same precision with which they had abandoned their sinking
U-boat. They ignored the military fanfare and, despite the gravity of their
plight, exhibited high morale. They received better treatment at the hands
of the enemy than they had been led to expect after listening to years of
German propoganda. (While in the water, the man who had lost his arm
waved his stump and begged not to be machine gunned.) Gerd Reussel was
"buried with full military honors in Post Section, grave No. 18, National
Cemetary, Beaufort, S.C."

According to the Office of Naval Intelligence, "A brief preliminary
interrogation was made shortly after the men were landed in the United
States. Thereafter they were taken to a place of temporary internment
where Rathke was permitted to maintain direct control over his men. A
stern disciplinarian, Rathke kept a strict surveillance over his men during
this temporary internment. Ample evidence of this can be found in the list
of punishments meted out to his men for various delinquencies."

After more thorough interrogation ONI found that, "though
courteous to a fault and cultivated, Rathke has been conspicuously arrogant
in complaining of his treatment as a prisoner and in assuming unwarranted
control of his men following their internment. He professes unqualified
admiration for Hitler and National Socialism." And, "Rathke spoke
of Hitler as a 'genius' who has unified all the German peoples of Europe.
... Rathke said Hitler was not only a military genius but 'a genuis in
everything.'"

The prisoners are marched off the deck of the *Icarus*. (Courtesy of the National Archives.)

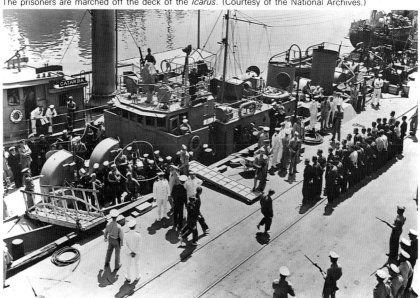

Rathke is the one wearing the mustache, goatee, and shorts.

The intelligence gained from Rathke and his crew left much to be desired. Hoping that it might learn more from steel than from flesh, the Navy decided to salvage the *U-352*: if not the entire hull then at least its log and code books and cipher machine. The Navy tug USS *Umpqua* (No. 25) left Charleston on May 19, but "it was not until May 23 that the submarine was located. Using a buoy anchor chain as a descending line, a dive was made by C.E. Meyer, TM2c, USN, who reported after coming to the surface that he had examined the bow of the submarine which had a deep gash in it. The submarine laid on its starboard side at the angle of about 60° but in as much as the diver had only enough line to give him a 20-foot radius of activity, a more thorough examination of the entire ship could not be made at that time.

"The following day diving operations were continued when it was hoped to enter the conning tower; however, it was impossible for the *Umpqua* to remain in one position and after many unsuccessful attempts to relocate the submarine, operations on this day were discontinued.

"There were no escort vessels available on May 25th to afford the *Umpqua* protection, but on May 26th and for the three following days further efforts to locate the wreck were not successful."

If the Navy seems to have given up too easily, it must be remembered that there was a war going on, and the services of tugs and escorts were sorely needed elsewhere. Besides, those in positions of higher authority were privy to the knowledge that German cipher machines had long been in Allied hands, and that German naval codes had long since been broken.

Nearly three months after the sinking of the *U-352*, on August 7, the British armed trawler HMS *Stella Polaris* "established a sharp metallic contact that was a submarine beyond doubt and with the excellent policy of 'shooting first—questions later,'" she went in to attack. This was in the vicinity of the *U-352*. She dropped three patterns of depth charges "which brought large air bubbles and additional oil to the surface. Then 5 minutes later a raft appeared. Excitement ran high when it was believed that another enemy submarine had been destroyed." The raft was covered with German writing, and contained "a red distress flag mounted on a 5-foot staff which could be broken in three joints.

"The *Stella Polaris* then dropped a pattern of 12 depth charges which brought more oil to the surface and then, developing a leak, stood by until 2030 when, after buoying the position, she departed for Morehead City. The following day the Coast Guard cutters *474* and *480* located the buoy and both dropped depth charges that failed to bring up wreckage or bodies, although oil came to the surface after each attack. It was at this time believed that a definite 'kill' had been made and the decision to conduct diving operations and search for the sunken submarine was reached."

The tug *P.F. Martin* was called in and a diver was put down. He found

Rathke leads his men to prison. It should be understood that the character references made by Naval interrogators pertained only to Rathke—not his men. So disliked was Rathke by his crew that after repatriation he was banned from the annual survivor's reunions. In May 1992, George Purifoy hosted a fifty-year reunion for the surviving crew members, in Morehead City.

"hard smooth sand with pock marks in the ocean bottom, and also depth charge arbors and a quantity of dead fish, but no submarine. The area was dragged with a grapnel and two hours later a solid object was hooked and buoyed; the following day a diver, using the buoy anchor line as a guide, located the submarine."

On the third dive "a piece of wreckage was brought to the surface. The wreckage consisted of a twenty foot section of upper deck grating, presumably the hatch over the upper deck torpedo storage containers." Diving operations were secured because of a two and a half knot current, and because of the discovery of five unexploded depth charges scattered around the wreck.

Unfortunately for the war record of the *Stella Polaris*, the divers also found entangled in the hull a three-inch wire hauser and a two-and-a-half-inch manila line, both of which had been lost in May during salvage operations on the *U-352*. The *Stella Polaris* had rediscovered the wreck and added to its destruction.

Thereafter the *U-352* remained dormant until located once again in 1975, this time by wreck divers who were bound and determined to find it. It was not an easy task. The story was told to me by George Purifoy. Among others, Claude Hall had already spent considerable energy in the search when he passed the torch to Purifoy and his friends Rod Gross and Dale McCullough. The trio chartered local fishing boats to take them to the coordinates recorded by the Navy. The position was given in lat-lons (latitude and longitude) and had to be converted to loran-A, the chain in use at the time and one known for lack of returnability. It often took three or four hours to find a *known* wreck. Week after week throughout the summer they ran grids with a fathometer. Eighty percent of the time they did not even get wet; sometimes they called it quits early enough to permit them to make a dive on the way home. The search was costly, time consuming, and frustrating in the extreme.

With a depth recorder for determining bottom contours it is necessary to drive exactly over top of a wreck before it shows up as a spike on the graph. Still the weeks went by, and still they had nothing to show for their efforts. The monitor showed no trace of any wreckage whatsoever: the oscilloscope was flatlined like an EEG on a dead person.

Finally, Purifoy bought his own boat and rented a loran-C just out on the market. Armed with this equipment he and his companions went out to begin running grid patterns in the suspected area. On the very first pass they ran over a target that showed promise. Then, because of the smooth hull, they had trouble grappling the wreck. When Purifoy went down the anchor line he knew that their quest was over. The grapnel's tines had caught in the conning tower. With two-hundred-foot visibility he could see both ends of the wreck, and knew for sure that it was a U-boat.

The *U-352* was a mile and a quarter from where the Navy had listed its position. Remember this the next time you use old lat-lons for hunting down a wreck. And remember how much time and money it cost Purifoy and his friends to find the wreck. Today's charter fee is cheap by any comparison.

Although the wreck had been worked over hard by successive depth charge attacks, the pressure hull remained unruptured. The outer skin was gone, either blasted or rusted away, as was the conning tower: the U-boat appeared like a stripped down model with the pumps and valves normally hidden under deck plates now exposed to the sea. The deck gun and periscopes were the most prominent features. White, hard sand provides a sturdy platform that not only kept the hull from settling into the bottom, but along with warm Gulf Stream currents helps maintain visibility in ranges that often exceed one hundred feet.

Soon the hatches were opened and divers began penetrating the darkened interior, either searching for artifacts or simply for the adventure of exploring. In 1978 George Purifoy recovered the deck gun; in 1979 Dave Bluett recovered the 1,500-pound port propeller, made of marine bronze. The wreck continues to yield German souvenirs to those willing to spend the time searching for them.

Although the *U-352's* hull had so far survived numerous depth charge attacks as well as natural ravages of the sea, it was in imminent peril of annihilation from a much more insidious force: bureaucracy. In 1978 Senator Lowell Weicker, a Republican from Connecticut, strayed into an area where he was definitely out of his state. Hearing that the sunken U-boat contained unexploded ordnance, and that divers visited the site regularly, he decided that the wreck should be placed off-limits. He called the *U-352* a "time bomb" waiting to explode. Exerting his senatorial influence, he eventually dropped a bomb where none had been before.

Under his direction the U.S. Navy was ordered to survey the wreck in order to assess its potential danger to sport divers. While national defense is more in the realm of the Navy's area of responsibility, it was forced to condescend to political pressures and conduct an investigation of the U-boat's live ordnance. What they found came as no surprise to local divers: exposed torpedoes and scattered 88-mm projectiles. Nor was this a situation with which the Navy had not dealt before.

Every once in a while a dragger hauls up in its net a lost mine or expended torpedo leftover from World War Two. Sometimes, concerned parents bring in warheads dug out of the beach near gun emplacements. The Explosive Ordnance Division handles these cases by delicately transporting all live (or suspected live) ordnance to a disposal range where it is covered with dynamite which is then detonated, thus destroying the old and supposedly unstable explosives. Never is anything disarmed. Reporters of these events describe the resultant blasts without bothering to mention that it was not the result of the old ordnance, but the dynamite used to destroy it. This has led people (and Senators) to believe that all antique ordnance can go off spontaneously, like some Jack-in-the-box waiting for someone to flip its lid.

Now there came the hue and cry that EOD might blow up the *U-352* as a way of discarding the ordnance it carried. The repercussions from Weicker's naivete were pronounced: local businesses and charter operators claimed that "this option may adversely impact the area's recreational assets;" the National Environmental Policy Act demanded an environmental impact statement because of the wreck's function as an artificial reef; and German nationals claimed that the U-boat was a war memorial that still entombed some of the U-boat's crew.

The loudest voice of protest was the latter, in the spokesperson of Captain Dieter Ehrhardt, the naval liaison for the German Embassy in Washington. "My government prefers to leave wreckage from World War II at the bottom of the sea, to give the dead sailors rest." He was further outraged over rumors that divers were removing from the *U-352* the bones of those dead sailors, and exhibiting them as curiosities. "Generally speaking, the boat is a cemetery, and nobody wants to disturb a cemetery. It is not good, if you are in a cemetery, to pull dead bodies out of the earth." That depends.

Land based cemeteries are often reclaimed for more useful purposes: housing, highways, and shopping malls. It is a common practice to disinter bodies and relocate them to newly established, out-of-the-way lots. Many warships have been demolished because they presented a hazard to navigation, and a way had to be cleared for safe shipping. In the case of the *U-853*, a U-boat sunk off Block Island, Rhode Island, bones were recovered and returned to the fatherland in piety toward the deceased. There is no overriding rule of human nature, cultural ethics, or political prerogotive that governs the disposal of human remains. Bodies can be buried, burned, or donated to science. Nor do people's beliefs concerning physical remains conform to any system of reason: whereas some individuals hold the corpse to be a sacrosanct receptacle with deep religious overtones, others regard it as nothing more than an inanimate object that was merely the carrier for the soul, persona, or consciousness.

Philosophical considerations aside, *which* German government had a proper claim on war graves: East Germany, West Germany, or the Third Reich to which the men and machines belonged but which no longer exists? Perhaps the only majority consent that can be counted upon is that skulls and skeletal parts should not be displayed as trophies. Yet, I have been to museums that highlighted skeletons in glass enclosures; and in one maritime museum I saw the skull of a passenger of a sunken ship in a lighted cabinet that was surrounded by other artifacts recovered from the wreck.

Although clearly out of his depth, Weicker gained a great deal of publicity for his cause (and for his image) by diving the wreck himself. Media attention focused on Weicker and his belief by claiming that the Navy was "worried" over the sunken U-boat. Such newspaper hype could not be farther from the truth; in actuality, the Navy had no concerns whatsoever concerning the *U-352*. It would rather have forgotten Weicker and his self-aggrandizing promotional stance, especially when he accused the Navy of foot-dragging when, after a year and a half, it had done nothing pursuant to his demands.

Finally, in the summer of 1980, senatorial will presided, and the Navy mounted an expedition to the wreck that was costly to the taxpayer, bothersome to the marine life, face-saving to German nationals, senseless to sport divers, and only partially gratifying to Weicker. Perhaps the only good that came of it was an exercise for Navy divers in which they could hone their skills.

After exhaustive administrative preparations that included the accumulation of equipment and the assignment of personnel, the USS *Hoist* (ARS-40) got underway on May 27, 1980 for an operation that lasted six full weeks. For two days and nights, working around the clock, the *Hoist* towed a side-scan sonar fish over four different positions found among Navy records. "However, no probable contacts were made." It was not until May 29 that the "decision was made to ask the Squadron to make arrangements for commercial assistance from Morehead City in locating the submarine." *Voila!* What insight. "Using loran charlie navigation, *Atlantis II* located and buoyed off *U-352* within 20 minutes." (I wonder how much money was spent on fuel and wages before someone thought of the obvious?)

Initial diving operations (on scuba) consisted of tying a series of radar buoys to the bow, conning tower, and stern of the wreck in order to determine its heading, which is northeast, so that a six-point moor could be established. This took two days. On May 31 the first survey was conducted. Using the MK 12 Surface Supplied Diving System with three hundred feet of hose, and taking pictures with a UDATS camera, they found that "the submarine is at rest on a sandy bottom, with a 65–75 degree starboard list. Divers reported soundings of 110 feet at the stern and amidship, and 116 feet at the bow. A variety of sea life linger in the vicinity of the submarine, including a school of barracuda. The forward 30 feet of the bow hull section is broken and down at an angle of 30 degrees. The entire submarine is heavily encrusted in barnacles, 75 percent of the decking is missing and only structural framing remains attached to the pressure hull. Approximately 20 per cent of the starboard hull is submerged in the sandy bottom, and an air lift or falcon nozzle could be used to remove this sand to gain access for a complete hull inspection. As previously mentioned, the submarine's outer shell is badly deteriorated and all that remains is the structural framing attached to the very accessible pressure hull which is in good shape. Because of the 65–75 degree starboard list, divers were unable to determine whether or not the two starboard forward torpedo tube outer doors are opened. Number two torpedo tube (upper port tube) is broken in half and number four tube (lower port tube) is intact but divers were unable to confirm the presence of any torpedoes. Although the external survey revealed that no torpedoes are stowed topside on the maindeck, a torpedo warhead was discovered wedged in the deck framing approximately 30 feet forward of

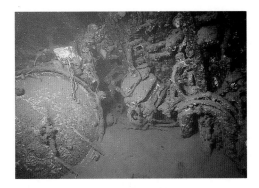 

Left: one of the tubes in the forwards torpedo room. Right:
the conning tower hatch is open.

the conning tower, above the forward torpedo room. The warhead is intact
with exploder removed. The forward torpedo loading hatch is open and the
hatch cover is missing. Divers passed survey of conning tower to continue
looking aft. The messdecks hatch and after torpedo loading hatch are both
open and both hatch covers are missing. Divers reported that after torpedo
loading hatch is blocked by two six inch diameter pipes, possibly vents.
Divers moved further aft and determined stern torpedo outer door is
opened and approximately 2.5 feet of a torpedo extends out the stern tube.''
They also found a single 88-mm shell in the sand twenty-five feet off the
starboard side.

The next day divers found that "the upper conning tower hatch is open
and is lying in the bottom of the conning tower. The lower conning tower
hatch, which allows access into the control room, is partially open. Divers
reported that the ready service aft of the 88mm gun mount is completely
deteriorated. Only the gun mount base remains intact . . . divers entered the
forward torpedo room through the forward torpedo loading hatch and
began the internal search. Divers reported the forward torpedo room
contains a considerable amount of mud, sand and silt. The presence of
unexploded ordnance could not be determined at this time. However, two
horizontal HP air flasks were identified extending between frames 26 and
37 on the port side, partially covered by mud and sand. A violet colored
Petroleum Oil Lubricant (POL) product is present in the overhead with a
depth of approximately 8 inches. A square water tight door (door missing)
provides access between the petty officer's compartment and the forward
torpedo room. At about frame 45 within the petty officer's compartment,
an approximate rectangular shaped 18 inch by 24 inch hole passes through
the pressure hull in the overhead and into the sea. Upon completion of the
brief internal survey of the forward torpedo room and the petty officer's

compartment, divers prepared for the X-ray of the stern torpedo. The radiation exposure device is heavy and required two divers to horse it around into position. ... An exposure was taken and the preliminary picture indicated the torpedo is unarmed.''

On June 2 divers commenced the removal of mud and sand from the forward torpedo room (in order to ''make the final determination as to the presence of unexploded ordnance'') by implanting a jet. Bad weather, strong currents, and hardpacked mud conspired to make this a difficult and time consuming job. Not until June 11 were they able to excavate down as far as the deck plates. Still, more torpedoes might be stowed below the deck plates. ''Several divers attempted to release the inner torpedo tube locking device using a 36 inch aluminum pipe wrench, but were unsuccessful.''

Then came a couple days of bad weather, one day of good, a couple more days of bad. ''Probing by hand in the bilges revealed no evidence of any torpedoes/unexploded ordnance in the excavation. Four air flasks, extended between frames 25 to 36, were positively identified within the forward torpedo room. Two lie end to end along the port side bulkhead and two lie end to end along the starboard side bulkhead.''

June 17: ''The lower port torpedo tube was found to be cracked and the battery section of a torpedo was visible. The lower port torpedo tube is cracked approximately 3 to 4 feet outside of the pressure hull which would indicate the torpedo inside is broken in the center section.'' Also, ''Alongside the starboard quarter, approximately 10 feet from the submarines side, divers located the end of a torpedo center section. ... Divers confirmed this torpedo was without an exploder.''

June 18: ''Two torpedoes were located in the bilges and confirmed, one directly underneath the port side air flasks and a second approximately 8 inches to the right of the first (as facing the bow). Both torpedoes are without exploders.'' The next day they found two more torpedoes in the bilges.

Part of June 22 was spent exploring. ''In the vicinity of the CO's cabin there is approximately 3 feet of clearance between the mud and sand level

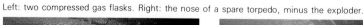

Left: two compressed gas flasks. Right: the nose of a spare torpedo, minus the exploder.

and the overhead. There is also a considerable amount of mud and sand in the mates compartment and the officers mess."

June 23: "Tubes one and four were drilled and probing revealed the presence of a torpedo in each tube. The two new torpedoes bring the total to ten torpedoes located thus far." So much for the veracity of the *U-352's* crew. They had stated that they started out with fourteen torpedoes and fired seven or eight.

"Divers reported the galley is approximately 2/3 full of mud and debris. The galley hatch door leading forward is present and partially open. Divers proceeded forward into the mates compartment and reported the space is approximately half full of mud and noticeably clear of debris, and that there is approximately five feet of clearance between the mud level and the overhead. A circular watertight hatch opens into the mates compartments and provides access into the conning tower control room. Divers then back tracked and proceeded aft through the engine room. However, the extreme starboard list, combined with the mud, debris and the port and starboard engines, made transit of the engine room very difficult. Divers continued through the engine room space and into the after torpedo room to investigate the two bars obstructing the after torpedo loading hatch. Investigation revealed the two bars appear to be securely in place and will probably require removal to allow easier access into the torpedo room. Like the forward torpedo room, the after torpedo room is full of a considerable amount of mud and debris. To complete a comprehensive survey all mud and debris will have to be excavated."

The next day they proceeded to torch through the bars, but then found that in MK II gear they could slip between them. After much excavation and time lost to bad weather, the determination was made on July 1 that no torpedoes were stored in the after torpedo room. Then they partially excavated the galley, where they removed the deck plates, and the CO's cabin. No unexploded ordnance was located.

July 3: "It was decided that any remote removal of the exploder from the torpedo in the stern tube is not considered a practical course of action." The next day "divers completed external excavation of sand alongside the entire length of the starboard side of *U-352*. No additional unexploded ordnance was found. However, communications problems developed with MK12 hats and diving had to be secured." When it developed that replacement communication assemblies were unavailable, survey operations were ended.

July 6: "Divers recovered all 88MM and loaded them on board. Divers then placed the torpedo warhead section into a cargo net lowered to the bottom ... lifted approximately 3 feet off the ocean floor and towed to a point 1500 yards away from the ship and submarine." Divers then attached an Incendiary Torch Remote Opening Device. "The first sign of the warhead burning was a large amount of smoke and bubbles on the surface. Approximately 5 minutes after commencing the burn, the warhead became

Above: A Navy diver examines the exploder on a torpedo found protruding from the stern tube. Below: The exploder is missing from this torpedo. (Courtesy of the U.S. Navy.)

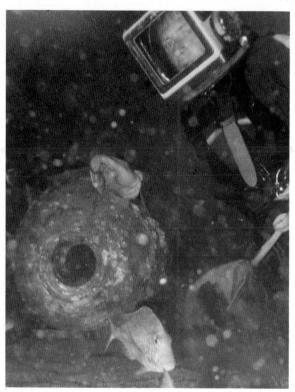

buoyant and ascended to the surface engulfed in flames. The warhead was recovered and lifted onboard along with 5 lbs of raw explosive and 7 lbs of residual.''

By July 7 it was all over. Navy divers had made one hundred thirty-seven dives for a total bottom time of three hundred sixty-one hours. A summary report stated that they had found numerous rounds from the ship's gun and an unexploded torpedo outside the submarine as well as eight torpedoes inside the hull (seven in the forward room and one in a stern torpedo tube).'' Inexplicably, the report failed to mention the torpedo trapped outside under the starboard hull. ''The torpedoes in the forward room do not pose a hazard as long as left undisturbed, i.e., if restricted from access they will not explode spontaneously but the torpedo in the aft tube does constitute a hazard as it can be approached from outside the hull.''

The recommendation was made that the torpedo in the after tube be burned by ITROD, while gratings could ''be welded on the entrances to the submraine to prevent access and accidental detonation of any of the torpedoes inside the hull or their associated exploders, six of which could not be located and could be anywhere inside the vessel.''

The results of the survey were pondered for a year. Navy divers returned to the wreck on June 18, 1991, stayed nine days, and made sixty-seven dives. Using ITROD, they succeeded in burning the torpedo protruding from the stern tube as well as the one trapped under the starboard hull in the bow. Then they proceeded to seal off the hatches. Instead of welding a grating across each hatch opening, as recommended, they opted to emplace on each a locking device that consisted of a steel T-bar that slipped inside the coaming and a smooth circular plate on the outside. The circular plate had a round hole in the middle, for the T-bar bolt, and two half-moon cutouts on opposite sides: so the T-bar could be held in place while the nut was run down the shaft from the outside. The nut was then welded in place. This was little more than an appeasement program for Weicker.

It took only weeks for sport divers to remove the hatch covers. The wreck has been open ever since.

Hand wheels and throttle control in the engine room.

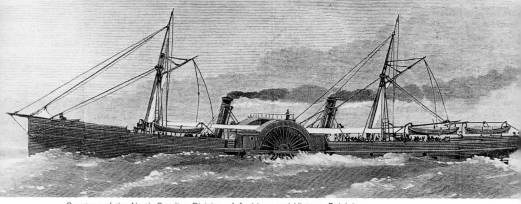

Courtesy of the North Carolina Division of Archives and History, Raleigh.

VIRGINIUS

Built: 1864
Previous names: *Virgin*
Gross tonnage: 441
Type of vessel: Side paddlewheeler
Builder: A. Akerman and Manson, Glasgow, Scotland
Owner: John F. Patterson
Port of registry: New York, NY
Cause of sinking: Foundered
Location: 45301.6

Sunk: December 26, 1873
Depth: 40 feet
Dimensions: 216' × 24' × 10'
Power: Two oscillating engines

59205.2

The history of the *Virginius* is perhaps the richest of any ship wrecked off North Carolina because she very nearly precipitated the Spanish-America War twenty-five years before the event. At the beginning of her career and at the end, the *Virginius* was the cause of trouble and embarrassment to the United States government.

The *Virgin* was built with a sleek, swept-back profile that presented an imposing picture of speed—speed that was required for her calling as a blockade runner. On her maiden voyage in 1864 she easily slipped through the ranks of the federal squadron blockading the Gulf of Mexico, and landed her valuable cargo at Mobile, Alabama. Before the *Virgin* could make good her departure to sea, however, the Union army swept into Mobile and captured the harbor. The Confederates managed to slip the *Virgin* north into the Tombigbee River. The *Virgin* sat uselessly at dock in Gainesville, Alabama until April 12, 1865, when federal forces took over that town. This time the *Virgin* did not escape; she was confiscated as a prize of war.

Throughout the year *Virgin* sat idle. Eventually, she was moved to Mobile where, on February 14, 1866, she was sold to C.M. Godbold and J.M. Moody. On June 23 they sold her to Miles T. Steele. In order to satisfy debts to the government, Steele sold her to the Treasury Department on May 14, 1867, for the nominal sum of $5. Then, on August 27, 1870, John T. Patterson purchased the *Virgin* from the government for $9,800. Shortly thereafter the newly named *Virginius* left for Curacao for her new occupation.

Ostensibly the *Virginius* worked as a tramp freighter between ports in the Caribbean and Central and South America. But her owner, John Patterson, was sympathetic to the cause of the Cuban patriots—some said he was an agent of the Cuban Junta. The Cubans had been fighting for independence from Spain since 1868. They were a desperate band of people without sufficient arms and ammunition. Patterson proposed to help them by "filibustering"—not the way it is done in the Senate, with words, but as "an adventurer who engages in a private military action in a foreign country." The *Virginius* was used to run guns into Cuba for the revolutionaries. Her shallow draft (eight feet) made her the perfect vessel for discharging military cargoes on desolate beaches.

It was no secret what the *Virginius* was doing. The Spaniards knew it, the Americans knew it. But as long as the *Virginius* flew the American flag—that is, was registered as a merchant vessel of the United States—she carried immunity from foreign aggression. Any Spanish warship that accosted her was in effect accosting the U.S. government. Spain protested vehemently that the *Virginius* was in actuality a pirate ship, and by July 1873 had had enough of what it perceived as interference with its internal affairs. Spain made a show of force by sending the frigate *Bazan* to detain the *Virginius* after leaving the port of Kingston, Jamaica.

Although the U.S. could not officially take sides in Spain's civil war, there were many American citizens who supported the rebellion by extending financial aid for the rebel cause. Their political influence was felt within the U.S. government. Besides this, since the *Virginius* was breaking no U.S. law and was a bona fide U.S. vessel, the federal government had no choice but to uphold her rights even had it felt otherwise. Thus the U.S. gunboat *Kansas* escorted the *Virginius* out of Kingston and stayed with her until she reached the high seas, where she effortlessly outran both the *Kansas* and the *Bazan*.

This uneasy state of affairs lasted for several months, with accusations against General Rafael Quesada, in charge of the gun running operation, reaching fever pitch. (Quesada resided in New York city.) Spanish dignitaries argued that the *Virginius* should have her register revoked, and should then be sent to the States for trial. The U.S. consol, while willing to admit that the *Virginius* was involved in smuggling, contended that she had to be caught in the act, not arrested before or afterward in a neutral port. Such rhetoric did not prevent the *Virginius* from continuing to land munitions on the Cuban coast.

On October 31, 1873, the daring *Virginius* approached Cuba as she usually did, from the south side. She was laden deep with weapons and ammunition. Of the one hundred fifty-five men aboard, one hundred three were free Cubans with American citizenship under the command of General Bernabe Verona. Assisting Verona in the campaign was General Washington Ryan, a Canadian with British citizenship, and Cuban patriots Pedor Cespedes and Jesus Del Sol.

About eighteen miles offshore the *Virginius* was spotted by the Spanish man-of-war *Tornade*. The Spanish captain recognized the notorious gun runner, and ordered full speed ahead.

Captain Joseph Fry, master of the *Virginius*, was no stranger to danger. He had a history of audacity that stretched back to the American Civil War, when he was the captain of the blockade runner *Eugenie*. While running the gauntlet of blockaders at Wilmington, North Carolina, his ship grounded off Fort Fisher within cannon shot of the federal fleet. With holds full of gunpowder, the *Eugenie* was in imminent peril of being blown to bits by a single stray shot. Yet Fry refused to abandon ship. With cannonballs splashing all around, he lightered some of the cargo, waited for high tide, then backed off his ship and brought her safely into port.

He tried a similar tactic now. He turned the *Virginius* for Jamaica, some one hundred miles away, and "ordered the engineers to get up all the steam possible, even if they burnt the boilers, and to drive the engines at their utmost speed."

The *Tornado* accepted the challenge. As the afternoon wore on the distance between the two ships closed. If Captain Fry hoped to escape under the cloak of darkness, he was thwarted by a brilliant moon that took the place of the sun. The masts and rigging of the *Tornado* sagged under the weight of extra lookout.

The *Tornado* was too fast, Jamaica too far off. Captain Fry ordered the cargo jettisoned: if no contraband were found on board, the *Virginius* could not legally be detained by the Spanish warship. When the *Tornado* steamed through the field of jetsam the Spaniards knew what the Americans were about. As soon as the warship got within firing range of the *Virginius* she brought her guns to bear. Being a merchant vessel the *Virginius* was unarmed. The projectiles that splashed around the blockade runner were not warning shots; they landed closer and closer with increasing accuracy. The Jamaica shore line was only six miles away, but, after a chase lasting eight hours, the *Virginius* was forced to yield to the *Tornado's* superior speed and firepower. The Spanish warship was about to blow the *Virginius* out of the water. The time was ten p.m.

The *Tornado* lowered two boats filled with marines; the men swarmed the decks of the *Virginius* and held her crew and passengers at gun point. In accordance with international treaty, Captain Fry smugly handed the ship's papers to the boarding officer. His was a neutral ship steaming in international waters, was hove to in British territorial water, and was backed by the authority of U.S. naval forces. Legally, he had nothing to fear.

The boarding officer had the American flag hauled down and replaced with a Spanish ensign. He placed Captain Fry and his men under arrest. With a prize crew aboard, the *Virginius* was turned around and escorted to Santiago de Cuba.

When news of the capture reached American shores the opinion of the media was that Spain "will doubtless be able to bring sufficient proof to procure her condemnation by a prize court." There was some debate about whether the ship's papers were in order, the concensus being that "registers granted to vessels continue until they are sold or change their names." Thus the *Virginius* should be afforded protection by dint of her American registry, and her passengers and crew by American sovereignty.

Imagine the shock of the American people when next they were informed that General Ryan, Bernabe Varona, Pedro Cespedes, and Jesus Del Sol had been executed! "The victims were shot in the back, and their bodies were afterward beheaded, the heads displayed on spikes and the trunks trampled by horses."

Great Britain was outraged at the effrontery of Spain in apprehending a British subject within British waters, executing him without due process, and violating his dead body with such a ghastly display of barbarity.

This was the beginning of an international incident. It was described in the American press as "a blot upon the civilization of the age, a disgrace to Spain, and an insult to our flag."

The sad saga that eventually unfolded was one that wrenched the emotions of even the most cold hearted. After the *Virginius* was brought to Santiago de Cuba her men were incarcerated aboard the *Tornado* and kept incommunicado. The local American Consul, Mr. Hall, tried to intervene in their behalf, but was himself confined to quarters under armed guard so he could not bring the situation to the attention of the Vice Consul in Havana. A newspaper reporter who tried to send out the story was jailed for his efforts. The telegraph cable between Santiago de Cuba and Havana was broken somewhere along its length—whether by accident or design was never determined.

The Cubans wasted no time in bringing about court-martial proceedings. The four leaders of the expedition were found guilty, and on November 4 they were summarily executed. "The four prisoners were shot at the place made famous by previous executions, and in the usual manner, kneeling close to the slaughter-house wall. All marched to the spot with firmness. Bembatta and Ryan showed marked courage, although the former was slightly affected toward the last. The two others quite broke down before they were bandaged; but Ryan kept up to the last, never flinched a moment, and died without fear or regret. Bembatta and Ryan were killed at the first volley." (Bembatta is Bernabe Varona.)

Only then were communiques issued about the capture of the *Virginius*. Upon receiving the news, Spain's President Castelar telegraphed instructions to Cuba that "no action should be taken in regard to the prisoners till a full report of the capture had been made to the Government at Madrid." The U.S. and England issued strong protests unaware that the executions had already been carried out. The government of Cuba, known as the Casino Espagnol, turned a deaf ear to the world and openly defied the home government at Madrid.

On November 6, sixteen others went to trial. Wrote Captain Fry to his wife, "Dear, Dear Dita: When I left you I had no idea that we should never meet again in this world. . . . I have been tried today, and the President of the court-martial asked the favor of embracing me at parting, and clasped me to his heart. I have shaken hands with each of my Judges, and the Secretary of the court and interpreter have promised me as a special favor to attend my execution, which will, I am told, be in a very few hours after my sentence is pronounced. I am told my death will be painless." The behavior of the Spanish inquisitors seems misplaced in light of the brutality of their actions, and hypocritical with regrad to their religious ceremony. "The priest who gave me communion on board this morning put a double scapular about my neck, and a medal which he intends to wear himself. A young Spanish officer brought me a bright new silk badge with the blessed Virgin stamped upon it to wear to my execution for him, and a handsome cross in some fair lady's handiwork. These are to be kept as relics of me."

The executions were carried out on November 7, and admitted in the press several days later. Cuban-Americans were incensed to riot. Thousands volunteered to march on Cuba in order to avenge their fallen comrades.

President Grant was not taking the matter lightly. While diplomatic relations between the U.S. and Spain continued on a political level, the U.S. Navy whipped the West India Squadron into combat readiness, and bolstered it with additional warships: the *Kansas*, *Ossipee*, *Worcester*, *Powhattan*, *Ticonderoga*, *Brooklyn*, and half a dozen monitors. If Congress made the decision to go to war, the Navy was prepared to carry out the task.

The true situation in Santiago de Cuba remained four days out of date because of the downed telegraph cables. This necessitated sending messages by railroad from Cuba to Batabario, then by steamship to Santiago—a distance of over five hundred miles, and a two-day trip each way. This suited the Casino Espagnol just fine.

On November 8 another thirty-seven men were "publicly butchered in open and flagrant violation of all international right or law, and in spite of the protests of all the competent foreign authorities. The execution was worthy of the people who planned and carried it out. The marines who composed the firing party were seven minutes putting the wretched prisoners to death. It seemed as if they never would finish, and when at last they marched off the troops defiled past the long row of corpses, and the dead-carts were hurried up and loaded with the mangled remains. Then all the spectators moved away, leaving the place silent and deserted, where only a few minutes before had stood thirty-seven men full of vigorous life." This brought the death toll to fifty-seven.

It developed that no less than sixteen men aboard the *Virginius* were British subjects. The HMS *Niobe* steamed into Santiago de Cuba in order to demonstrate a British presence, and to facilitate comminication between Mr. Hall and the outside world.

Spain's twofold positions were diametrically opposed: on one hand it was adament in refusing to back down to military threats made by the United States and Britain, while on the other hand it offered reconciliation for the *Virginius* affair by making reparations for loss.

The ship could be returned or paid for, but there can be no substitute for human life. The wives and children of those men murdered would be forever widows and fatherless.

Meanwhile, Spain was undergoing political upheaval within its ranks. There was talk of an overthrow of the government and the establishment of a dictatorship. The control Spain exercised over the Casino Espagnol was doubtful—especially in light of recent experience. Spain's President Castela was forced to bear the responsibility for the actions of those who ignored his executive prerogative. Cuban insurrection was threatening to tear the country apart. The United States was amassing its fleet in Key West. There were British warships *in* Havana.

The world was on the brink of war, and Cuba was the focal point.

Washington, November 29. "The formal protocol, embracing the terms of settlement of the *Virginius* affair, was drawn and signed today by Admiral Polo, the Spanish Minister, and Secretary Fish. Spain agrees to deliver immediately to the United States the *Virginius*, and all the survivors of the persons captured with her by the *Tornado*. Spain further agrees to salute the American flag on the 25th day of December, provided, that if the United States shall become satisfied before that date that the *Virginius* was not entitled to carry the flag, or in other words, if the display of the American flag is proved to have been simply a fraudulent device, the salute will not be required, but instead, Spain will disclaim any intentional disrespect to the flag. Spain engages on her part to apprehend and bring to trial and punishment any persons who have done wrong or violated treaty stipulations."

Spain also agreed to indemnify the families of the deceased, or, if the two countries could not agree upon the amount of settlement, it agreed to arbitration. In this manner war was narrowly averted.

The *Virginius* and her survivors were moved to Havana to await their deliverance. Imagine their horror when they learned that instead of carrying out the orders of the Madrid Cabinet, Captain General Jovellar, head of the Casino Espagnol, issued this proclamation: "Gen. Jovellar respectfully resigns his position, and demands that another person be sent to take his place, who can carry out the orders of the Government, considering the excited state of public opinion, and the impossibility of overcoming the difficulties." Jovellar assured Madrid that the delivery of the *Virginius* to the United States "will instantaneously cause a frightful commotion throughout the island, which would be sure to result in successive catastrophes."

Cuba prepared itself for war against the United States rather than yield to submission. It was a collective decision based on emotion, not reason. After more negotiations, however, Cuba agreed to surrender the *Virginius* but only to a neutral nation—a face-saving condition that avoided direct contact with the country that was providing Cuban rebels with men, materiel, and financial backing.

The American response? No dice. "The United States Government will still press for a complete and satisfactory vindication of our rights. Whatever consideration may be shown to the Spanish Government, on account of its peculiar situation, the United States cannot and will not yield the substance of its just demands." More than a hundred members of Congress called on the Secretary of the Navy to show their support. American warships headed out to sea and converged on Cuba. The USS *Juniata* and the USS *Wyoming* slipped into Santiago de Cuba; the HMS *Woodlark* joined the *Niobe* there. The British demanded that their subjects be released at once.

"United States naval officers at Santiago de Cuba report officially that the number of men captured on the *Virginius* was 155. Fifty-three were executed." An investigation into the circumstances now revealed that "four were shot on Nov. 4. Thirty-seven (Capt. Fry and crew included) were shot on the 7th, and twelve passengers on the 8th." Four executions less than the number originally reported did nothing to mitigate American public opinion, nor did Cuba's pooh-pooh of the affair. "Their concessions are slender, and are evaded at every chance. When a promise has been obtained it has been very necessary to remind them of it, and appeal to their Castilian honor before they think of fulfilling it."

The Secretary of the Navy caught the Congressional pass and ran with it for the touchdown. "I have taken measures to put every available iron and wooden ship of our navy in a condition for immediate duty. I have ordered all the ships of the various squadrons within reach to rendezvous at Key West. I am enlisting men to supply and fill up the crews of all our vessels. I have accumulated materials, provisions, and supplies for their maintenance and support, and ordnance, ammunition, and all the weapons of naval warfare for their use."

It was further stated that "Rear Admiral Scott, at Key West, will have the strongest naval force under his command that has been collected by the Government at any American port since the termination of the war." (The Civil War.) In Santiago de Cuba, Commander Braine presented his position concerning the *Virginius* people to the governor: "If any more were ordered to be executed ... I will sink every Spanish gun-boat and other Spanish men-of-war here that I can get at."

That the U.S. meant business did not go unnoticed. The Casino Espagnol very wisely backed down from its hard stance. The *Virginius* left Havana harbor escorted by the Spanish man-of-war *Isabella la Catolica*. She was officially turned over the U.S. representatives at Bahia Honda on the morning of December 18. Under the command of Lieutenant Rogers the *Virginius* steamed to the Tortugas to take on coal before beginning her journey north.

On December 19, the surviving prisoners boarded the USS *Juniata*, which left Havana immediately for New York.

Once again it seemed that war was averted.

However, the British government was not satisfied with Spain's handling of the matter. It demanded punishment for General Burriel, the man who ordered the executions. British warships filled Cuban harbors. The Casino Espagnol countered by demanding that the *Virginius* and her passengers be returned to Cuba. The protocol between Spain and the U.S. did not permit this. There were riots in Havana because the people felt that their government had let the U.S. and Britain intimidate them.

Then came the fillip that crowned the entire affair. Spain submitted documents proving that the *Virginius* flew the American flag illegally, and therefore should not have been afforded protection by the U.S. government. After careful perusal and consideration, Attorney General George Williams agreed that the evidence was preponderant. In order for a ship to be duly registered in the United States she had to be wholly owned by U.S. interests. Patterson, it developed, was merely the straw man for Quesada; the money for the purchase of the *Virginius* had come from the Cuban Junta. Since the register had been obtained by fraud, it was invalid. *But—*

"Spain, no doubt, has a right to capture a vessel with an American register and carrying the American flag, found in her own waters, assisting or endeavoring to assist the insurrection in Cuba, but she has no right to capture such a vessel on the high seas."

What this ultimately signified was that Spain did not have to salute the American flag as stipulated in the original agreement, but it did have to acknowledge that the failure to do so meant no disrespect.

If this diplomatic give-and-take sounds like a grown-up version of "Oh, yeah? My father can beat your father," welcome to the world of international politics. It just goes to prove that groups of adults can feel as insecure as individuals. The difference is that instead of exchanging vulgar invectives and throwing a couple of punches, countries couch their language with rhetoric and drop gunshells and bombs. The result is mass murder instead of a black eye.

Cuba continued to insist that the *Virginius* be returned, now that it had been proven that she was indeed a revolutionary vessel. How far this protestation might have gone will never be known because of a fortuitous but unanticipated course of events.

While coaling in the Tortugas the *Virginius* began taking on water through a hole in her stern. The bilge pumps alone were not enough to stem the flood so a bucket brigade was established. The crew eventually got the leak under control. It was then decided that rather than proceed under her own steam, the *Ossipee* should tow the *Virginius* to New York.

For three days the pair worked north along the coast. The crew in charge of the *Virginius* toiled ceaselessly day and night to keep the incursion of water down to an acceptable level. Lieutenant Commander David Woodrow, assigned to command the *Virginius* for the voyage, signalled to the *Ossipee* that his ship could not make it to New York without repairs, and recommended that they put in at Charleston. For reasons unexplained, his recommendation went unheeded. By the time they reached Frying Pan Shoals the *Virginius* was in imminent peril of sinking because the rising water had doused the boiler fires, thus knocking the steam pumps out of action. Woodrow signalled for help.

The *Ossipee* sent boats to remove those on the *Virginius*. Heavy seas made the rescue a memorable one, but there were no casualties. The *Ossipee* then stood by to witness the gun runner's final moments. The *Virginius* took her time going down—about eight hours. "A little after 4 o'clock P.M. she began to settle down in the water. At first she went down by the head, her forward compartments being stove and open. After the water had reached to above the paddle-boxes, it rushed backward into the cabin, and, tearing out the compartment partitions, carried the ship down on an almost even keel."

The date was December 26, 1873. It signified the end of an intense and trenchant episode in U.S.-Cuba relations. The British begrudgingly did not promulgate war against Spain. Cuba reportedly paid $80,000 in reparations to the families of the deceased. The revolution went on just as bloody as ever.

About three feet of the topmasts of the *Virginius* remained above the surface of the sea. The *Ossipee* attached a buoy to the end of the tow rope, as a marker in case of a decision to salvage. This was never done.

While the *Virginius* affair has become a memorable part of history, the wreck is largely forgotten. Lying close to shore in forty feet of water, diving conditions are poor and visibility generally murky, averaging five feet. Most of the hull is sanded in. Yet on those rare days of clarity one can be rewarded with a remarkable sight of the engine block and shafts, the remains of the paddlewheels, and the two boilers—one forward, one aft.

Perhaps one can see better through the mind's eye—to conjure an image of a ship not in glory, but as a portrait of all that is base and tragic in the unfolding human drama. The *Virginius* is best beheld not for how she looks but for what she represents: the folly of man's past.

Courtesy of the U.S. Coast Guard.

W.E. HUTTON

Built: 1920   Sunk: March 18, 1942
Previous names: *Portola Plumas*   Depth: 70 feet
Gross tonnage: 7,076   Dimensions: 435' × 56' × 32'
Type of vessel: Tanker   Power: Oil-fired steam
Builder: Bethlehem Ship Building Corp., Alameda, California
Owner: Pure Oil Company
Port of registry: Baltimore, Maryland
Cause of sinking: Torpedoed by *U-124* (Kapitanleutnant Mohr)
Location: 27143.2   39524.3

     No seaman headed toward the Diamond Shoals in the early months of 1942 could have done so without feeling the fear of dread anticipation, particularly during the month of March. Hardly a day passed without some merchantman going to the bottom in flames. Some days two or three ships (and twice, four ships) fell prey to the perdition meted out by soulless German U-boats. It was a horrible time to go to sea, a horrible time to work the coastal pipeline. Not all the innocent men survived the gautlet.

     The *W.E. Hutton* left Smith's Bluff, Texas on March 12, her tanks brimming with bunker C fuel oil bound for Marcus Hook, Pennsylvania. She proceeded independently across the Gulf of Mexico, through the Florida Straits, and north along the east coast. According to Captain Carl Flaathen, "regular watches were kept, and a sharp lookout maintained, with the officers on watch and the seamen on lookout ever on the alert." The ship followed a course "close inshore and in line with navigational buoys along the way." Furthermore, when the sun set, the running lights were left off and black-out covers were sealed tight against their gaskets. The staunch bow cut through the waves at a steady ten knots.

     Such strict precautions did not help the heavily laden tanker, however. No one saw the gray wraith lurking in the darkness on the night of March

18 (some sources say March 19.) But Able Bodied Seaman James Cosgrove spotted the approaching torpedo a split second before it struck the ship's stem. There was a deafening roar of spuming oil and twisted shrapnel. "The explosion caved in the bow, flooded the forepeak tanks, and resulted in a fire of a few second's duration which apparently did no appreciable damage." The time was ten p.m.

The radio operator transmitted an SOS, followed by a continuing series of SSS's: the signal for submarine attack. The ship listed to starboard but slowed only slightly. The crew "was mustered on deck and lowered the lifeboats about three-fourths of the way down. But since the ship gave evidence of remaining afloat and also due to the fact that she had on too much headway to safely launch the boats, it was decided to head the vessel more inshore rather than to abandon ship."

The lumbering tanker could not outrun the U-boat. The *U-124* stuck to the *W.E. Hutton* like a wolf harrying a wounded caribou. Eight minutes after the first explosion, another torpedo struck the tanker "on the port side amidships, in way of #3 tank, and her amidships section caught fire, which started to spread quickly."

One report stated that the pilot house was overturned "as decks just aft of the bridge were ripped open and buckled. The third mate and an unknown member of the crew were killed by the second explosion, while Captain Flaathen was cut by shattered glass and bruised by the concussion. Cosgrove, also was among the casualties, sustaining a fractured eardrum and severe bruises when thrown from atop the pilot house to the main deck. The ship and cargo were set afire and soon the amidships section was a raging inferno, with blazing oil streaming down all the alley ways."

Although no order was given to abandon ship, men began leaping overboard in order to escape the flames. Many drowned. Through the cacophany of burning oil and hissing steam, little communication was possible. Captain Flaathen helped lower one lifeboat, then cut away a raft. Elsewhere on the tanker, another lifeboat and raft were successfully launched in the moments following the second explosion. A third lifeboat "capsized several times when some of the crew attempted to get aboard and finally was dashed against the ship."

Stated Captain Flaathen, "I was covered with oil, and the vessel was surrounded with fire and smoke of the burning oil and superstructure. . . . I saw a life raft being launched from the after deck, which contained the wireless operator and the seamen who were assisting me. They advised me that all men were off the boat, so I jumped in the water and swam to the raft."

Jorgen Bauner later testified that "we heard four or five members yelling for help . . . but none could be located."

Captain Flaathen witnessed the sinking of his ship. "We drifted on the raft and watched the vessel burning. She was down by the head with her stern sticking out of the water. After about 45 minutes when we were about one-quarter of a mile from the vessel, the fire seemed to be extinguished suddenly, and we lost sight of the vessel in the darkness."

It must have been a sad and lonely moment.

Adrift upon the silent sea were twenty-three crew men: four in each raft, three in one lifeboat, and twelve in the other. Thirteen men were gone forever.

The various craft stayed in close proximity throughout the night. "At daylight the next day all survivors joined in one lifeboat and started rowing toward land." After a few hours, however, they were spotted by the British vessel *Port Halifax*, which stopped and took them all aboard.

The *W.E. Hutton* was insured for $1,250,000 dollars. No value can be placed upon the lives of the men who were lost.

This was an active night for Johann Mohr, captain of the *U-124*, for he torpedoed the *W.E. Hutton* only half an hour after doing in the *Papoose* (q.v.). Also covered in this book are Mohr's attacks against the *E.M. Clark*, *Esso Nashville*, and *Naeco*. See *Shipwrecks of North Carolina: from the Diamond Shoals North* for his sinking of the *Kassandra Louloudis*. On the night of April 2–3, 1943, Mohr and all hands on the *U-124* were lost west of Gibralter.

A ship as large as the *W.E. Hutton* presented quite a high profile. Because it lay in such shallow water it was a definite hazard to navigation. This fact was brought eminently to light on March 26, 1943, when the *Suloide* (q.v.) crashed into the sunken hulk, and sank.

As a direct consequence of this the Coast Guard cutter *Vigilant* was called into action. On June 29 she anchored near the site and the Navy Salvage Service began blasting down the hull and superstructure. By autumn it was reported that the least depth over the wreck was "in excess of 40'." There must have been some doubt, however, for operations continued on and off until January 11, 1944. By that time some thirty tons of dynamite had been used in the demolition process. "A wire drag party of the U.S. Coast and Geodetic Survey visited the wreck on 3 February 1944 and determined the least depth at mean low water to be 41 feet."

The result of such extensive use of explosives is evident today, for the *W.E. Hutton* can be described as hardly anything more than an underwater junk yard: a tangled mess of rusted steel spread out over more than an acre of sea floor. Because there are no recognizable parts, orientation on the wreck is practically impossible. A muddy bottom coupled with visibility averaging twenty to thirty feet ensures that a diver exploring only a short distance from the anchor line is unlikely to find his way back.

The few good reference points are the two large Navy anchors in the bow, the rudder in the stern, the huge crankshaft and connecting rods of the engine, and a pair of boilers. The bow points to the north, and if one looks in the area some seventy-five or eighty feet forward of the boilers one can find the remains of the galley. Toilets in the sand are the giveaway reference. China and silverware have been found here. Bon apetit!

SUGGESTED READING

Anonymous (1838) *Narrative of the Loss of the Steam-Packet Pulaski*, H.H. Brown, Providence, Rhode Island.

Berman, Bruce D. (1972) *Encyclopedia of American Shipwrecks*, The Mariners Press, Boston, Massachusetts.

Bright, Leslie S. (1977) *The Blockade Runner Modern Greece and Her Cargo*, Archaeology Section, Division of Archives and History, North Carolina Department of Cultural Resources, Raleigh, NC.

Caram, Ed (1984) *U-352: Pictures and Reports*, privately printed.

_____ (1987) *U-352: The Sunken German Uboat in the Graveyard of the Atlantic*, privately printed.

Eastern Sea Frontier (1944) *Report of Wrecks Surveyed by USCG Gentian in Fifth Naval District*, Naval Historical Center.

Gentile, Gary (1992) *Shipwrecks of North Carolina: from the Diamond Shoals North*, Gary Gentile Productions, P.O. Box 57137, Philadelphia, PA 19111 ($20 postage paid).

_____ (1989) *Track of the Gray Wolf*, Avon Books, New York, NY.

Harker, Jess, and Lovin, Bill (1976) *The North Carolina Diver's Handbook*, Marine Grafics, Box 2242, Chapel Hill, North Carolina 27514.

Heyl, Erik (1952–1969) *Early American Steamers* (six volumes) Erik Heyl, 136 West Oakwood Place, Buffalo, New York 14214.

Horner, Dave (1968) *The Blockade-Runners*, Dodd, Mead & Co., New York.

Howland, S.A. (1840) *Steamboat Disasters and Railroad Accidents in the United States*, Dorr, Howland & Company, Worcester.

Keatts, Henry, and Farr, George (1986) *Dive into History: U-boats*, American Merchant Marine Museum Press, Kings Point, New York.

Lonsdale, Adrian L., and Kaplan, H.R. (1964) *A Guide to Sunken Ships in American Waters*, Compass Publications.

MacNeil, Ben Dixon (undated) *Torpedo Junction*, Time Printing Co., Manteo, North Carolina.

McEwen, W.A., and A.H. Lewis (1985) *Encyclopedia of Nautical Knowledge*, Cornell Maritime Press, Centreville, Maryland 21617.

Naisawald, L. Vanloan (1972) *In Some Foreign Field*, John F. Blair, Winston-Salem, North Carolina.

National Ocean Service, *Automated Wreck and Information System* (AWOIS), National Oceanic and Atmospheric Administration.

Naval History Division, (1959–1981) *Dictionary of American Naval Fighting Ships*, (eight volumes) Department of the Navy.

Navy Department, Office of Naval Records and Library, Historical Section (1920) *German Submarine Activities on the Atlantic Coast of the United States and Canada*, Publication Number 1, Government Printing Office.

Newton, John; Pilke, Orrin; and Blanton, J.O. (1971) *An Oceanographic Atlas of the Carolina Continental Margin*, North Carolina Department of Conservation and Development, Raleigh, NC.

Regan, Dennis C; and Worthington, Virginia (1978) *Wreck Diving in North Carolina*, UNC Sea Grant, Raleigh, North Carolina.

Shomette, Donald (1973) *Shipwrecks of the Civil War*, Danic, Ltd., Washington DC.

Spence, E. Lee (1991) *Shipwreck Encyclopedia of the Civil War: North Carolina, 1861–1865,* Sullivan's Island, South Carolina.

Sprunt, James (1920) *Derelicts: an account of ships lost at sea in general commercial traffic and a brief history of blockade runners stranded along the North Carolina coast, 1861–1865*, Wilmington, North Carolina.

Standard Oil Company (1946) *Ships of the Esso Fleet in World War II.*

Stick, David (1952) *Graveyard of the Atlantic*, The University of North Carolina Press, Chapel Hill, North Carolina.

Treasury Department, Life-Saving Service (Annual Report from 1876 to 1915) *Operations of the United States Life-Saving Service*, Government Printing Office.

Octopus.

LORAN NUMBERS — ALPHABETICAL

1250 Rocks	26810.0	40410.0
14 Buoy	27040.5	39572.4
1700 Rock	27043.0	39709.8
18 Fathom Wreck	45138.6	59398.2
210 Rock	27069.7	39493.1
240 Rock	27079.0	39495.3
43 Fathom Wreck	26864.9	40217.5
Aeolus (439′ cable layer)	27081.4	39489.7
Alexander Ramsey	27268.0	39106.5
Alton Lennon (150′ barge)	27217.7	39082.9
Amagansett	27025.3	39724.3
Anchor Wreck	45314.6	60179.0
Ann R. Heidritter	26965.5	40197.0
Arabian	45332.4	59046.0
Ario	27043.2	39712.9
Artificial Reef	27128.2	39661.5
Ashkhabad	27037.1	39617.6
Asphalt Barge	26868.5	40458.8
Aster	45329.7	59048.6
Atlas	27023.6	39721.5
Australia (stern)	26883.3	40250.4
Australia (bow)	26883.5	40250.2
Barge	45463.7	59761.1
Barge	45464.8	59762.1
Barge	45463.0	59763.0
Barge	45411.8	59881.1
Barge	45411.4	59881.5
Barge (130 feet long)	26975.1	40689.1
Barge (130 feet long)	26975.0	40690.0
Barge (130′)	27019.4	40133.0
Barge (60 feet long)	27127.5	39660.2
Barge (60 feet long)	27127.3	39662.5
Barge, Bridge Span, YSD	27300.7	57421.7
Barges (3)/111,000 Tires	27275.5	57508.5
Bedfordshire	27048.6	39562.1
Bedloe/Jackson	26940.8	40687.3
Big Rock	26990.0	39535.0
Big Rock	26985.0	39585.0
Big Rock	45138.0	59975.0
Big Ten Fathom	27079.6	39555.2
BK Barges (8) & Tires	45424.0	59402.6
BP-25	45306.0	59551.5
Brick Wreck	45252.4	59202.6
British Splendour	26976.7	39957.4
BT-6400 (104′ barge)	27019.4	40132.4
Buarque	26863.7	40932.9
Buarque	26863.9	40933.2
Bubble Rock	45084.0	60024.0
Byron D. Benson	26923.6	40864.9
Camel	45426.8	59741.3
Caribsea	27042.5	39741.0
Cassimir	27128.6	39250.1
Chenango	26872.3	41104.8
Chenango	26872.2	41105.0
Ciltvaira (false)	26847.8	40450.8
City of Atlanta	26894.8	40399.7
City of Houston	45170.6	59281.6
City of Richmond	45343.8	59925.6
City of St. Helens	44890.8	59761.5
Civil War Wreck	45333.6	59483.4
Classroom	27217.7	39082.9
Coast Guard Cutter	26940.8	40687.3
Concrete (480 tons) 200′s	27267.4	39161.0
Concrete (930 tons)	27303.0	57426.8
Condor	45332.0	59048.6
Consols	27042.8	41011.2
Consols	27042.8	41011.7
D Wreck	27042.5	39740.8
D. Howard Spear	44931.9	59336.3
Danny's Wreck	26943.7	40560.2
Diamond Tower	26875.2	40278.8
Dionysys	26940.7	40575.7
Dirfys	45247.0	59211.9
Dixie Arrow	26949.7	40038.3
Dixie Arrow	26951.5	40038.6
Doris Kellogg	44954.2	59566.8
Dredge Barge (100′ long)	45363.2	59996.2
Dredge Wreck	27241.2	39046.0
Dredge Wreck	27241.2	39046.8
E.M. Clark	26905.3	40062.2
Ea	27063.2	39623.1
East Tanker	26981.8	39793.0
Eastern Slough Buoy	27075.0	39670.4
Ed's Lobster Wreck	27110.7	39236.3
Empire Gem	26903.3	40172.7
Empire Gem (stern)	26903.5	40172.6
Empire Gem (bow)	26903.5	40173.0
Equipoise	26843.5	40999.3
Equipoise	26844.1	40999.8
Esso Nashville	27156.3	39163.8
F.W. Abrams	26967.3	40073.6
Far East Tanker	27981.3	39788.9
Feather	45330.3	59051.6
Fenwick Island	27064.0	39607.9
Fishing Vessel	26904.5	40148.6
Frederick W. Day	45429.6	60473.7
Freighter	27133.2	39180.0
Frying Pan Tower	27190.0	39025.0
Frying Pan Tower	45165.2	59220.0
General Sherman	45413.3	59455.7
George MacDonald	44996.5	59851.5
George Summerlin (130′)	27062.2	39683.3
George Weems	45216.5	59190.9
Georgetown Rock	45136.0	59968.0
Georgiana	45498.3	60454.1
Golden Liner	45481.8	59792.2
Grainger Wreck	27160.0	39175.0
Green Buoy Wreck	26847.8	40450.8
Hang	45181.9	59236.9

Hebe	45237.4	59612.7
Hector	45379.0	60027.1
Hector	45380.3	60027.1
Hector	45379.6	60027.2
Hector (part)	45379.6	60026.8
Hesperides	26910.1	40236.5
Houston	45170.6	59281.6
Hyde (215' dredge)	27218.2	39081.9
Jackson/Bedloe	26940.8	40687.3
John D. Gill (bow)	27198.5	39085.3
John D. Gill (stern)	27199.5	39083.5
John Rose	44994.4	59269.2
Juan Casiano	44892.6	59806.4
Kassandra Louloudis	26886.9	40274.7
Keshena	26959.8	40085.2
Knuckle Buoy	27061.2	39618.7
Lancing	26897.2	40182.3
Landing Craft	45385.9	59414.0
Landing Craft	45386.9	59417.4
Landing Craft	45386.5	59418.5
Landing Craft	45426.4	59742.3
Landing Craft	45464.1	59763.2
Landing Craft (2)	45457.0	59814.0
Landing Craft (2) & Tires	45456.9	59814.9
LCM (55 feet long)	27267.5	39160.8
LCU–1468, 100' S of buoy	26941.4	40685.5
Liberator	26888.7	40218.8
Liberty Ship	27268.0	39025.0
Little Ten Fathom	27081.1	39560.6
Liverpool	45471.2	59933.1
Louisiana	45331.6	59046.3
Malchace	26941.1	39881.4
Manuela	26945.2	39916.8
Marie Palmer	45261.2	59219.7
Marore	26885.2	40504.2
Marore	26885.6	40505.3
Mary B. Barid	44653.4	59178.8
Mary Barry	44830.2	59144.8
Merak (?)	26869.7	40273.1
Mercel	26894.6	40502.3
Mirlo	26847.0	40450.8
Modern Greece	45333.5	59042.3
Monitor	26887.4	40174.5
Monitor	26887.6	40174.7
Monitor	15760.6	58268.2
Moorefield	45331.1	59047.4
Moriana 200	26868.5	40458.8
Mount Dirfys	45247.0	59211.9
Mr. J.C. (105' long tug)	26957.0	40155.0
Mt. Dirfys	45247.0	59211.9
Naeco (bow)	27053.7	39422.8
Naeco (stern)	27065.4	39387.8
Nevada	26940.1	40191.4
New River (80' vessel)	27225.7	39403.7
Norlavore	26878.3	40237.6
Normannia	27142.8	39180.5
Normannia	27143.3	39180.5
Northwest Place #1	27090.4	39577.6
Northwest Place #2	27089.1	39574.8
Northwest Place #3	27089.1	39570.0
Northwest Rock	27037.2	39595.4
Norvana	26913.6	40817.0
Novelty (140' menhaden)	27138.5	39636.9
Old Wreck	26887.2	41372.3
Ore Freighter	45138.6	59398.2
Oriental	26949.3	40559.1
Panam	26975.5	39585.0
Papoose	27074.0	39431.1
Peterhoff	45323.0	59075.9
Phil's Wreck	26857.1	40340.5
Pinnacle	26953.5	40039.9
Pocahontas (105' tug)	27240.4	39048.3
Point Shoals Buoy	26891.4	40250.0
Portland	27056.5	39652.0
Powell	26949.4	39997.4
Prince of Wales	45471.2	59933.1
Proteus	26949.6	39960.6
R.R. Stone (86' tug)	27241.4	39045.8
Ramsey	27268.0	39106.5
Raritan	14539.5	
Raritan	45248.2	59275.2
Regulus	26942.5	40159.0
Rock Pile	27903.0	40070.0
Rock South of 13	27134.3	39470.0
Rose	45481.5	59899.4
Rosin Wreck	45170.2	59156.7
Rover	45481.8	59792.2
Russian Freighter	27037.1	39617.6
Russian Trawler (130')	26849.5	40886.1
San Delfino	26810.2	40622.6
Schurz	27067.7	39463.8
Screw Steamer	45314.6	60179.0
Semaeco	27035.0	39391.0
Senateur Duhamel	27092.8	39633.3
Shad	27025.3	39724.2
Slick Wreck	26897.2	40182.3
Smell Wreck	26903.5	40173.0
Socony 8	27268.7	39106.8
South Wreck	27143.2	39524.3
South Wreck	27143.6	39524.3
Southeast Naeco	27035.0	39391.0
Southeast Rocks	26861.0	40234.0
Squirrel's Rock (220')	26891.1	40160.9
St. Cathan	45238.1	59616.6
Steel Framing	27127.7	39661.9
Steel Scaffolds	45410.5	59882.0
Steel Scaffolds	45410.4	59882.3
Steel Scaffolds	45411.1	59882.7
Steel Scaffolds	45411.4	59882.9
Stone Brothers (105' tug)	27269.4	39105.7
Stonewall Jackson	44711.1	59322.1
Stormy Petrel	45330.0	59052.1
Suloide	27146.1	39550.1

T.A. Ward	44844.9	59006.0
T.J. Don	44567.9	59608.6
Tamaulipas (stern)	26980.7	39773.9
Tamaulipas (bow)	26981.3	39788.8
Tarpon	26946.0	39959.2
Ten Mile Reef Wreck	45427.1	59741.3
Tenas	26888.8	40219.2
Theodore Parker	27127.8	39660.9
Thistleroy	27078.8	39656.8
Tires (16,280)	26950.0	40280.0
Tires (48,700)	27256.9	39252.5
Torungen (90 feet long)	45410.3	59882.1
Torungen (90 feet long)	45410.3	59882.8
Train Cars (10)	27340.7	57350.1
Train Cars (10) 200' SW	27177.0	39549.8
Train Cars (10) 250' W	27160.2	39524.8
Train Cars (10) 275' SW	27210.0	39324.4
Train Cars (10) 300' SE	26995.9	39998.0
Train Cars (10) 300' SW	27261.0	39068.7
Train Cars (10) 350' SW	27162.4	39545.3
Train Cars (10) 350' SW	27139.7	39569.5
Train Cars (10) 350' SW	26975.0	40690.0
Train Cars (10) 400' S	27325.9	57362.0
Train Cars (10) 400' SW	26987.0	40024.0
Train Cars (10) 450' S	27312.6	57375.5
Train Cars (10) 500' SW	27211.7	39195.0
Train Cars (10) 525' W	27217.7	39082.9
Train Cars (10) 550' SW	27233.1	39224.5
Train Cars (10) 550' SW	27214.7	39226.0
Train Cars (10) 350' SW	26979.1	40726.0
Train Cars (5) 250'		
SW	27243.1	39077.2
Train Cars (5) 300' NE	27243.1	39077.2
Train Cars (7), Concrete	27316.4	57390.2
Train Cars (8), Concrete	26945.0	40175.0
Train Cars (9), Concrete	26951.0	40182.0
Trawler	27092.3	39633.3
Tug (65 feet long)	27267.8	39161.6
Tug, Tanker, Two Barges	27268.0	39107.0
U–352	27063.5	39491.5
U–85	26917.0	40713.6
Unis	26940.1	40191.4
Unknown	26900.3	40403.6
Unknown (Norman Miller)	26928.8	39922.6
Urn Wreck	26940.1	40191.4
Valley Moon	27028.7	39995.7
Vermillion	45266.2	59834.8
Veturia	26895.6	40246.4
Virginius	45301.6	59205.2
W.E. Hutton	27143.2	39524.3
W.E. Hutton	27143.6	39524.3
West Rock	27072.1	39515.7
West Rock	27077.4	39521.5
Western Slough Buoy	27083.3	39654.9
Whistling Wind	44487.5	59124.9
WR–2	27128.6	39250.1
WR–4	27198.3	39085.4
Wreck	26906.2	40242.3
Wreck	26906.8	40242.8
Wreck	45014.8	59111.0
Wreck	44402.9	59140.4
Wreck	44803.2	59273.1
Wreck	44668.5	59292.8
Wreck	44532.1	59362.5
Wreck	45216.0	59419.0
Wreck	45299.8	59733.5
Wreck	45109.6	59967.8
Wreck	44859.5	60003.1
Wreck (165 feet long)	45201.8	59334.7
Yard Oiler (174')	27039.3	39574.6
YDS–68	45167.0	59368.0
YDS–68	45166.4	59369.4
York	26913.6	40817.0
Zane Grey	26940.7	40574.3

LORAN NUMBERS — DESCENDING 4 AND 3 LINES

Old Wreck	26887.2	41372.3
Chenango	26872.2	41105.0
Chenango	26872.3	41104.8
Consols	27042.8	41011.7
Consols	27042.8	41011.2
Equipoise	26844.1	40999.8
Equipoise	26843.5	40999.3
Buarque	26863.9	40933.2
Buarque	26863.7	40932.9
Russian Trawler (130')	26849.5	40886.1
Byron D. Benson	26923.6	40864.9
York	26913.6	40817.0
Norvana	26913.6	40817.0
Train Cars (10) 350' SW	26979.1	40726.0
U-85	26917.0	40713.6
Train Cars (10) 350' SW	26975.0	40690.0
Barge (130 feet long)	26975.0	40690.0
Barge (130 feet long)	26975.1	40689.1
Jackson/Bedloe	26940.8	40687.3
Coast Guard Cutter	26940.8	40687.3
Bedloe/Jackson	26940.8	40687.3
LCU–1468, 100' S of buoy	26941.4	40685.5
San Delfino	26810.2	40622.6
Dionysys	26940.7	40575.7
Zane Grey	26940.7	40574.3
Danny's Wreck	26943.7	40560.2
Oriental	26949.3	40559.1
Marore	26885.6	40505.3
Marore	26885.2	40504.2
Mercel	26894.6	40502.3
Moriana 200	26868.5	40458.8
Asphalt Barge	26868.5	40458.8
Mirlo	26847.0	40450.8
Green Buoy Wreck	26847.8	40450.8
Ciltvaira (false)	26847.8	40450.8
1250 Rocks	26810.0	40410.0
Unknown	26900.3	40403.6
City of Atlanta	26894.8	40399.7
Phil's Wreck	26857.1	40340.5
Tires (16,280)	26950.0	40280.0
Diamond Tower	26875.2	40278.8
Kassandra Louloudis	26886.9	40274.7
Merak (?)	26869.7	40273.1
Australia (stern)	26883.3	40250.4
Australia (bow)	26883.5	40250.2
Point Shoals Buoy	26891.4	40250.0
Veturia	26895.6	40246.4
Wreck	26906.8	40242.8
Wreck	26906.2	40242.3
Norlavore	26878.3	40237.6
Hesperides	26910.1	40236.5
Southeast Rocks	26861.0	40234.0
Tenas	26888.8	40219.2
Liberator	26888.7	40218.8
43 Fathom Wreck	26864.9	40217.5
Anna R. Heidritter	26965.5	40197.0
Urn Wreck	26940.1	40191.4
Unis	26940.1	40191.4
Nevada	26940.1	40191.4
Slick Wreck	26897.2	40182.3
Lancing	26897.2	40182.3
Train Cars (9), Concrete	26951.0	40182.0
Train Cars (8), Concrete	26945.0	40175.0
Monitor	26887.6	40174.7
Monitor	26887.4	40174.5
Smell Wreck	26903.5	40173.0
Empire Gem (bow)	26903.5	40173.0
Empire Gem	26903.3	40172.7
Empire Gem (stern)	26903.5	40172.6
Squirrel's Rock (220')	26891.1	40160.9
Regulus	26942.5	40159.0
Mr. J.C. (105' long tug)	26957.0	40155.0
Fishing Vessel	26904.5	40148.6
Barge (130')	27019.4	40133.0
BT–6400 (104' barge)	27019.4	40132.4
Keshena	26959.8	40085.2
F.W. Abrams	26967.3	40073.6
Rock Pile	27903.0	40070.0
E.M. Clark	26905.3	40062.2
Pinnacle	26953.5	40039.9
Dixie Arrow	26951.5	40038.6
Dixie Arrow	26949.7	40038.3
Train Cars (10) 400' SW	26987.0	40024.0
Train Cars (10) 300' SE	26995.9	39998.0
Powell	26949.4	39997.4
Valley Moon	27028.7	39995.7
Proteus	26949.6	39960.6
Tarpon	26946.0	39959.2
British Splendour	26976.7	39957.4
Unknown (Norman Miller)	26928.8	39922.6
Manuela	26945.2	39916.8
Malchace	26941.1	39881.4
East Tanker	26981.8	39793.0
Far East Tanker	27981.3	39788.9
Tamaulipas (bow)	26981.3	39788.8
Tamaulipas (stern)	26980.7	39773.9
Caribsea	27042.5	39741.0
D Wreck	27042.5	39740.8
Amagansett	27025.3	39724.3
Shad	27025.3	39724.2
Atlas	27023.6	39721.5
Ario	27043.2	39712.9
1700 Rock	27043.0	39709.8
George Summerlin		

(130')	27062.2	39683.3
Eastern Slough Buoy	27075.0	39670.4
Barge (60 feet long)	27127.3	39662.5
Steel Framing	27127.7	39661.9
Artificial Reef	27128.2	39661.5
Theodore Parker	27127.8	39660.9
Barge (60 feet long)	27127.5	39660.2
Thistleroy	27078.8	39656.8
Western Slough Buoy	27083.3	39654.9
Portland	27056.5	39652.0
Novelty (140' menhaden)	27138.5	39636.9
Trawler	27092.3	39633.3
Senateur Duhamel	27092.8	39633.3
Ea	27063.2	39623.1
Knuckle Buoy	27061.2	39618.7
Russian Freighter	27037.1	39617.6
Ashkhabad	27037.1	39617.6
Fenwick Island	27064.0	39607.9
Northwest Rock	27037.2	39595.4
Panam	26975.5	39585.0
Big Rock	26985.0	39585.0
Northwest Place #1	27090.4	39577.6
Northwest Place #2	27089.1	39574.8
Yard Oiler (174')	27039.3	39574.6
14 Buoy	27040.5	39572.4
Northwest Place #3	27089.1	39570.0
Train Cars (10) 350' SW	27139.7	39569.5
Bedfordshire	27048.6	39562.1
Little Ten Fathom	27081.1	39560.6
Big Ten Fathom	27079.6	39555.2
Suloide	27146.1	39550.1
Train Cars (10) 200' SW	27177.0	39549.8
Train Cars (10) 350' SW	27162.4	39545.3
Big Rock	26990.0	39535.0
Train Cars (10) 250' W	27160.2	39524.8
W.E. Hutton	27143.6	39524.3
W.E. Hutton	27143.2	39524.3
South Wreck	27143.6	39524.3
South Wreck	27143.2	39524.3
West Rock	27077.4	39521.5
West Rock	27072.1	39515.7
240 Rock	27079.0	39495.3
210 Rock	27069.7	39493.1
U-352	27063.5	39491.5
Aeolus (439' cable layer)	27081.4	39489.7
Rock South of 13	27134.3	39470.0
Schurz	27067.7	39463.8
Papoose	27074.0	39431.1
Naeco (bow)	27053.7	39422.8
New River (80' vessel)	27225.7	39403.7
Southeast Naeco	27035.0	39391.0
Semaeco	27035.0	39391.0
Naeco (stern)	27065.4	39387.8
Train Cars (10) 275' SW	27210.0	39324.4
Tires (48, 700)	27256.9	39252.5
WR-2	27128.6	39250.1
Cassimir	27128.6	39250.1
Ed's Lobster Wreck	27110.7	39236.3
Train Cars (10) 500' SW	27214.7	39226.0
Train Cars (10) 550' SW	27233.1	39224.5
Train Cars (10) 500' SW	27211.7	39195.0
Normannia	27143.3	39180.5
Normannia	27142.8	39180.5
Freighter	27133.2	39180.0
Grainger Wreck	27160.0	39175.0
Esso Nashville	27156.3	39163.8
Tug (65 feet long)	27267.8	39161.6
Concrete (480 tons) 200'S	27267.4	39161.0
LCM (55 feet long)	27267.5	39160.8
Tug, Tanker, Two Barges	27268.0	39107.0
Socony 8	27268.7	39106.8
Ramsey	27268.0	39106.5
Alexander Ramsey	27268.0	39106.5
Stone Brothers (105' tug)	27269.4	39105.7
WR-4	27198.3	39085.4
John D. Gill (bow)	27198.5	39085.3
John D. Gill (stern)	27199.5	39083.5
Train Cars (10) 525' W	27217.7	39082.9
Classroom	27217.7	39082.9
Alton Lennon (150' barge)	27217.7	39082.9
Hyde (215' dredge)	27218.2	39081.9
Train Cars (5) 300' NE	27243.1	39077.2
Train Cars (5) 250' SW	27243.1	39077.2
Train Cars (10) 300' SW	27261.0	39068.7
Pocahontas (105' tug)	27240.4	39048.3
Dredge Wreck	27241.2	39046.8
Dredge Wreck	27241.2	39046.0
R.R. Stone (86' tug)	27241.4	39045.8
Liberty Ship	27268.0	39025.0
Frying Pan Tower	27190.0	39025.0

LORAN NUMBERS — ASCENDING 5 AND 6 LINES

Train Cars (10)	27340.7	57350.1
Train Cars (10) 400'		
S	27325.9	57362.0
Train Cars (10) 450'		
S	27312.6	57375.5
Train Cars		
(7)/Concrete	27316.4	57390.2
Barge, Bridge Span,		
YSD	27300.7	57421.7
Concrete (930 tons)	27303.0	57426.8
Barges (3)/111,000		
Tires	27275.5	57508.5
Monitor	15760.6	58268.2
T.A. Ward	44844.9	59006.0
Modern Greece	45333.5	59042.3
Arabian	45332.4	59046.0
Louisiana	45331.6	59046.3
Moorefield	45331.1	59047.4
Aster	45329.7	59048.6
Condor	45332.0	59048.6
Feather	45330.3	59051.6
Stormy Petrel	45330.0	59052.1
Peterhoff	45323.0	59075.9
Wreck	45014.8	59111.0
Whistling Wind	44487.5	59124.9
Wreck	44402.9	59140.4
Mary Barry	44830.2	59144.8
Rosin Wreck	45170.2	59156.7
Mary B. Baird	44653.4	59178.8
George Weems	45216.5	59190.9
Brick Wreck	45252.4	59202.6
Virginius	45301.6	59205.2
Dirfys	45247.0	59211.9
Mount Dirfys	45247.0	59211.9
Mt. Dirfys	45247.0	59211.9
Marie Palmer	45261.2	59219.7
Frying Pan Tower	45165.2	59220.0
Hang	45181.9	59236.9
John Rose	44994.4	59269.2
Wreck	44803.2	59273.1
Raritan	45248.2	59275.2
City of Houston	45170.6	59281.6
Houston	45170.6	59281.6
Wreck	44668.5	59292.8
Stonewall Jackson	44711.1	59322.1
Wreck (165 feet long)	45201.8	59334.7
D. Howard Spear	44931.9	59336.3
Wreck	44532.1	59362.5
YDS–68	45167.0	59368.0
YDS–68	45166.4	59369.4
18 Fathom Wreck	45138.6	59398.2
Ore Freighter	45138.6	59398.2
BK Barges (8) &		
Tires	45424.0	59402.6
Landing Craft	45385.9	59414.0
Landing Craft	45386.9	59417.4

Landing Craft	45386.5	59418.5
Wreck	45216.0	59419.0
General Sherman	45414.3	59455.7
Civil War Wreck	45333.6	59483.4
BP–25	45306.0	59551.5
Doris Kellogg	44945.2	59566.8
T.J. Don	44567.9	59608.6
Hebe	45237.4	59612.7
St. Cathan	45238.1	59616.6
Wreck	45299.8	59733.5
Camel	45426.8	59741.3
Ten Mile Reef Wreck	45427.1	59741.3
Landing Craft	45426.4	59742.3
Barge	45463.7	59761.1
City of St. Helens	44890.8	59761.5
Barge	45464.8	59762.1
Barge	45463.0	59763.0
Landing Craft	45464.1	59763.2
Golden Liner	45481.8	59792.2
Rover	45481.8	59792.2
Juan Casiano	44892.6	59806.4
Landing Craft (2)	45457.0	59814.0
Landing Craft (2) &		
Tires	45456.9	59814.9
Vermillion	45266.2	59834.8
George MacDonald	44996.5	59851.5
Barge	45411.8	59881.1
Barge	45411.4	59881.5
Steel Scaffolds	45410.5	59882.0
Torungen (90 feet		
long)	45410.3	59882.1
Steel Scaffolds	45410.4	59882.3
Steel Scaffolds	45411.1	59882.7
Torungen (90 feet		
long)	45410.3	59882.8
Steel Scaffolds	45411.4	59882.9
Rose	45481.5	59899.4
City of Richmond	45343.8	59925.6
Liverpool	45471.2	59933.1
Prince of Wales	45471.2	59933.1
Wreck	45109.6	59967.8
Georgetown Rock	45136.0	59968.0
Big Rock	45138.0	59975.0
Dredge Barge (100'		
long)	45363.2	59996.2
Wreck	44859.5	60003.1
Bubble Rock	45084.0	60024.0
Hector (part)	45379.6	60026.8
Hector	45379.6	60027.1
Hector	45380.3	60027.1
Hector	45379.6	60027.2
Anchor Wreck	45314.6	60179.0
Screw Steamer	45314.6	60179.0
Georgiana	45498.3	60454.1
Frederick W. Day	45429.6	60473.7

HANG NUMBERS — DESCENDING 4 AND 3 LINES

26853.9	41638.5	26898.0	41293.9	26873.8	41107.8
26913.7	41495.7	26865.4	41292.9	26995.3	41106.6
26914.1	41494.2	26901.0	41290.0	26876.1	41105.3
26916.0	41493.6	26854.4	41281.9	26872.2	41105.2
26912.0	41493.0	26886.4	41280.2	26870.0	41099.5
26905.0	41491.5	26850.4	41278.9	26866.5	41090.7
26911.6	41489.8	26864.7	41277.5	26866.4	41090.7
26892.0	41485.0	26864.4	41277.2	26863.5	41084.7
26884.9	41485.0	26864.7	41276.9	26868.4	41073.4
26901.8	41482.2	26951.0	41276.5	26868.4	41073.0
26918.0	41480.0	26857.9	41270.4	26869.3	41064.3
27004.1	41478.7	26876.6	41267.6	26864.3	41064.3
26871.8	41437.0	26876.0	41267.6	26869.4	41062.5
26895.1	41424.7	26902.7	41261.4	26866.0	41060.9
26902.7	41421.2	26846.0	41258.0	26857.3	41040.3
26882.1	41413.1	26900.0	41250.0	26853.9	41038.6
26880.8	41409.6	27887.0	41248.0	26857.8	41038.5
26879.7	41402.5	26887.0	41248.0	26863.2	41033.9
26889.4	41385.0	27877.0	41244.2	26833.0	41033.8
26885.6	41372.6	26875.5	41244.2	26863.9	41033.2
26885.0	41372.0	26875.4	41240.9	26865.3	41030.4
26887.3	41371.8	27869.9	41239.5	26854.7	41029.9
26887.1	41371.2	26869.9	41239.5	26871.1	41021.6
26883.4	41369.0	26837.6	41236.8	26855.2	41011.2
26901.6	41368.9	26863.5	41231.7	26878.0	41010.8
26864.5	41367.8	26839.0	41231.0	26977.3	41003.5
26886.7	41366.7	27104.9	41226.2	26858.2	41000.8
26902.0	41365.3	26984.7	41224.7	26888.4	40992.4
26881.2	41362.9	26982.7	41224.7	26866.5	40991.4
26857.2	41362.7	26982.4	41224.7	26827.0	40977.4
26881.2	41361.0	26844.0	41222.0	26843.8	40968.7
26875.0	41355.0	26850.0	41218.0	26866.5	40964.7
26864.2	41348.3	26845.0	41217.0	26858.0	40955.0
26884.6	41347.8	26890.9	41216.9	26861.2	40953.2
26892.0	41345.9	26843.0	41210.0	26865.2	40953.0
26864.9	41345.5	26843.0	41208.0	26858.4	40949.8
26888.0	41343.0	26886.7	41198.7	26862.6	40941.9
26878.5	41342.5	26989.7	41194.8	26821.1	40936.8
26888.0	41342.0	26852.0	41191.6	26861.1	40936.7
26855.1	41339.9	26875.0	41190.0	26862.5	40933.3
26865.9	41332.8	26988.4	41186.5	26859.8	40933.3
26885.0	41332.6	26988.2	41185.3	26863.8	40932.8
26882.5	41329.0	26999.1	41174.4	26863.5	40932.3
26856.0	41322.0	26864.0	41169.0	26855.4	40932.3
26869.0	41317.6	26842.5	41168.4	26594.6	40929.9
26869.0	41312.0	26815.3	41154.7	26934.6	40916.0
26900.4	41310.0	26874.3	41149.5	26864.9	40914.9
26852.0	41307.0	26855.7	41140.2	26865.7	40906.2
26896.1	41304.1	26869.5	41137.6	26865.9	40903.6
26882.0	41299.5	26851.3	41137.3	26866.5	40897.5
26896.1	41299.4	26857.6	41127.0	26869.5	40886.0
26842.7	41299.2	26868.0	41125.5	26842.4	40886.0
26896.1	41299.1	26867.3	41125.5	26849.4	40885.1
26885.0	41299.0	26877.7	41123.5	26877.3	40878.8
26882.0	41295.5	26859.6	41120.0	26877.3	40873.6
26855.8	41295.3	26978.0	41114.0	26929.2	40872.6
26897.0	41294.5	26886.3	41109.0	26875.0	40867.0
26999.7	41294.0	26877.3	41108.6	26867.0	40841.0

26853.8	40832.8	26954.7	40221.2	26979.5	40139.4
26854.0	40832.0	26954.4	40221.1	26992.0	40135.0
26882.2	40828.1	26888.6	40219.0	27990.2	40131.7
26863.0	40822.0	26958.4	40214.5	26973.0	40131.1
26876.0	40818.0	26962.9	40201.8	26938.5	40128.9
26852.8	40818.0	26949.7	40200.3	26995.8	40122.4
26855.7	40817.4	26961.2	40199.6	26989.7	40122.0
26913.0	40586.7	26965.5	40197.0	26955.5	40121.4
26936.8	40586.1	26965.0	40197.0	26991.1	40099.8
26930.0	40580.0	26964.2	40196.2	26987.0	40094.0
26932.0	40556.5	26965.7	40195.2	27005.9	40090.9
26931.7	40555.5	26968.7	40193.2	26991.7	40090.3
26931.0	40555.1	26965.7	40193.2	27105.9	40090.1
26946.3	40550.0	26951.0	40189.9	27005.9	40090.1
26939.3	40550.0	26967.7	40189.2	26993.0	40085.1
26929.7	40547.6	26967.2	40189.2	27008.8	40065.2
26935.2	40543.0	26963.8	40189.0	27002.1	40064.8
26918.5	40513.0	26964.4	40188.7	27002.9	40055.9
26937.3	40511.2	26965.9	40183.3	27011.3	40048.8
26915.0	40511.0	26951.3	40182.5	27011.7	40043.9
26931.2	40507.0	26967.6	40181.8	27015.3	40041.6
26928.2	40506.0	26945.0	40180.0	27015.6	40040.8
26934.0	40504.6	26968.1	40179.2	27015.0	40040.3
26913.8	40501.7	26968.1	40179.1	27014.7	40040.3
26934.8	40501.0	26769.0	40177.4	27019.1	40039.6
26928.3	40498.7	26961.7	40176.6	26974.0	40039.0
26926.7	40496.7	26967.6	40174.9	27017.9	40038.7
26932.8	40496.0	26969.1	40174.7	27076.9	40038.5
26929.7	40491.8	26969.1	40174.4	27017.5	40038.5
26929.6	40491.0	26765.1	40174.4	26951.9	40038.0
26930.5	40490.5	26969.5	40173.7	27021.3	40036.8
26905.2	40487.7	26903.5	40173.2	26978.2	40036.8
26913.4	40487.4	26913.0	40173.0	27075.6	40032.0
26924.1	40487.3	26969.6	40172.6	27024.5	40029.4
26912.8	40483.0	26969.6	40172.4	27021.3	40026.0
26913.7	40458.0	26965.0	40172.0	26952.8	40025.8
26913.1	40458.0	26959.5	40172.0	27015.7	40020.3
26907.8	40449.3	26945.0	40172.0	27029.2	40013.4
26932.1	40435.3	26971.0	40169.9	27028.7	40012.5
26922.0	40435.3	26977.8	40168.1	27014.0	40012.0
26928.0	40430.0	26971.4	40167.7	27029.0	39995.4
26921.8	40335.0	26970.0	40167.5	27026.8	39987.2
26916.0	40335.0	26975.0	40167.0	26980.4	39924.0
26922.0	40334.5	26905.0	40164.0	27013.6	39772.2
26921.8	40331.0	26764.6	40164.0	27017.5	39740.0
26921.0	40331.0	26974.6	40163.3	27019.5	39737.0
26919.0	40331.0	26911.0	40155.7	37016.0	39730.3
26916.0	40331.0	26946.2	40154.3	27024.3	39726.4
26923.1	40328.4	26979.7	40153.1	27025.3	39724.3
26923.4	40324.9	26973.1	40153.1	27023.7	39721.6
26920.0	40318.0	26973.0	40153.1	27027.2	39712.8
26918.0	40318.0	26962.9	40151.9	27028.4	39712.1
26917.0	40316.0	26920.9	40151.9	27027.0	39699.0
26922.0	40301.0	26978.9	40151.0	27020.3	39679.8
26923.0	40294.1	26978.2	40150.8	27017.8	39672.0
26921.8	40294.1	26904.5	40149.0	27023.0	39663.0
26936.0	40252.0				

Books by the Author

Fiction

Underwater Adventure
The Peking Papers

Action/Adventure
Mind Set

Supernatural
The Lurking

Vietnam
Lonely Conflict

Science Fiction
Entropy
Return to Mars
Silent Autumn
The Time Dragons Trilogy:
A Time for Dragons
Dragons Past
No Future for Dragons

Nonfiction

Advanced Wreck Diving Guide
Shipwrecks of New Jersey

Track of the Gray Wolf
Wreck Diving Adventures

Available (postage paid) from: GARY GENTILE PRODUCTIONS
P.O. Box 57137
Philadelphia, PA 19111

$25   *Andrea Doria: Dive to an Era*
$20   *Shipwrecks of Delaware and Maryland*
$20   *Shipwrecks of North Carolina: from Hatteras Inlet South*
$20   *Ultimate Wreck-Diving Guide*
$20   *USS San Diego: the Last Armored Cruiser*
$25   Video (VHS): *The Battle for the USS Monitor*

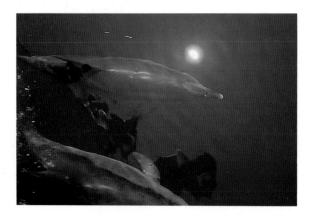